T0354136

The Secrets From Your Subconscious Mind

How to Interpret the Code for Changing Your Life!

Ryan Elliott, MSW
Medical Hypnoanalyst

iUniverse, Inc.
Bloomington

The Secrets From Your Subconscious Mind
How to Interpret the Code for Changing Your Life!

Author Credits: Wide Awake, Clear-Headed and Refreshed

iUniverse books may be ordered through booksellers or by contacting:

iUniverse
1663 Liberty Drive
Bloomington, IN 47403
www.iuniverse.com
1-800-Authors (1-800-288-4677)

ISBN: 978-1-4759-3627-8 (sc)
ISBN: 978-1-4759-3628-5 (ebk)

Printed in the United States of America

iUniverse rev. date: 09/06/2012

Contents

"Ryan Elliott's sessions took me from a confident kid to a confident adult! It might not seem earthshaking, but it's a big thing to me. Thanks Ryan!"

Steve Beck, author of
"How to Have a Great Day Everyday!"

"Ryan is an incredible therapist. He has walked me through a number of challenging times in my life. What I like best about him is that he is present with me, has incredible integrity and helps me go to the level I need to be at to find solutions. He also has a great sense of humor, which helps in difficult times. If you really want to create a different life—he's the therapist!"

Lynne Murray

"Ryan is a highly skilled practitioner and pioneer in the field of hypnoanalysis. His book on medical hypnoanalysis was groundbreaking. I highly recommend him."

Dan Lippmann, Owner, Counseling
& Wellness Innovation

"Ryan has been providing hypnosis services to clients for over twenty years. He is competent with a wide range of client issues such as stopping smoking, emotional problems, stress management, and performance enhancement."

Lawrence Todryk, President/ Owner,
Integrative Psychological Services, Inc.

"I had completed having one knee replacement and was scheduled for a second one. Although the first procedure went well, I was a bit apprehensive about the second one. I scheduled an appointment with

Ryan for some hypnotherapy, hoping it would ease my anxiety. What a difference! The surgery went smoothly, my incision healed very swiftly and I actually looked forward to my physical therapy sessions. I believe this all happened because of hypnotherapy and wished I had thought of it the first time around. I am pain-free, back on the golf course and active with my family. Pretty good for someone seventy-eight years old! Thanks, Ryan."

Ruth Femali

"Ryan Elliot is a good person in the true sense of the word. He is sincere in all he does with me. Ryan allows me to accept myself and to feel "good enough" about who I am. When I am around him and people he knows I am safe. His world is open to me any time I need him and he is very good at staying connected with me. I feel calm around him. Therapy for me is hard work and always evolving. If you are willing to do the work of therapy and you need non-judgmental support Ryan Elliot can provide it."

John Holden, hired Ryan for mental and physical health issues relating to eating disorders and divorce

"Ryan Elliott is one of the best hypnotherapists specializing in hypnoanalysis and biofeedback. His practice is not just your typical hypnosis, he finds the source of your concerns, which includes going back to previous lives. With this system the issues are dealt with successfully. I have personally seen the results several times where the party has turned themselves around to some wonderful healing. His practice of hypnoanalysis and biofeedback alleviates concerned issues. Therefore, I highly recommend Ryan Elliott for your problems."

Renee Page, Interior Designer/owner, Simply Design

"I visited The Lightheart Center and worked with Ryan Elliott experiencing his expertise in Hypnoanalysis and Neurofeedback. We worked with enhancing my ability to 'Speak Up' and 'Set Boundaries' with very favorable results that are still in existence six months later. His Neurofeedback is a detailed representation of brain wave patterns . . . allowing the evidence of healthy or non healthy activity. I trust Ryan's expertise in both fields and his ability to put you at ease with his compassionate and relaxed manner. I highly recommend Ryan."

Peggy Kinst

"Ryan is a very compassionate, competent professional who uses state of the art therapeutic techniques. I am very impressed with the results I have been able to achieve with Ryan. Day after day he proves that positive results can definitely be achieved without prescription drugs. I will definitely continue to take advantage of Ryan's services if needed in the future and would recommend him to anyone. Top qualities: Great Results, Personable, Expert."

George Beahan

"Ryan is a talented man in many ways and he uses his talents to help people improve their lives. He truly understands the workings of the mind. I highly recommend him."

Carole Dean

"Ryan is very knowledgeable as a Hypnoanalyst and Therapist. As a business owner, Ryan helps his clients get down to the root of their issues and then does what he can to work with them to feel better. As a very energized individual, Ryan learns new skills constantly developing himself across many areas of business. This has helped him keep his business on top and running smoothly. What I like about Ryan is his creativity. He is always brainstorming new ideas with his staff or others, which I feel has helped him to experience several new ventures. Mostly, Ryan has a desire to really help others feel better about themselves and to succeed. He strives to motivate people to find better ways to live a healthier lifestyle both physically and spiritually. Ryan has great integrity. He has always been there for others. He has a passion to live life. As a Hypnoanalyst/Therapist, Ryan is very trustworthy. Ryan has a very positive attitude on life and really enjoys his work in doing what he can for others."

Diane Tetens

"Ryan is a true professional from A to Z. He recommended his12 session Hypno-Analysis and I gave it a try. It was amazing!!! It took me to the next level of confidence. I am a motivational speaker and I have a lot of confidence yet his sessions seemed to give me a boost I wasn't even expecting. I HIGHLY recommend his 12 session Hypno-Analysis. It is well worth it! He is also a great guy with a fabulous sense of humor."

Steve Beck

The *Secrets From Your Subconscious Mind:*
How to Interpret the Code for Changing Your Life!

Library of Congress Catalogue Card Number: TBA
Elliott, Ryan, MSW
The Secrets From Your Subconscious Mind
1. Hypnosis—Psychology 2. Hypnoanalysis

ISBN # 0-9754817-1-1

Copy Editor: Anne M. Schwab

The Secrets from Your Subconscious Mind: How to Interpret the Code for Changing Your Life! Hypnoanalysis: A tested and proven system for unlocking the secrets and the power they have over us, secrets that limit behaviour, negative feelings, and destructive thoughts while strengthening skills, boosting performance, learning to love, connecting with God (or your higher self), and improving all dimensions of your life. Hypnoanalysis reveals, examines, and ends the power our subconscious secrets have over us.

Secrets vary from person to person, some burn slowly over a lifetime causing all kinds of pain. Others pack a powerful punch, which if ignored for long, have consequences to the body. Some secrets are shaded in shame and operate at the boundaries of consciousness making their presence known only in relationships. Many secrets feel benign until reality hits the fan and we come face to face with the notion that "something must be wrong here." Nevertheless, all secrets can be changed, that's the beauty of living on earth at this time as a human being.

Ryan Elliott, M.S.W.
The Lightheart Center
165 S. Church St.
Winfield, Illinois 60190 www.thelightheartcenter.org

Dedication and Intention

This book is dedicated to easing the pain of life, increasing the acceptance of joy and happiness innately available, and creating the life you were meant to live, The author of this book hopes you will join the evolutionary process of healing not only your life, but also that of your relatives and ancestors that you have inherited through the various timelines in your subconscious. Never before in human history has a time existed where human beings could heal the subconscious mind the way we can now.

Your subconscious mind has produced four symbols—your unwanted feelings, thoughts, behavior, and life circumstances. By decoding those symbols into information understandable by your conscious mind, a basic healing almost always happens. Consequently, revealing the secrets from your inner mind exposes the operating code in your life. Exposing this code and understanding it so that you may change your life is the primary intention and goal of this work.

Acknowledgements

I feel very thankful to my stepparents, Harry Rose and Jan Elliott, who supported me unconditionally in my early years. Without their help this book never would have been written. Rosemary Bell, L.C.S.W., for her help in healing my past, and finally, thank you to all the others who have been there for me over the last sixty years, including the late Dr. George Honiotes and Pat Honiotes and of course Dr. William Jennings Bryan, Jr., M.D.

Most of all, I thank my clients who have volunteered their stories, backgrounds, and the intimate details of their lives, especially those who have had the guts to stick out the long-dark night of the soul, because it was through their courage that contributed to this writing.

Due to the confidential nature of the material, names have been changed and other telltale facts distorted in order to protect clients identities without diluting the basic elements of their cases. In several situations, the third person personal pronoun *he* is used generically.

Author's Notes

My intention is to present an overall description of the hypnoanalytic and subconscious analysis processes, focusing on the underlying subconscious diagnosis which is vastly different from a psychological diagnosis. It is also my intention to present information on subconscious management of external forces that affect one's mental state. For more information on the underdeveloped concepts, research the bibliographic sources cited in the chapter notes.

However, it is important to note that *Secrets* is only one of two books written about The Bryan Method of Medical Hypnoanalysis, and the only one designed for the layperson and prospective client. The other book, *The Handbook of Brief Psychotherapy by Hypnoanalysis,* written by John Scott Sr., describes the process in detail for professionals.

I have made every effort to document my sources, but some quotations (which I especially treasure) are not cited in the chapter notes as I have gleaned them over the years from books, articles, speeches, and seminars, while others I discovered on the internet or in correspondence sent to me and saved but, nevertheless, lost over time.

Preface

The purposes of this book are to share therapeutic techniques to unlock the secrets in our subconscious mind, secrets that cause dysfunction and disruption in our lives as long as those secrets remain buried in our subconscious; to share natural, viable remedies as an alternative to standard medication generally offered to clear up our confounded subconscious minds. The chemical model for easing unhappiness seems based on the idea of the body, mind and spirit as machine—much as when your car breaks down, it needs a new part, an oil change, or tires inflated. Human beings are not human "doings" or machines but are much more complicated.

About the historical and current treatment for mind/body health and imbalances, William Bengsten, Ph.D. says, "I discovered that in most societies, except for ours, the preferred medical model has been holistic. Both tribal and Eastern healers traditionally diagnose disease as an imbalance in a person's mind/body/spirit, or in that person's relationship to his or her society and environment." This man has to his credit many documented cases of curing cancer and proves it in his book, *The Energy Cure*, through the laying of hands on a patient.

Finally, for all those individuals wounded from the consequences of neglect, abuse, trauma, incest, death, sorrow and (as Shakespeare referred to it) "the slings and arrows of outrageous fortune," it is my intention to inspire hope by showing how to unlock the secrets in your subconscious mind, interpret the code and change your life!

On the subject of quick cures: espousing the simple method of only changing one's thinking supplies, at best, limited symptomatic change for some folks. At the worst, this method can cause more suffering and frustration for those who have suffered enough. Many gurus advocate the notion that a simple change in one's thinking will cause one's life to change. I say, "show me the proof" because it's more complicated than that. If the truth were told in quick-fix books, the books wouldn't sell.

M. Scott Peck nailed the notion down in the title of his first book, *The Road Less Travelled.*[1]

This book grew out of my last thirty years in practice and reflects a ripening and maturing of my practice orientation from a strict medical hypnoanalysis model to an approach combining medical hypnoanalysis with two other natural methods of problem solving.

One method I especially appreciate and use regularly is Eye Movement Desensitization Reprocessing (EMDR) due to its compatibility with hypnoanalysis. After training with Francine Shapiro, PhD, during 1994-95, I began using EMDR with my hypnoanalytic clients. To my delight, I discovered, how effectively it helped de-condition extreme negative thoughts and feelings subconsciously associated with childhood trauma. EMDR works by changing the neural network and synaptic connections in the brain to allow new, healthy associations, much like developing a new trail in the forest. The EMDR Institute offers information about the eight-phase treatment method on their web site[2].

The other method I really appreciate is *The Trauma Model* by Dr. Colin Ross.[3] This model has been extremely helpful in redirecting the energy and effects of childhood abuse and trauma. I often combine EMDR and The Trauma Model with the hypnoanalytic secrets method for a more powerful and dramatic conclusion for my clients. With neurofeedback, which I describe later, as a brain back-up method, I use these three methods with my clients to both heal the mind and change the brain. It's powerful and amazing to witness the changes in my clients.

One of the more dramatic influences came from 5,000 miles away in a small town of Abadiania in the State of Goias, Brazil.[4] Meeting and getting to know Joao de Deus (John of God), convinced me that the spiritual world is real. Before meeting Joao, I "only believed in me"(as John Lennon sang). Participating in and witnessing the miracles in Brazil at the Casa de Dom Inacio, encouraged me to change my mind about my own life situation. The outcome was learning—and eventually believing—that we are all spiritual beings having a physical experience and understanding that we become wounded by our vulnerability in a physical environment that is spiritually antagonistic, an environment (namely, this planet earth) on which we are held captive since there's only one way to leave it!

This book also arose because my own life had been anything but calm. I've had just about every symptom myself—anxiety, depression, shame, suicidal thoughts, phobias, crushing guilt, an ulcer, IBS, panic attacks, self sabotage, childhood trauma and functional brain damage. As a teen, I tried to become an alcoholic and drug addict but failed because I couldn't tolerate substances—I would simply pass out. I was kicked out of high school once and finally quit altogether, lost most of my family to alcoholism, have seen two brothers die from drug use, been divorced, bankrupt, arrested (and acquitted) on politically motivated charges. I was beaten up, stalked by an obsessed woman with a hit list, set up as a patsy by a money-hungry couple, audited by the IRS for years until I nearly lost my marbles and subsequently moved to another state.

Besides discovering my own co-dependence and how it operates in relationships, I have worked diligently to overcome these problems. I've had my share of negativity, but you know what? The best revenge is to live a fulfilled life—and I'm living it! Most of the traumatic things happened in my first fifty years and those years are behind me.

Over the next fifty years, I know . . .

The Best Is Yet To Come!

In therapy circles, the concept of "You spot it, you got it" signifies how well a therapist can help his or her clients heal. We can help our clients only what we ourselves have healed. The wounded-healer images in Greek Mythology of Chiron and Asclepius come to mind as well as the mandate "physician heal thyself". I include an overview of my forty-year history with the therapy process and episodes from my own personal growth to inspire hope in others who are searching for answers that can be found. It is my wish that this book will be more accessible to readers so that more people can heal, as I've been healed. Much has been left out because this book is not about me but about how healing is possible.

Introduction

Although the last decade of my life has been peaceful, the first 50 were anything *but*! I grew up in an Irish-Catholic, alcoholic family, the oldest of 6 children. I began checking out treatment as young as age twenty. Realizing something was wrong but not knowing what, surrounded by drugs, alcohol, hippies, the threat of dying in Vietnam, watching the war and mayhem on TV, I knew I wanted something better. My father would have been proud had I died for my country in Vietnam. I was a disappointment to him. He also wanted a son for a drinking buddy and once again I was a disappointment to him. Then there was LSD.

Thank you Timothy Leary

At 21, my friends and I dropped acid (aka LSD), the psychedelic drug most common in the sixty's. And thanks to the insights while tripping, I quit drinking alcohol and coffee, smoking cigarettes, and taking drugs all at once. I can still remember my vision of the black gymnast, dressed in a red suit and swinging on a trapeze, laughing as he discussed the probable life I was going to experience if I kept going the way I was. Also, I want to thank the late Steve Jobs for mentioning his experience with LSD, which reminded me of my own, and gave me the courage to print it.

As a child I never had aspirations to be anything specific when I grew up. It was only as an adult that I discovered that most trauma survivors (of which I was one) just want to get through the day, much less consider having a future. I knew I felt depressed, guilty, ashamed, paranoid, abandoned and I was sure I was a loser. To feel good I tried the common ways to escape but would pass out after experimenting with my alcoholic legacy or the hippie solution most of my peers used. I basically slept away all the "sex, drugs, & rock 'n roll" adventures I heard so much about.

I thank God I couldn't tolerate alcohol (it tastes terrible to me and gives me nausea to boot) or substances (drugs knocked me out cold). My brothers weren't so lucky.

My two years in high school destroyed what little self-esteem I had. I remember one guidance counsellor telling me how there must be some occupation I was suited for, although she couldn't tell me what it might be. I was ill suited for sports—re-enforced by gym coaches constantly reminding me how terrible I was at beating on other kids and how lousy I was at driving myself relentlessly into a frenzy of mindless competition. It just didn't seem like much fun to me, and now I view high school and college sports as pre-paramilitary training.

As I see it, team sports taught boys (and now girls) to honour a military mindset based on the original Olympic games that were intended to keep warriors in shape during brief periods of peace. I found my niche working at a speedometer shop and playing pool, a game at which I excelled, winning my first car before I could legally drive. Later, I decided I needed a college education if I wanted a different life so I enrolled at the College of DuPage (COD), a local community college. Although I assumed I was stupid, I believed I could actually learn something there. After a couple of years at COD, I transferred to Elmhurst College and paid the (expensive) tuition by starting my own import company.

During my time at Elmhurst College, I applied to American Mensa just to see how my IQ rated. Much to my surprise, Mensa allowed me into their organization—I had scored in the upper 1% on the IQ tests. Since I struggled with a self-image of "stupid," I thought there must be some mistake. (Groucho Marx's motto, "I don't care to belong to any club that will have me as a member" was my motto too.) Later, in graduate school while studying IQ, I discovered that I was not an impostor. What an incredible discovery!

As a therapist I discovered the Myers-Briggs Type Indicator and learned my personality preferences scored as an ENFP/INFP—a type shared by only 4% of the population. In the Myers-Briggs classification, 16 personality types are possible. The letters in these types represent four pairs of opposite preferences:

- extroversion vs. introversion,
- intuition vs. sensation,

- feeling vs. thinking, and
- perception vs. judgment.

The dominant personality type—composing about 50% of the population—is E or I at the beginning, ST in the middle and J or P at the end. Society, in general, values the "left brain type" more so than those "right brain" types, which is where my personality type lies. This amazing discovery helped me understand why high school was so difficult and why the sports/military mindset disagreed so strongly with my values. Talk about a round peg in a square hole! Now back to the story . . .

Driving to COD in Glen Ellyn, Illinois, during the late 1960's, I often listened to Stan Dale's radio show, *I'm Ok—You're Ok*. I was fascinated by promises of freeing my inner child and feeling happy, something I knew little about due to my shame and insistence on proving I wasn't a loser. My psychiatrist at the time had given me an ominous diagnosis, leaving me cold and embarrassed, so Stan Dale's ideas appealed to me. I joined his Transaction Analysis Group.

One particular group experience left me sobbing for an hour after it ended. Certain that I had embarrassed myself for no good reason, I left the group mortified. From there I was directed to Reparenting Therapy ala Jacqui Schiff—which I subscribed to one hundred percent—and to which I give much credit for helping me get the life I desired.

During and after graduate school, I continued therapy of various kinds, finding some good and some just OK. However, I still had problems with over-emotionality, impulsivity, and a huge dose of shame, not to mention how difficult it was for me to love anyone, much less myself. My thoughts turned to suicidal ideation, at other times to joy and wonder, yet the help I was in need of seemed unattainable.

Driven by a desire to understand myself, in 1978 at age 30 I entered George Williams College in Downers Grove and graduated 2 years later with a degree in social work and continued my career as a people helper. In 1984, having discovered medical hypnoanalysis that helped me release underlying trauma, I knew I wanted to offer medical hypnoanalysis to others.

After becoming board certified, I continued my work and discovered how colic affected me as a child. However, due to my seemingly intractable impetuousness, I still needed to work on myself.

I spent a week at the Light Institute in New Mexico (the one Shirley MacLaine made famous) reviewing my past lives. I also spent much time in training seminars offered by Dick Sutphen. Eventually it was the help of a special social worker that allowed me to grieve the loss of my childhood, the loss of everyone I loved, the projection of my emptiness on to others—but still therapy missed certain parts of me.

Then in 2008, I finally discovered what was wrong with me. I had three hyperactive areas in my brain, malfunctioning areas that were secondary to an "accident" I sustained as a 5 year old. I had been told that a trunk lid fell on my head. Later I learned my trauma was actually from a car crash. In 1953, I was in the front seat of the car my mother was driving when we hit a tree. I was thrown from the car and ended up on the street unconscious (seat belts hadn't been invented yet). The ER doctors worked valiantly on me but I actually died for a while and then returned. I had survived!

What I've finally come to understand is that when I experienced stress, it would retrigger the feelings connected to that trauma and I would relive the near-death experience over and over again—reacting out of the fear for my life—regardless of the situation or who was involved. Even mild conflicts would create the fight-or-flight syndrome in me—a racing heart and a flood of adrenaline. I could turn on "gorilla mode" in a flash and be ready for a fight that would make any action/adventure director proud.

Regular Neurofeedback treatments helped my situation. Neurofeedback[5] is a biofeedback therapy technique that presents the user with real-time feedback on brainwave activity as measured by sensors on the scalp, typically in the form of a computer screen with sound reinforcing the desired outcome. In my case, lowering high beta frequency in my frontal lobes and increasing alpha frequency in the same areas restored normal function to my brain activity levels. I now sleep better and have the wherewithal to think about my emotions without freezing, fleeing, or fighting first. I have stabilized my moods, lifted my depression and decreased my combativeness. People with whom I have relationships rave about my changes, but not as much as I do.

Siegfried Othmer, Ph.D., one of the founders of EEGInfo.com and who pioneered neurofeedback along with his wife, Sue, explains how traumatic brain injury and emotional trauma affect a person's brain thusly: ". . . Traumatic Brain Injury and emotional trauma both disturb network functional integrity and, if anything, emotional trauma disturbs it more pervasively and more globally." Certainly in my case, Othmer's description applies. Now I offer neurofeeedback to my clients along with EMDR.

Discovering neurofeedback was not an accident: I kept searching for answers for myself, never giving up until I found an answer that worked. My secrets had kept me "in the dark" about my own life and hypnoanalysis unlocked the code that allowed those negative suggestions to surface. Neurofeedback finally helped me diagnose and treat the problem underpinning the problem—namely that my brain couldn't sustain the changes I desired.

During treatments, the memories and feelings associated with the car crash began returning to consciousness, feelings and memories that had not been available to me even under hypnosis. I always felt defective and did my best to overcome those feelings, frequently by over-achieving and going well beyond the norm in most endeavours, hoping that some day I would feel like a winner—sure signs of growing up around alcoholism.

During my 40-year odyssey, I tried just about every form of treatment I could find. Each worked for a while but I still felt like a train wreck. Now, the train has come to the end of the line without crashing and I am able to love both others and myself. I am forgiving the injuries I sustained at the hands of ignorant caretakers and have created meaning for my life that once seemed meaningless, a very important component of healing childhood trauma.

Helping others heal has provided structure to my life. But it's done more than that—from understanding I've gleaned from my subconscious and my higher self, I know that I chose this life in order to experience a challenge, to learn about pain, and to overcome these problems as well as give of myself in the form of hope to others.

I have not yet mentioned my search for the meaning of God. My Catholic indoctrination taught me to pray that someone would come along and love me. I did all the necessary rituals but nothing changed until much later when I discovered reparenting and decided that the "someone to love me" was me! What an amazing discovery! I recommend it.

After having explored different forms of Christianity, and even considering becoming Jewish, I realized that I preferred Neopaganism, a nature-based spiritual orientation, and Spiritualism.

Neopaganism appealed to me because it is a one-law system: *Do what thou wilt, but hurt no one.* The chief characteristic of Spiritualism is the karmic nature of existence in that whatever one does comes back to the doer. To me, life would be more pleasant if we all practiced according to the karmic law—if we, as a culture, believed that our lives would be far better here and now by acting lovingly towards others rather than waiting for the reward of sitting at the right hand of God in the afterlife.

In these complimentary belief systems, I discovered a benevolent, energetic God and a philosophic way to deal with life that works for me. Frequently, modern pagans (i.e. most Eastern Religions, Native American Religions, shamans, and polytheistic religions) are viewed as undesirable or unclaimed by the Abrahamic monotheistic triad of Christianity, Judaism, and Islam. Or, worse, they are simply non-Christian heathens. What a shame! In my experience some very good people who are living according to a philosophical alternative to the Abrahamic theology are shunned. (If the reader requires more information about the beginnings of religion, look to the works of Zecharia Sitchin, "The 12th Planet" and information left for us on the Sumerian Clay Tablets as well as "The Gods of Eden" by William Bramley.)

One of my goals here is to inspire hope and viable remedies in a time when medication (drug therapy) only allows clients to feel a little less miserable. Television spots tell us there's a drug for just about everything. I wouldn't be too surprised if the future of medication holds drugs for loneliness, homelessness, and social isolation. Had I listened to "authority" and taken medication for my problems, I would be as dead as my two brothers. Doomed shortcuts to health and happiness on planet Earth are simply too good to be true. Why else is our planet called Earth rather than Happiness? That said, I have witnessed some clients get help through medication as a temporary measure along with some form of emotional support, therapy and/or spiritual healing.

We *can* walk the road toward wholeness and wellness.

Some Change Occurs by Changing One's Thinking, But Primary Change Occurs by Feeling Changes

In the mental health field, the Cognitive Behavioral Therapy (CBT) faction promotes the idea that change can occur simply by thinking. This idea though overlooks (by omission or commission) the irrefutable fact that emotional power is stronger than mental power and can flood consciousness instantly. Of the 40,000 or so neurons in the heart's nervous system (called sensory neurites) the vast majority of these neurites are afferent and send information from the heart to the head. The minority of these neurites flow in reverse, from the head to the heart. This is why cognitive prescriptions for emotional issues tend to be ineffective and cumbersome.

Emotions connect us to our beliefs and, ultimately, to our memories. The energy stored in our emotions/feelings creates the world we live in and, therefore, change first requires finding, reviewing, and nullifying the first time the negative suggestions and emotions were generated. This is accomplished by thoroughly examining the memory and associated feelings locked in the subconscious mind.

Platonic in its origin, the CBT camp seems to view emotions and thought as separate dimensions of the soul in constant combat for control over the psyche. Christian Theology followed Greek thinking by likening emotions to sin and temptation which are to be overcome by willpower and the voice of reason. Yet, to me, the real truth is that a cooperative balance is more likely to produce the goals we have for living happily.

For example, Daniel Goleman in his book *Emotional Intelligence* makes a case that people with a high degree of self-awareness, motivation, altruism, and compassion indicates an emotional intelligence which allows them to deal with life more successfully. Consequently, a high "EQ" rather than a high IQ gives bearers an edge in life. In keeping with this concept, knowing one's motivation, weaknesses, and strengths gives credence to what Socrates said at his trial: "The unexamined life is not worth living." Karl W. Palachuk, author of *Relax, Focus, Succeed*, a book focusing on workaholism, states it thusly:

> "People who do examine their lives, who think about where they've been, how they got here, and where they're going, are much happier people. No one has all the answers. And no one's life is free from trouble and strife. But those who have some sense of where they belong in the universe also have a context for understanding how all the elements of their life fit together."

This concept is not rocket science—it is intuitively natural. While I do believe a small portion of the population *can* actually change their lives by simply thinking differently, the vast majority of us—especially those who have endured childhood trauma or trauma later in life—need to reveal the secrets created by that trauma, secrets which most often hide in symptoms of anxiety, depression, addictions, etc. Then the negative suggestions associated with that trauma must be removed before their minds can process the emotions and intake the desired positive suggestions and create new outcomes. This is supported by the evidence presented in this book, which evidence is the culmination of case histories and freely given testimonials in my thirty-five years of practice.

I also want to direct the reader's attention to page 6 of *The Science of the Heart* published by the Institute of HeartMath in 2001 which supports the point I am making:

> "The latest neuroscience research confirms emotion and cognition can best be thought of as separate but interacting functions . . . each with its unique intelligence. Our research is showing that the key to successful integration of the mind and emotions lies in increasing the coherence (ordered, harmonious function) in both systems and bringing them into phase with one another."

In simpler words, this means that in order to be a fully functional human being living without symptoms of emotional and intellectual disabilities, the subconscious secrets must be integrated with the conscious mind, not blocked, repressed, or denied.

Switching to Another Idea, Noam Chomsky Says it Well

In addition, please indulge my paraphrasing of a familiar phrase in order to provide additional meaning to this book: "*Happiness cannot exist when the right to be free is not guaranteed.*" I feel deeply about this concept, especially in today's world when events seem so dark. Noam Chomsky remarks,

> "For those who stubbornly seek freedom, there can be no more urgent task than to come to understand the mechanisms and practices of indoctrination. These are easy to perceive in the totalitarian societies, much less so in the system of 'brainwashing under freedom' to which we are subjected and which all too often we serve as willing or unwitting instruments."[6]

Consequently, I believe that our system promotes a social consciousness of "manufactured consent" through media, political correctness, social consciousness, and guilt about the sins of our ancestors. Since I have been a freedom seeker all my life, I tend to resist these notions permeating current social consciousness and hope to plant seeds for your further consideration.

The Many Meanings of Freedom

Freedom from one's limiting beliefs and freedom from one's history are the most important kind of freedoms one can attain. Thus these freedoms top my list of desirable experiences, equal to political liberty. I believe being able to enjoy our liberty is only truly possible when we experience freedom from our historical proscriptions, both personal and societal.

My reasoning for this is simple: if we have not matured beyond dependency on an outside force to take care of us, make life better, protect us from evil, etc., then we remain as vulnerable as children to manipulation, subsequent disappointment, and the continued erosion of the liberty guaranteed by our Bill of Rights.

As an aside, the words *freedom* and *liberty* are used interchangeably these days but have vastly different meanings. Liberty is what God has given us—the right to be free of arbitrary control. Our founding fathers understood this and that's why the phrase "Liberty and Justice for all" is contained in our Pledge of Allegiance. One does not find "Freedom and Justice for all" in the pledge because freedom denotes what governments give their citizens. Once it's given, governments generally have no compunction about taking freedom back.

I desire to help humanity find freedom from their, heretofore unchangeable habits, thoughts, or feelings, and hope to inspire the next step: to find liberty in their lives. Moreover, the concept of taking back one's power sits comfortably in my mind when thinking of both personal freedom and political liberty. Many of us have been living under a power restriction or dysfunction.

Most of us operate from a subconsciously programmed level of inhibiting beliefs (the code or programming which stems from our hidden secrets). These are beliefs that we unknowingly incorporated before we were six years old or younger. Thus, to live the creative life we desire, we must examine and take responsibility for that code or programming and change it. Recovering from our power dysfunction by decoding, unlocking, or deprogramming our mind is what *The Secrets from Your Subconscious Mind* will demonstrate.

Chapter One

Are You in Control of Your Life?

Let us define mental health
as the adjustment of human beings
to the world and to each other
with a maximum of effectiveness and happiness.
Not just efficiency or just contentment
or the grace of obeying the rules of the game cheerfully.
It is all these together.
It is the ability to maintain an even temper,
an alert intelligence,
socially considerate behavior,
and a happy disposition.
This, I think, is a healthy mind.

Dr. Karl A. Menninger

Frequently, people ask me for help in controlling their lives. What people most want to know is how to stop or change unwanted feelings, thoughts, and actions that come up in response to both internal and external conditions in their lives.

My response is usually: Life is a do-it-yourself project. Our thoughts and feelings are the tools with which we construct our lives, and our circumstances are the products of those thoughts and feelings—especially those that have long been forgotten and buried deep in our subconscious minds.

In a sense, our feelings are like children. If we ignore our children, what happens? In a short time, the child becomes upset because adults are needed to survive. In severe cases, neglect equals child abuse. Therefore, it follows that ignoring our feelings can constitute self-abuse. Some people even punish themselves for having feelings!

We must carefully examine and control what we think and pay attention to how we feel because we set ourselves up for what we get. We do, in fact, create reality in our minds. In other words, we get what we expect to get, especially when our expectations originate in fear. Fear creates conditions that shape our "reality" from the very things we are afraid of.

Much of this happens in the mind on the subconscious level, which is the mechanism behind everyday existence. If you think about it, you will discover that everything you believe and emotionally embrace, whether positive or negative, has manifested itself in your life—everything! We create our realities based on how we feel, think, and how we program our minds.

Our subconscious, fear-based programming influences the events in our lives here and now, accepting suggestions and dictating our feelings and behaviors, both wanted and unwanted. This is where the philosophy of personal responsibility comes into play. "Personal responsibility" means accepting that others—parents, society, friends and lovers—are not responsible for your circumstances. Personal responsibility means that the buck stops with you.

One caveat here: this does not mean that shit won't happen because it will. Many things are outside of our control and so discretion must be used when considering and applying these ideas to situations over which you have no control.

Let's get back to the question—how do we take control of our emotions and thoughts? We begin to take control of our emotions and thoughts when we bring into our awareness programming from earlier periods of life, by understanding and reinterpreting that programming, and nullifying it. Once we let go, we free ourselves to be the way we really want to be. We can take control of our personal "do-it-yourself project". We can exert control over our lives.

To develop personal control over your life requires both a commitment and a decision to follow through with whatever action is necessary to achieve your goals. The most important part is the decision to do it. Once that decision is made, the "how" follows almost as if by magic, generated by your subconscious, intuition, and conscious knowledge.

Dan Kennedy[7], who possesses one of the most authoritative marketing minds in the United States, says that the principle of *massive action* is what gets things done and achieves goals more powerfully than any positive mental attitude, affirmation, and thought patterns. His principle states that you must do everything in your power to achieve your goals. I agree. In order to make life work, the principle of massive action must be employed. Dan uses a military battlefield analogy: generals use air strikes, ground forces, psychological operations, the navy, reconnaissance, etc. to win their objectives. Similarly, you must employ massive action to solve whatever is troubling you.

You develop personal power by balancing and directing your creative energy. You can make your life different if you want to because you have the power to bring about the desired changes in yourself and in your environment. You have created what you have now, knowingly or unknowingly. If you don't like it, you can un-create it, then re-create it to make your life come out the way you want.

Uncovering *The Secrets from Your Subconscious Mind* will help you discover why you are where you are and give you a model of how to get where you want to be. Utilizing this process combined with developing your mind power, you can make the necessary changes in your life.

Twenty-One Reasons Why You Need This Book:

1. You have a habit or behavior that is getting the better of you.
2. Your self-esteem isn't what it should be.

3. You have good habits you would like to strengthen.
4. You are depressed, anxious, or fearful.
5. You want to become more competent, confident, and successful in your life.
6. You experience useless or excessive guilt.
7. You want to be more at ease in situations that currently make you uncomfortable.
8. You want to unlock mental powers that you have never used.
9. You are having difficulty discovering who you are.
10. You want to know more about how your past plays out in your present.
11. You are dedicated to connecting with your higher self or God but have been unable to do so.
12. You feel as though a piece of you is missing or is suspended in animation somewhere you can't reach.
13. You're tired of hearing about how chicken soup or some universal law is affecting you.
14. You've read all the self-help books—your shelves are full of them—and yet you are unfulfilled.
15. You've tried NLP, EST, EFT, ESP, HFT, TA, RET, and still your demons taunt you.
16. The wonderful works of Deepak Chopra, Louise Hay, Wayne Dyer, Jack Canfield, and other visionary material hasn't helped you affect the change you want.
17. You've tried drugs, alcohol, prescriptions, Tai Chi, affirmations, bodywork, various spiritual philosophies, yet your basic identity remains unmoved.
18. You've been to churches, read scripture, prayed, sung hymns, asked the saints, spirit guides, and angels for help and yet life still feels the way it always has.
19. You've stretched as far as yoga could stretch you and Paramahansa Yogananda failed. Card readers have said many positive things but your cards seem to still be off the table.
20. You've sought out chiropractic care, macrobiotic diets, fads and fakes, teachings and teachers and you still feel unfulfilled and your goals unrealised.
21. Though you are as frustrated as I was in your struggle for answers to your seemingly intractable problem, you are feeling

as motivated as I was and will never give up until you find the help—and the answers—you need.

If any of the above applies to you, then you must continue reading.

Please understand the comments above are not meant to berate those practices or practitioners for each fulfils many needs. I love much of what the alternative community offers, have used their material and services on numerous occasions, and still do. But for conscious alternatives to work, you first have to have the subconscious room. If the subconscious is blocked, then most procedures will continue to fail until the subconscious negativity, self-punishment, shame, etc., is released.

Although I was only using hypnoanalysis when I was writing the first edition of this book, I have since incorporated several other types of subconscious analysis into my treatment: EMDR techniques, neurofeedback, and different forms of body and energy work along with the help of John of God, who I mentioned in the section on my journey. When a client is committed to moving forward but has a problem that doesn't respond, I will sometimes send a picture of the individual to John of God for spiritual help, usually with good response.

Hypnoanalysis breaks down subconscious programming through the use of hypnosis, which is a natural state of mind. Hypnosis opens the door to the subconscious; analysis then opens a person's understanding to the cause of the problem. The analyst redirects the client's energy toward a solution—hence, the term "hypnoanalysis."

Hypnosis was recognized by the American Medical Association in 1958 as a legitimate approach to solving medical problems.[8] Today, more and more doctors, health professionals and patients accept the idea that the mind and body interact to cause physical illness as well as psychological, emotional, and behavioural problems. Mind, emotions, and body are integrated parts of a whole, and a change in one part affects the other—the circular cause and effect discussion, also known as which-came-first-the chicken-or-egg dilemma.

My answer to the chicken or egg question is that it is both and not one or the other. Here on planet Earth, pain is part of the deal. Feelings of pain, sadness, fear, etc. are inseparable from joy, happiness, wonder, lust, love, etc. As the old song says, love and marriage go together like a horse and carriage. And so, too, pain and suffering go together with joy and happiness.

Our human condition dictates that we suffer—life on planet earth is not hospitable to humans. Cockroaches have a much better chance of survival on this planet. With food and shelter plentiful, cockroaches thrive. I am amazed humans have lasted this long. Due to our brain size, we have overcome many of our limitations—except for the problems associated with living as humans. Most mental and emotional problems arise out of attempting to escape the pain and suffering inherent in the human condition.

How Changing Energy Vibrations Are Affecting You

Those conditions of attempting to escape the pain and suffering inherent in the human condition seem to be escalating and accelerating on planet Earth due to changing energy vibrations. Science has determined that all matter vibrates, though the vibrations are at different speeds. You vibrate, I vibrate, the earth's cavity vibrated (the latter at a rate of 7.8 cycles/second or Hz). The vibration rate of the earth's cavity, the Schumann Resonance, is named for physicist Winfried Otto Schumann who mathematically predicted this global electromagnetic resonance phenomenon in 1952.

The Schumann Resonance occurs because the space between the surface of the Earth and the conductive ionosphere acts as a wave-guide. (It has increased to 11 Hz. or so in the past few decades—which has allowed more subconscious material to become conscious in human beings.)[9]

In contrast to its vibratory increase, the Earth's magnetic field is decreasing due to the gradual slowing of the planet's rotation. In the last twenty-five years, 22 "leap seconds" have occurred—meaning we have lost a second almost every year. The International Atomic Clock that is the official timekeeper has adjusted the "official" clock to accommodate this decrease. Twenty-two seconds doesn't sound like much, but in terms of astronomical time over thousands of years, it adds up to a lot of lost time.

But wait—there's more! A study published in April 2008 in the *New Scientist* indicates a direct connection between the Sun's solar storms and human biological effect.

"The most plausible explanation for the association between geomagnetic activity and depression and suicide is that geomagnetic storms can desynchronise circadian rhythms and melatonin production," says Kelly Posner, a psychiatrist at Columbia University.

Even NASA recently produced a report stating that the solar radiation hitting the Earth is now over 200% greater than it was a hundred years ago!

Wow! All this stuff is happening, but what does it mean for you and me? Here's what Mr. Gregg Braden, author of *Awakening To Zero Point* says: "The consequence is that the subconscious mind is becoming closer to consciousness. In terms of brain wave frequency, the boundary between conscious and subconscious was very close to 7.8 Hz."[10] In other words, the vibration speeds of both the conscious and subconscious are now almost identical. Further, our conscious and subconscious is now vibrating at speeds closer to the earth's cavity.

I believe we are all being affected by these planetary changes. At this point, you are probably asking . . .

How Do Changing Vibration Speeds Affect Me?

A friend of mine living in Croatia sent me an article about the symptoms of **ascension**. (In this discussion, I am not referring to the Christian belief of Christ's Ascension; I am referring to the general concept of ascension.) Ascension is the belief that as our solar system moves through the universe, it encounters increasing amounts of gamma wave. In the electromagnetic spectrum, gamma waves are the energy possessing the shortest wavelength and the highest frequency. The gamma waves are affecting not only the Earth and planets in our solar system, but are affecting all inhabitants as well.

The symptoms of ascension include depression, disorientation, dissociation, forgetfulness, fear, cognitive dissonance, feeling out of place and out of time, unusually stressed out, weight gain, wild dreams, friends leaving, the Law of Attraction magnified in your life, and the sense that time is speeding up. Sound familiar?

These are symptoms commonly associated with mental illness and other diseases. (For more information about what's happening in our solar system, please search the works of David Wilcock, David

Icke, and SheldonNidle). And, as Gregg Braden and others assert, the subconscious is becoming conscious. In other words . . .

Reality Is Becoming a Dream and Our Dreams Are Becoming Reality

Barbara Marciniak and The Pleiadians effectively sum up what's happing on Earth:

> "The spiritual awakening that is unfolding on Earth is well under way in birthing a new type of consciousness . . . on psychic-spiritual levels of reality, a collective initiation is occurring that is testing everyone's spiritual resolve . . . the process of the initiation involves cleansing and purging the use of fear as a means for managing life . . . *The signature of the times is that all repressed energies will surface for a healing.*"[10]

The signature of the times shows symptomatically as an increase in personal problems, alcoholism, cancer, drug addiction, and the host of other dysfunctional solutions for killing pain. Pain, sadness, fear, emptiness, anger are among the repressed energies surfacing for healing. If these emotions are blocked, then dysfunctional solutions manifest.

Very often, blocks to our emotional and spiritual energy interfere with our ability to live life creatively. Once these negative suggestions, ideas, or blocks are nullified, then life beyond mediocrity can be achieved. Dr. Walter Russell says it this way:

> "Successful men of all the ages have learned to multiply themselves by gathering thought energy into a high potential and using it in the direction of the purpose intended. Every successful man or great genius has three particular qualities in common.
>
> *"The most conspicuous of these is that they all produce a prodigious amount of work. The second is that they never know fatigue, and the third is that their minds grow more brilliant as they grow older, instead of less brilliant.*

> "Great men's lives begin at forty, where the mediocre man's life ends. The genius remains an ever-flowing fountain of creative achievement until the very last breath he draws.
>
> "The geniuses have learned how to gather *thought energy* together to use for transforming their conceptions into material forms. The thinking of creative and successful men is never exerted in any direction other than that intended.
>
> "That is why great men produce a prodigious amount of work, seemingly without effort and fatigue. The amount of work such men leave to posterity is amazing. When one considers such men of our times As Thomas Edison, Henry Ford, or Theodore Roosevelt, one will find the three characteristics I have mentioned common to every one of them."[11]

This description is one of my favorites. I believe everyone should aspire to greatness and greatness should be the model for children to emulate. Aim for the stars; if you miss the stars, you'll still hit the moon.

Aspiring to mediocrity is the theme song of failure. Henry Ford went bankrupt multiple times before his Ford Motor Company began rolling. Author J.K. Rowling was an unemployed single mother before writing the Harry Potter series. Michael Jordan was cut from his high school basketball team the first time he tried out. They failed at first, but because they did not succumb to mediocrity and aimed for the stars instead, they ultimately succeeded. Maybe you are not interested in being J.K. or MJ or having a car named after you, but your goals are just as important and can be reached. There is help for you and a way to reach your goals.

If you've tried other methods and failed, more options exist than giving up.—I encourage you to still shoot for the stars. Many methods exist to help the seeker and hypnoanalysis is one. Hypnoanalysis provides a comfortable, reassuring way to help you change your beliefs about yourself, about the people you relate to, and about the world. It is evolution in process. Through hypnosis, we concentrate our minds and affect our realities. It is a circular cycle—by affecting our minds and by changing ourselves, we can change our evolution.

In my opinion, hypnosis is one of the best tools to accomplish personal understanding and change—virtually a pen with which you can write a new life plan.

Using hypnosis to harness your mind power, you can raise yourself out of poverty, unhappiness, misery, alcoholism, sexual problems, and drug addiction. You can quit smoking; lose weight, and overcome fears and phobias. It is possible not only to overcome maladies such as depression and anxiety disorders, but to also balance your mind and body chakra system, simply by learning the ancient method of relaxation.

But . . .

The Real Power and Beauty of the Method

is that *it trains your subconscious mind that is working against you to instead work for you* by producing conscious awareness of the negative suggestions causing your troubles. And once your subconscious works *for* you, we can solve emotional and psychological problems by going after the underlying causes.

It is, however, a process of analyzing the subconscious, reaching into the subconscious mind, pulling out negative suggestions that have lodged there, nullifying them, and replacing them with positive suggestions. Memories are not readily available to waking consciousness and the hypnotic state creates an inroad to the subconscious.

Because it is a process, doing it on your own may not achieve the desired outcome. That's where a qualified professional hypnoanalyst can help. And although hypnoanalysis is neither magic nor snake oil, it is a powerful method for improving the human condition and still requires work, mostly on the part of the hypnoanalyst who is trained in the process.

Remember the subconscious automatically remembers events from early periods of our lives—memories that affect who we are, what we do, what we think, and what we feel today.

Bruce Lipton, author of *The Biology of Belief*[2], states that EEG (electroencephalography) activity in children six years of age and younger operate in the Alpha, Theta, and Delta range of cycles per second. In these ranges, then, children are <u>always</u> in a hypnotic state. Consequently, children under 6 have been receiving hypnotic suggestions, both positive and negative in nature. That means that by the time we were six, each of us had already decided answers to the following three questions

1) Who am I?
2) Who are all those others?
3) What am I doing here?

The problem is that when we were six years old, we lacked the proper information to decide such important existential questions. A professional hypnoanalyst can help you to recall and review these suggestions, memories, and decisions that you might not be able to recall on your own. It is important to remember that subconscious memories are not readily available to waking consciousness. The hypnotic state creates an inroad to the subconscious.

Recognition vs. Removal

"Isn't it enough to know where the problem came from to stop it from bothering me?" asked a seminar attendee. My answer is "Yes and no."

Recognizing the underlying cause of a problem, attitude or feeling may be all that is needed to erase its power over us. However, the simple understanding of <u>*why*</u> you eat too much, why we smoke, why we are afraid of heights, may not be adequate to eliminate your more intense problems, feelings or behaviors. It is comparable to breaking your ankle after tripping over an obstacle, then expecting to get up and walk on the broken ankle. Yes, it can be done, but it does nothing to heal your ankle.

Problems such as alcoholism, addictions, childhood trauma, depressive states, personality disorders, mind control, and sexual abuse symptoms require more than recognition. In such cases, hypnoanalysis can be helpful. When you are in a hypnotic state, you are more receptive to change and to a therapist's positive suggestions to reprogram our thinking. Moreover, treatment of severe and diagnosable conditions may take some time to resolve. Sometimes, such conditions need prescribed medication for short-term relief.

Healing the mind, emotional body and spirit takes time, patience, and—most of all—love. My practice philosophy is that if I do not really care for a client, I will not accept him or her as a client and offer referrals to other therapists. This, in part, reflects my belief in the Pygmalion Effect[13] that states that students or clients do better when they are expected to do better by people in power positions for whom they have respect. Because I truly want my clients to do better, then I must care about them to generate the most positive expectations.

Therapy is phenomenological, not static, and difficult to quantify. The difference between a hero and heroism is that even though we know that heroism exists, we cannot see it. In that respect, heroism is a phenomenon similar to the process of therapy. Something happens between client and therapist that cannot be completely quantified, measured, or even seen except by the experience of the client; but its results are felt and observed. When people are in pain and anguish, confiding in a trusted observer lessens that pain and is a necessary ingredient of the therapy phenomenon to succeed.

At a seminar years ago, I heard Jean Houston discuss the origin of the word "therapy" as being derived from the Greek word *therapeia*, which means, literally, "the work of the gods." Doing the work of the gods is not the same as being a god—living up to godhood is very difficult, indeed. In my opinion, though, the work of the gods includes helping people change by providing a loving environment, one that creates conditions for the inner mind to recalibrate, through the deliberate use of one's self—a formidable, but hugely rewarding task!

Ofer Zur, Ph.D., an acquaintance of mine who taught at the California School of Professional Psychology at the time I was writing *Wide Awake*, states that effectiveness of treatment resides in the relationship between client and therapist. In his own words,

> "Research that has examined 'common factors' in effective therapy across orientations, therapists, and patients may be more illuminating. These 'common factors' are ingredients in all effective therapy. The

most critical of these factors is the presence of a positive therapeutic alliance between therapist and patient. This alliance includes warmth, mutual understanding, trust, and respect.

"What disparate therapists such as Freud, Jung, Kohut, Ellis, Rogers, Perls, and Haley have in common is obviously not their theoretical orientation or any specific intervention. To complement their knowledge and expertise they allow the power of personality and their passion to guide them in their relationships and interventions with their patients. They did not use techniques or interventions as if they were tools drawn mechanically from a toolbox. What they drew upon flowed flawlessly from their relationship with their patients in a way that was congruent with their individual personalities and styles. In this light, therapeutic skills are seen as not merely tools, but part of the therapist's essential being."

In accordance with Zur's beliefs, my work is based on the belief that effective hypnoanalysis must proceed with a trained therapist using gentle suggestion to help remove limiting beliefs and thereby allowing constructive, positive, life-affirming ideas to form naturally. Whatever therapeutic goal is decided upon is self-directed by the client with the therapist acting as a guide. Through the following steps, a hypnoanalyst guides the client in uncovering the origin of a problem, undoing the subconscious negative feeling and corresponding beliefs, and freeing the person to live a healthier, more productive life.

1. **Relaxation**

By learning to relax and let your mind go, you can concentrate on and allow an opening to your subconscious. The next step then becomes possible.

2. Realization

Difficulties stem from negative suggestions to your thinking and feeling. In this step, you recognize the source and understand how mindless programming has had power over you so that in the next step, you can learn to restructure those problem attitudes and create the outlook you desire.

3. Re-education

Re-education helps you recognize the difference between the underlying cause arising from the past and the conscious problem and belief you have in the present. When the underlying cause is part of your past, it can be removed by direct suggestion—and by realizing the past is past and that the behaviors you needed in dealing with the problem have passed, too.

4. Rehabilitation

Through hypnoanalysis, you will receive new information and positive suggestions, will work on correcting mindlessness, and work on rehabilitating your thinking and practice your new thought patterns.

5. Reassurance

You will gain reassurance that you are on the right track through a number of avenues. Family or friends may indicate that you're getting better or you may experience a decrease in symptoms. Your analyst should take advantage of reminding you of your improvement, no matter how slight.

6. Repetition

Repetition is necessary to implant positive suggestions in the fertile soil of your subconscious. The more you repeat something, the more permanently implanted it becomes in your mind.

7. Reinforcement

By developing your skill in self-hypnosis, you will be able to support the positive suggestions you've received from the analyst, enabling you to continue the growth begun in the office.

8. Responsibility

Once the first seven steps have been accomplished, accepting personal responsibility for your life is the natural outcome. And did I mention happiness? From accepting personal responsibility, self-confidence and a sense of accomplishment will bloom.

This approach to problem solving owes a debt to Freud, Mesmer, Erickson, and mainly to Dr. William Jennings Bryan, Jr. Their concepts have been validated by the clinical observations of other researchers.

You can make this simple exercise of reading this book into a transformational experience. This book will . . .

1. Acquaint you with the process of hypnoanalysis and provide instructions for inducing yourself into a self-hypnotic state.
2. Show you how to program your mind for improved, increased performance.
3. Challenge you to take control of your circumstances and create change in as little as 30 days.
4. *The Secrets from Your Subconscious Mind* will show you how to make things happen for you instead of just watching them happen to others. While some problems will require aid from a qualified hypnoanalyst, you can effect many changes in your life through the practice of hypnotic self-suggestion offered in this book. As you learn more about the power of your subconscious mind, you will see and feel how suggestion and self-hypnosis can improve the quality of your life, both physically and emotionally.

It' is up to you, just as your entire life is up to you—this is a do-it-yourself project. Remember, you are in control. Or are you?

If you are not in control of your life, then now is the time to take control.

Chapter Two

The First Step to Discovering Your Secrets: *Understanding Your Subconscious*

The
Purpose
of life
after all,
is to live it,
to taste the experience
to the utmost, to reach out
eagerly and without fear for
newer and richer experiences

Eleanor Roosevelt

You Are a One and Only—and the Master Copy

Have you wondered what makes you "you?" Wondered why you like or dislike certain foods, music, films, TV shows, books, political ideas, or people? Why you behave in certain way in one situation and in an opposite way in another situation? Think the thoughts you think one day and other thoughts another day? Why specific holidays trigger certain feelings?

On a larger level, have you contemplated why you are here and what you are doing with your life? What about other people in your life—how do they figure in? Do you feel free or somehow programmed to be, think, or feel a certain way? Throughout this book, I intend to show you how others have discovered answers to those questions and how you might do the same. This discovery starts with understanding your subconscious mind.

As a fetus, you came into existence without any conscious awareness of yourself. Not yet having a developed conscious mind, your subconscious mind immediately began absorbing, collecting, and inputting data. Notwithstanding genetic considerations, you were similar to other fetuses in your ability to perceive and respond to your reality while still in the womb. As a fetus, your subconscious began downloading information from the moment of conception.

Then, at the moment of birth, you experienced two immediate fears: the fear of falling and the fear of loud noises. You were also born with physical needs: the need for warmth, food, hunger, stimulation, and nurturing. Along with your subconscious programming from the womb, life was either peaceful and pleasant, or stressful and anxious or, more likely, some mixture of the two.

Once you emerged from the birth experience, change began to happen rapidly. The first nine months of your life began with a unique, individual journey. Your mind started recognizing and retaining memories of your varied experiences. From infancy through the present, your mind's "slate" has filled with thoughts, feelings, beliefs, and memories, one day after another. More importantly, before the age of 6 when your mind is nearly always in the hypnotic state, input is much more powerful than input received after the conscious mind develops.

By now, you've accumulated tens of thousands of yesterdays and a wealth of knowledge to apply to your future. Those cumulative experiences are what make you a unique person. You are a one and only—and the master copy!

While people in a given peer group might share similar experiences, no two people in the world have perceived their pasts identically, even individuals sharing the same developmental experience. Twins for example, often walk away with different perceptions. Three witnesses to an automobile accident might sound as if they were describing three totally different events. The reality of the accident does not change, but reality is perceived differently by each of the three witnesses.

The oft told story of five blind men describing an elephant is an apt example. The first blind man held the elephant's trunk and declared the animal to resemble a hose. The second blind man held its tail and insisted that an elephant was really like a rope. The third touched the leg and concluded that the animal was like a tree. The fourth touched an ear and believed that the creature amazingly resembled a huge leaf. The fifth, touching the massive side, concluded that his companions were all wrong: An elephant, obviously, was like a wall. None of them changed the reality that stood before them but each perceived the reality from a different perspective based on his own limited experience.

Because each person's perception of reality is different, reality can be likened to a trance (daydream, reverie, fog, fantasy, illusion, nightmare) of sorts. And, as such, many of the experiences and beliefs about who you are, who all those others are, and what you are doing here have been implanted in your mind, whether you are consciously aware of it or not. And in our six-year-old mind, reality was already formed—not by our own volition—but by parents, caretakers, teachers, the popular culture, religion, social consciousness, government propaganda and all the other outside influences as well as what we decide about what happens to us.

Consequently, your trance—your perception of reality—has, to a large extent, been determined by others and may, or may not be, to your liking. If your life is not working the way you desire, it may due to faulty ideas and beliefs formed as a child when you were literally in trance 24/7, which faulty ideas and beliefs have been reinforced by feedback from reality, which then confirms your mindset. Therefore the basis of change begins with examining how you became the "who" you are and that starts with understanding your subconscious mind.

> *The intuitive mind is a sacred gift and the rational mind is a faithful servant. We have created a society that honors the servant and has forgotten the gift.*
>
> —Albert Einstein, 1929

The Workings of the Subconscious Mind

Since you are the product of your experiences, your past plays a strong part in determining how you perceive life. Your subconscious mind is the storehouse of all your experiences recording every hurt and trauma you experienced, even while the conscious mind forgets. Your subconscious mind is a warehouse of memories and lessons that you automatically apply to the present and future. Even more important than the memories you have accumulated is the *power of the subconscious mind* in which they are stored.

Although the subconscious is subservient to the conscious mind (whether or not one consciously decides to make it so), it is much more than a storage container for memories. The subconscious also controls your central nervous system, which controls the operation of your body's involuntary functions. Often called the irrational or reactive mind, it is what keeps you alive. Without your subconscious at work behind the scenes, your heart, lungs, kidneys, and other vital organs would not function.

The subconscious can also lure the body into unhealthy coping actions. Most people's lives are run by programs stored in their subconscious mind. Unless the programs are changed, people inevitably sabotage themselves with their restricting programs. Since the conscious and subconscious operate outside of one another (meaning one doesn't observe the other), the obstructive and destructive programs of the subconscious are free to do what they do best, namely, to stop you from living the life you desire.

Frank, a 50-year-old, two-pack-a-day smoker, started puffing as a teenager because it was "cool" at the time. Now, of course, he's hooked. His nicotine addiction is a physical reality, but there's something else that makes cigarettes so hard to give up. Every time he lights up, Frank's subconscious still tells him he looks like James Dean—that cool, idealized image he tried to live up to as a teenager. Because he lacked the support and feedback from his family when he was a teenager, he instead sought affirmation from popular culture, which included smoking. But the smoking "solution" only partly solved Frank's self-esteem problem. It was a temporary fix. The old memory buried in his subconscious kept playing over and over again, causing him to light up one cigarette after another. Once the archaic "solution" became a problem and he felt his health was at risk, Frank came for help. Smoking is frequently a substitute for other unmet needs. Smoking is described in greater depth in Chapter 7.

The subconscious also is responsible for how we experience life through our five senses as well as our intuition. We see, hear, taste, touch, smell and perceive. We may, or may not, enjoy our experiences, which experiences trigger our emotional subconscious reactions.

The subconscious includes a third, lesser known level of awareness. According to Swami Kriyanada:

> "There is a third, less well-known state of awareness: the superconscious. The hidden mechanism at work behind intuition, spiritual and physical healing, successful problem solving, and finding deep, lasting joy, super-conscious awareness is the missed link to living richer, more meaningful lives. Though many of us have experienced fleeting moments of raised consciousness and enlightenment, few know how to purposely enter such an exalted state." [14]

The superconscious is commonly referred to as the connection with the mind of God. It is also referred to as residing in the right side of the brain. Although not conclusively located in the right hemisphere of the brain, the superconscious is responsible for our creativity. All literary and musical compositions, inventions, and original ideas are the outputs of the creative part of the subconscious mind: namely, the superconscious. Albert Einstein, Nicola Tesla, and Wolfgang Amadeus Mozart[15] all described how their genius appeared to them as a force of non-ordinary reality.

The same is true for intuition. When an incident occurs that you sensed beforehand, your extrasensory perception (ESP)—that is to say, your superconscious right hemisphere through the subconscious—has been at work.

Does this mean that the subconscious has magical powers? Yes and no, depending upon how you define "magical." The subconscious does have a lot of power—more power than most people can even imagine.

Creativity, intuition, and imagination are functions of the subconscious mind which produce your physical reality. The reality it produces depends upon the information stored in your subconscious (or consciously programmed by you). When your intuition leads you to predict someone's next move, it is because your subconscious mind reviewed its knowledge of that individual and alerted you of the anticipated action.

When you use your imagination, you are creating a thought based on your knowledge of similar settings. For example, even if you've never been to the Adirondack Mountains, you still could develop a mental picture of what they may look like, based on your experience with other mountains. Whether your mental image really looks like the Adirondacks is not important here. Right or wrong, your imagination—in your subconscious—still creates a visual image. Albert Einstein is credited with saying, "*Imagination is more powerful than knowledge.*"

With 90 percent of your mind devoted to the subconscious, imagine how much information you can store in it! Some experts believe that the average human being has enough brainpower to master some 40 foreign languages, commit a complete set of encyclopedias to memory, and even complete full-course requirements from a dozen universities. This is because the average brain, which weighs just under four pounds, is able to house up to two quintillion bits of information. Numerically, that is 2,000,000,000,000,000,000. To put that number in perspective, it would take McDonald's at its current rate another 875 million years to sell that many hamburgers—give or take a few centuries, of course.

According to Bruce Lipton, Ph.D., the *subconscious mind is one million times more powerful than our conscious mind* as an informational processing machine. It can process and digest *forty million bits of data per second*—warp speed compared to the poor conscious mind turtle-like processing of forty bits of data per second. And *you* have the ability to tap into that power.

How the Conscious Mind Works With the Subconscious

Generally, before anything can be stored in your subconscious mind, (however there are exceptions when the conscious mind is basically turned off) it must first pass the objective or conscious mind. The conscious mind, which deals with the physical world, is logical, mathematical, and orderly. Because the conscious mind filters information to the subconscious, everything you've ever learned or experienced consciously is stored in your subconscious mind. Since 90 percent of the brain is devoted to the subconscious mind, only 10 percent is involved with conscious thought.

One can't help but develop an appreciation for the power of the subconscious. The conscious mind is analytical by nature and controls conscious activities such as thinking, speaking, writing, arithmetic, planning, organizing, judgment, and reading. The conscious mind, through imagination, is often called the gateway to the subconscious because only the conscious mind can access information stored in the subconscious and bridge the gap between reality and the subconscious mind. You are using your conscious mind right now to read the words on this page. When you recall this information tomorrow, it will be because your conscious mind has retrieved it from your subconscious storage department, commonly called memory.

Because the conscious mind can retrieve information from the subconscious, we can function as productive human beings. Even though reading requires conscious activity, the knowledge of vowel sounds, phonetics, and word definitions stored in your subconscious allows you to read without consciously thinking about it. The same applies to mathematics. It requires conscious ability, for instance, to multiply 365 by 4. If you've committed multiplication tables to memory (your subconscious) you remember that 5 times 4 equals 20, 6 times 4 equals 24, and 3 times 4 equals 12. After adding and carrying the appropriate figures, your conscious mind calculates the answer: 1,460.

Almost everything we do involves cooperation between our conscious and subconscious minds. Although the subconscious is receptive to suggestion, in general nothing goes into the subconscious against the will or evaluation of the conscious mind. However, a couple exceptions exist: emotions generated by trauma or joy, and informal hypnosis. Your subconscious cannot make comparisons or judgments. It does not reason through information or determine truth, but simply reacts to impressions transmitted to it from the conscious mind.

The formula or instructions for any action you execute repeatedly become fixed in your subconscious, and the information becomes available upon conscious command. Routine actions from tying your shoelaces to operating a motor vehicle become second nature through the power of the subconscious. Second-nature operations include typing on a keyboard, computer protocols, riding a bicycle, or any other activity in which you regularly engage. If you can recall things you learned in grade school, it is because the conscious mind has retrieved it from the subconscious. Here are a few examples of how a subconscious becomes programmed.

Did you know that every time you watch TV, you go into a hypnotic trance? Advertisers depend on it. The advertising industry implants its messages in your subconscious mind through repetition. This is why you can remember popular commercials years after the media have stopped running them. (Winston tastes good like a cigarette should! Timex takes a licking and keeps on ticking, etc.)

Television should be considered "Tell A Vision" because it is basically a mind-control machine. Television presents a version of reality that the networks want disseminated to the viewing public. For example: as I write this page, there is a global economic downturn. What if no one watched TV, preferring instead to listen to nature? Would the general public have the same emotional response to the downturn? Along those same thought lines: what if the government declared war and nobody showed up because they did not watch TV? This topic requires much discussion, but, I'm sure you get my point—that people are hypnotized daily by the "tube" and have no fear of turning it on.

Push the Right Button, Activate the Right Association and Out Comes the Information

Why do you sometimes have trouble recalling something? For example, in your conscious mind you have a clear picture of the face of a former schoolteacher, even though you can't recall the teacher's name. Or sometimes you can remember the first two lines of a poem or a song, but you can't remember the rest. Does that mean that the information is no longer stored? No. Considering the almost limitless storage capacity of your subconscious mind, it's highly unlikely it will ever be filled to capacity.

Similarly, the information about your past may not be readily available, because the conscious mind does not have the proper stimulus to retrieve it. For example, the name of the instructor might come to you instantly if someone gave you the initials. Or you might remember the rest of the poem if someone gave you the first word or two of the forgotten portion. No information in your subconscious is ever "forgotten"—it is simply obscured deep in your subconscious and just needs a "hint," a priming, to bring it back into the conscious mind. When you push the right button, the association is activated and your conscious mind remembers the information.

In contrast, there are experiences you can easily remember happy and sad, pleasant and miserable, that never seem to fade. That is because information of high emotional impact is instantly and firmly committed to your subconscious mind.

However, emotionally troubling memories or information can be, and often are, blocked from consciousness due to its painful nature. Basically, two motivations exist to block memories: one is spurred by a pain-avoidance imperative and the other motivates you towards the pleasure principle. Escaping pain is one of the primary culprits when it comes to understanding undesirable thoughts, feelings, and behaviors.

Cravings and the Subconscious Mind

Adults who crave sweets usually acquired the craving as a child. Without self-discipline, such a craving can lead to a weight problem. An obese person might consciously decide to avoid sugar whenever possible. After years of feeding the craving, though, the subconscious may be hooked. Cutting out sweets isn't easy any more.

This is similar to what happens when a person starts smoking, except that nearly all smokers will tell you that cigarettes tasted terrible at first. Still, new smokers consciously light up (for reasons that we'll discuss in detail in Chapter Seven). In time, the cigarettes begin to taste good until one day they are too good to give up. Even without considering the twenty minute half life that nicotine is in the blood, the subconscious is hooked.

Many of my clients who wanted to give up sweets or cigarettes came to me when they believed that they couldn't win the battle without professional help. Although they had consciously decided to kick their psychological—if not physical—addictions, they found that their subconscious minds put up a tough battle. Once your subconscious mind establishes a bit of information as a "truth"—that sugar or cigarettes are good, for example—there is often hell to pay if you try to change that truth.

The psychological torture, referred to as "cold turkey", that the subconscious inflicts can be too much for the conscious mind to bear. Many would-be sugar or nicotine quitters eventually cave in and indulge themselves with a vengeance. While they consciously realize the undesirable consequences of resuming their habits, that realization makes no difference to the subconscious, mainly because the pain-killing ability of the addiction is too tempting. Only a dose of what it is accustomed to receiving can satisfy it.

When the conscious and the subconscious minds are in conflict, the conscious mind will almost always lose the battle. In the next passage Susan illustrates the personal trauma she experienced in her attempt to lose weight.

Sweets Were Her Fix

"Dear God . . . PLEASE make this the last time," I thought, as I drove to the local bakery. I was already stuffed from a full lunch at a nearby restaurant. But being stuffed was irrelevant. I wanted more. I knew a few sweet rolls would go down real well and I'd still be on time for my 3 P.M. appointment with Ryan Elliott.

I was desperately hoping the yo-yo cycles would end, but I was VERY skeptical. How could Ryan help me do what I had been unable to do since the age of 7?

But I had made up my mind that this was to be the last binge. I bought two doughnuts, two cream horns and one petit-four pastry and zoomed back to the car. I headed toward Winfield, shoving the 'illegal' goodies into my mouth, watching crumbs flying everywhere as I ate.

What an awful trip. Sweets were my fix. For me the 'drug of choice' was Hostess Suzy-Qs and anything from the bakery. Compulsive eating—or compulsive binging—had become a way of life. I wanted OUT.

Why couldn't I be normal, eat normally and control my weight like the rest of the world? I was plenty miserable by the time I pulled into the parking lot and entered the office.

I'd tried therapy before. "What would make this time different?" I wondered, as I was escorted to a small consultation room.

His secretary took some pretty mundane information, which she wrote on my file folder, and told me to wait for Ryan. Several minutes elapsed and I really wondered, "What am I doing here?" I had a real uneasy feeling. "Maybe I'm coming down from my sugar high. I'm an invincible person. I can stand anything . . . even this." I was already frightened at the thought of admitting I was out of control and as `superwoman' I couldn't solve my own eating problem.

Ryan began to take my case history, probing all sorts of areas that I, quite frankly, would rather not have talked about. He asked about my childhood, my parents (both deceased), siblings (none), and my sex life.

What sex life? People who are fat and ugly don't have sex lives. He should know better.

Finally, he explained that the program would take 30 sessions, twice a week for 15 weeks. He strongly recommended an up-front payment so when the 'going got rough' I'd have a financial investment and would continue the program. I made a mental note that I'd have absolutely no problem. I'm strong. I'm invincible. He wouldn't get to me—others, yes—me, no.

The first hypnosis treatment followed.

Blindfolded, headset in place, vibrating chair turned on. I was ready. That first session was an introduction to hypnosis and how to do self-hypnosis to support the office treatments.

I made two appointments for the coming week before leaving.

I wanted to succeed more than anything. And, I was MOTIVATED. I stayed on a very reasonable eating plan and dropped two pounds by my next visit.

Then came the visit that was to change my life.

It was Friday. Time for the word-association test. I was hypnotized as usual. By now, the blindfold, headset, and vibrating easy chair were becoming routine. Then, oh! Oh! The chair stopped its normal vibrating and there was an awful silence. And, I heard Ryan's voice.

Simultaneously, my stomach tightened and I had a sickening feeling. "Oh, no! This guy is going to get to know the real me."

I can't describe how terrifying the thought of full self-disclosure was. Ryan gave me a word and I was to respond with the first word or thought that came to mind. And, oh, the words! I was mortified at my responses.

I left the office thinking, "I NEVER want to come back."

"Awkward," "embarrassed," "horrified" only hint at the way I felt. My depression grew with every passing hour. I drove home. Had dinner. Went to bed. I was even more depressed when I awoke. I struggled to get out of bed. "If I go to my exercise class, I'll feel better," I thought. My body was sluggish. I didn't want to exercise. I didn't want to eat. I didn't want to do ANYTHING. The feeling in my gut was awful—a feeling I'd never experienced before.

This had to be a severe case of depression: I certainly had all the symptoms. I sat on the stairs by the phone and stared into space for an hour.

Two voices were fighting in my head: Superwoman kept saying, "This is ridiculous. You can control any situation. Get hold of yourself."

The other voice said, "You feel awful. You need reassurance. Call Ryan."

I picked up the phone. And put it back. The pattern repeated for several minutes.

Finally, I realized that I was not Superwoman that I very, very much needed someone, and that someone was Ryan. He was the only person who would know what was going on in my head and heart.

Finally, I made probably the most significant phone call of my life. Being Superwoman is an awesome responsibility to carry all the time. It was wonderful to have someone be there and take the burden.

Ryan assured me I wasn't crazy and the depression would go away. He asked what I was feeling. I'd just begun to learn what it was to FEEL anything.

At that moment, I realized that I ate to hide from the world and from my own feelings. Food was my only friend. I used food to escape from life and to keep people and experiences out.

When the overeating was removed from my life, I began to experience emotions and feelings—like other people experience every day.

Suddenly, it occurred to me that if I could feel depression, I could also feel joy—a delightful thought to consider.

Ryan got through the wall of fat and emotion. At times the process was painful, but it was a necessary part of making me well. Although the therapy was not always pleasant, the benefits were a thousand fold better than the pain, so I continued with the treatment, gaining insights into my reasons for eating. Negative suggestions, which contributed, to my desire to overeat were removed through hypnosis. I ate reasonable-to-small quantities of food, and, surprise, I was FULL!!!

Through hypnosis, Ryan also worked on improving my self-esteem and confidence. Very slowly I began to emerge from behind the wall of fat. My outlook shifted to POSITIVE. I started loving myself. I learned to give and receive emotional feelings.

Does the story have a happy ending? Well, this is real life, but I think so. Working with Ryan, I lost 27 pounds, making me a total of 50 pounds thinner than last year. I feel wonderful. Compliments abound from others who have noticed.

The best part of the change, though, is what I gained: self-love and self-esteem. I'm not perfect, but I don't expect to be. I just have to be me, and now, I know that's ok.

I certainly don't need food in the addictive way I did before. Therapy is a slow process—a little bit of insight at a time. The benefits have been overwhelmingly positive in my life. It's fun to get high on people and friends rather than on food.

The world looks different and wonderful because together Ryan and I changed ME! God heard my prayer. Thank you, God.

Susan[16]

During her hypnoanalysis, Susan revealed many secrets that had been hidden in her subconscious. Her most penetrating feeling was of seeming undesirable to her mother. First she "recalled" how unhappy her mother felt while pregnant with Susan. Compounding Susan's intrauterine sensations was the subsequent indifference her mother held toward Susan's need for warmth and acceptance. To fulfill her need, Susan turned to food. Regardless of how her mother actually acted, Susan felt, experienced, and believed her secrets to be true. This, and only this, is what counts in recovering from serious emotional and psychological problems.

If You Think It's True

Much like Susan, many people go through life acting on "beliefs" that may or may not be true. Reality isn't as important as *perceived* reality. Individual reality is an extension or projection of consciousness. Many people in the world today do not live up to their potential because they believe they lack certain qualities. They believe they aren't intelligent, capable, skilled, or talented enough to achieve their ambitions. Individuals who believe they are inadequate usually act that way. A conscious belief eventually becomes committed to a person's subconscious mind—regardless of whether the belief reflects true or false information.

Once an erroneous belief is developed, an individual will either react or adapt to it. People who suffer from anorexia nervosa, for example, commit a slow form of suicide. They literally starve themselves to death because they believe they are too fat. Among tribes and cults that practice voodoo, there are documented cases of people who died within a half hour after a witch doctor placed a spell or curse upon them. There was no foul play involved. The individuals simply believed they were going to die while under the spell of the curse, and they did. These people programmed their minds to engineer their own deaths.

So doesn't it stand to reason that if the mind can be programmed to engineer death, that it can also be programmed to enhance life? Most emphatically, it can! The subconscious mind is strictly impartial. It doesn't discriminate between right and wrong, life or death, success or failure. It will simply function the way it's programmed to function given its hierarchical nature.

The Mandatory Hierarchy of Human Needs

An appropriate point is to examine what motivates human beings. Psychologist Abraham Maslow identified five levels of motivation, which he called the "hierarchy of human needs."[17]

According to Maslow, every person starts at the bottom of this hierarchy and works upward through the levels as they progress through life. Only after mastering the lowest level will a person focus the next level. If at any time the person's security on a lower level is threatened, the individual will drop back to that level and reestablish there before moving up the ladder. Let's take a look at these five levels.

1. **Survival.** When our physical survival is in question, nothing else matters. People will work long and hard to obtain food, water, clothing, and shelter. These are the basics of life, and it's hard to become excited about lofty ambitions or social standing when you are hungry and need money for your next meal.
2. **Security.** Once survival is assured, people usually concentrate on their security—survival on a long-term basis. Security translates into peace of mind, safety, stability, savings, and a financial nest egg so that survival is not threatened. It is difficult to acquire this level if you are constantly concerned with whether you and your family will eat regularly.
3. **Social.** Only after assuring their survival and establishing security do people turn toward developing relationships for social gratification, for love, and for a sense of belonging. Most people develop "support systems" for emotional needs ranging from spiritual growth to recreational activities.
4. **Ego**. Once people satisfy their basic physical and social needs, they are ready to turn their attention to gratifying their egos and gaining recognition. They direct their efforts toward becoming good at what they do so others will notice and approve. People work to satisfy ego needs on the job, in their relationships, and in community and volunteer arenas.
5. **Self-actualization.** Once all other needs are met, people are free to turn their attention toward self-fulfillment, satisfying their greatest ambitions, doing not just what it takes to survive or even to have a good life, but what they really want to do. Not everyone in life reaches a level at which he or she can do the things that give him or her most pleasure.

Generally, a person's rise through these levels will not be steady but will involve stops and starts—a couple of steps forward, then one or more backward. Also, there is no guarantee that once an individual achieves a certain level, he or she can forget about that one and focus on challenges further up the developmental ladder. Jerky progress is the norm. For example, a person working toward self-actualization might fall all the way back to survival if his or her financial nest egg is wiped out in a stock market crash or a bad investment.

Which levels you have reached in the hierarchy is not as important as being continually challenged, evolving and forward moving toward self-actualization. Your motivation will be controlled by the difference between where you feel you are in your climb and where you would eventually like to be.

The Order of Importance

The late Dr. William Jennings Bryan, Jr., M.D., co-founder of the American Institute of Hypnosis and originator of the Bryan Method of Hypnoanalysis, also developed a hierarchical scale. Bryan's assessment of what is important to human beings varied greatly from Maslow's, however.

Bryan, a medical doctor, psychologist, lawyer, and hypnoanalyst, stressed the following forms of survival and their relative importance to human beings:

1. **Spiritual survival.** An individual's connection to God, to an infinite power, or to a universal intelligence topped Bryan's list of important factors. While admitting that earthly physical well being is important, Bryan insists that physical security pales in comparison to spiritual well being. He contrasted Maslow's basic survival level of security to spiritual well being through Jesus Christ's words, "What good will it be for a man if he gains the whole world, yet forfeits his soul?"[18] Even if you don't believe that your spirit will survive for all eternity, there is still value in respecting and practicing truth, he contended. People will give their lives for someone or something they love, whether it is a person, a country, or a belief. The most miserable people in any society, Bryan said, are those who live lives that are based on physical survival only.
2. **Analytical or psychological survival.** Next in importance is our ability to make our way in the world, develop self-esteem and establish personal identity. The ability to reason, to discern, and to exercise judgment is of utmost importance, second only to our spiritual survival. As mentioned earlier, the conscious

mind is analytical by nature. It controls such activities as thinking, speaking, writing, arithmetic, planning, organizing, judgment, and reading. For many people, a fear much worse than death is the loss of analytical powers, effectively turning them into "vegetables."

3. **Physical survival.** With our mental and emotional faculties assured, physical survival is next on the list of priorities. A major fear with people as they age is that they will lose their physical abilities while their minds are still alert. Physical survival was Maslow's number-one priority, you will recall. The fact that smoking is a threat to physical survival does not prevent people from puffing away. Using Bryan's order of importance, the personal enjoyment or emotional satisfaction gained from smoking would not outweigh the activity's potential physical harm. Physical survival has three components: air, water, and food. A person can go without air for only moments, water for a few days, and food for a month or so.
4. **Territorial survival.** As we go through life, we stake out certain "territories" that become very much a part of our identities. Our homes, our jobs, and our social outlets are territories that we won't give up without a fight—unless we have already secured new territories to replace them. This motivational level corresponds to Maslow's security and social levels.
5. **Sexual survival**. Surprisingly, sexual survival is lowest in importance to most people. Despite America's apparent obsession with sexual activity as manifested by the mass media, it ranks on the bottom of the list. Although we might not like the idea of survival without sex, most people would agree that they would give up sex before giving up their identities, their bodies, their minds, or their spirits. Given the choice between food, water, or sex, a starving person will opt for the food and water first.

Now, with the above ideas in mind and considering what you hold important, let me ask you a question: Could your life be better than it is now? If you answered yes, you are the only person who can change it. External events that affect your life often are beyond your control. However, the quality of your life is of your own making. Your personality, your health, your marital and employment status, and your social standing are all within your control.

With hypnosis and the God-given power of your mind, you can change undesired behaviors, feelings, and thoughts, or whatever you choose. Whether it is getting up early in the morning or developing greater creativity, learning to love yourself more or changing addictive behavior, hypnosis and self-suggestion can help you change your way of life for the better.

First, however, it's important that you know more about what hypnoanalysis is and about the exciting symptomatic and personality changes that you can make once the awareness of the true cause of a problem surfaces. Recognizing and releasing negative suggestions, repressed emotions, and the secrets from your subconscious will result in great changes in your life. Chapter Two explains more about the art and science of making that happen.

Code Concepts

- Disregarding genetics, at birth you were similar to other newborns in your ability to perceive and respond to reality, and in your capability to develop your God-given ability to choose.
- Since you are the product of your experiences, your past plays a strong part in determining how you perceive subsequent incidents in your life.
- Your subconscious mind has stored all your experiences. It records every hurt and trauma a person experiences, even when the conscious mind chooses to forget negative incidents.
- The subconscious, which includes the superconscious, is responsible for creativity.
- Creativity, intuition, and imagination are functions of the subconscious mind, and the results of these functions depend upon the information stored in the subconscious.
- The conscious mind is analytical by nature and controls conscious activities, such as thinking, speaking, writing, arithmetic, planning, organizing, judgment, and reading.
- When the conscious and the subconscious minds are in conflict, the subconscious mind will almost always win out.
- Reality is not as important as *perceived* reality.
- The impartial subconscious mind doesn't discriminate between success and failure. It will simply function the way it has been programmed, or the way you program it based on the order of importance of things.
- Through hypnosis and natural mind power, you can change undesired behaviors, feelings, and thoughts and initiate and adopt new ones.
- Our lives are lived according to survival in the following areas, in descending order of importance:

    - 1. Spiritual (love)
    - 2. Identity (self-esteem)
    - 3. Physical (food, water, air)
    - 4. Territorial (property, money, social position, etc.)
    - 5. Sexual

Stimulate Your Understanding

1. Cite examples of how your past experiences that you know about influence your life now.
2. Cite examples of how your past experience that you do not know about might be influencing your life now.
3. Remember a time when your subconscious mind solved a problem with a spontaneous creative solution.
4. Have you ever had an ESP experience?
5. Name a feeling, thought or behavior pattern you have that goes against your rational thought.
6. What or for whom would you give up your life?
7. When you were 6 years old, how do you think you answered the questions: Who are you? Who are all those others? And what are you doing here?

Use your answers to gain understanding of your subconscious at work.

Chapter Three

The Truth Is Safer Than Fiction

To look is one thing;
To see what you look at
is another.
To understand what you see
is a third.
To learn from what you understand
is still something else.
But to act on what you learn
is all that really matters.

Anonymous

Dispelling the Myths Surrounding Hypnosis *Dracula, Dr. Mabuse, and "The Black Mantled Hypnotist"*

There are many myths surrounding hypnosis, most as a result of Hollywood melodramas where a corrupt and unscrupulous hypnotist is the stock villain.

The plots are more or less the same: a scheming hypnotist coerces an unwitting subject to do his evil bidding, most often the crime is murder. The unwitting subject is hypnotized without his consent or even his knowledge. Then the hypnotist hands him a knife and instructs him who to stab. The subject carries out the deadly instructions. With the victim dead, the hypnotist brings the subject back to reality. The subject emerges with no memory of having committed murder, thus making the subject the perfect stooge.

These myths have been perpetrated by a series of movies beginning with a film based on the 1897 Gothic Horror novel, *Dracula*, by Bram Stoker. In this novel, Count Dracula oozes a veneer of aristocratic charm that disguises his incomprehensible evil that includes hypnotic and mind-control abilities, especially with women and nocturnal animals.[19]

In the 1957 movie *The Blood of Dracula*, the elegant, appealing, innocent Nancy Perkins, falls under the spell of the evil chemistry teacher Miss Branding. Using hypnosis, Miss Branding converts the innocent damsel to vampirism, committing murders without memory. The villianess' karma comes full circle when Nancy refuses to awaken from her hypnotic trance, transmuting into a vampiric savage.

The "evil hypnotist" theme was not limited to Hollywood. In 1933, the Nazis outlawed *The Testament of Dr. Mabuse*, a film by Fritz Lang about an ingenious criminal and hypnotist who ten years earlier went mad. Mabuse spends his days writing detailed plans for crimes, his *Testament*; at the same time, a felonious gang commits crimes according to "the plans of the Doctor," with whom they confer.

Similarly, *The Manchurian Candidate*, the 1959 thriller written by Richard Condon, adapted to film in 1962 and 2004, involves the son of a prominent political family who is hypnotized into becoming an unaware assassin for the Communist Party. (Actually, Dr. Bryan who is considered to be the father of modern day hypnotherapy served as a technical consultant on the film.)

While these films misrepresent hypnosis, that does not mean that the world is devoid of evil people who use mind-control techniques for their own evil purposes. Several of my clients have experienced a coercive variety of hypno-torture used in conjunction with sensory deprivation, colored lights, threats, and physical and sexual abuse to prejudice their mind toward their handler's directions. However, programming such as this breaks down eventually and causes symptoms similar to Post Traumatic Stress Disorder (PTSD). To learn more on that subject, research Dr. Colin Ross's work on mind control, the CIA, and the military.[20]

Thank goodness most of the above is outrageous fiction. The average hypnotherapist has no clue about how to create a Manchurian Candidate nor does he or she even want to. Because of these melodramas and flamboyant stage shows, which should be billed as "*hype*-nosis," several classic hypnosis myths persist today.

Back To Reality—What Hypnosis IS

Hypnosis is not a sleepwalking state nor is it total submission to the caprice of a hypnotist. It is an altered state of consciousness in which the body can be very relaxed and the mind highly focused. A hypnotized person is aware of everything that is happening. In fact, hypnosis is a state of increased awareness. (See Figure 2.1.)

ORDINARY STATE

Only a few "units" affected by suggestion; therefore, effect is weak.

Suggestion

Units of Mind Power
Scattered units of mind power untouched by suggestion

HYPNOSIS

Units of mind power concentrated and all affected by suggestion; therefore, strong effect. No mind power left to take notice of anything apart from the hypnotic suggestion; therefore, even pain is ignored.

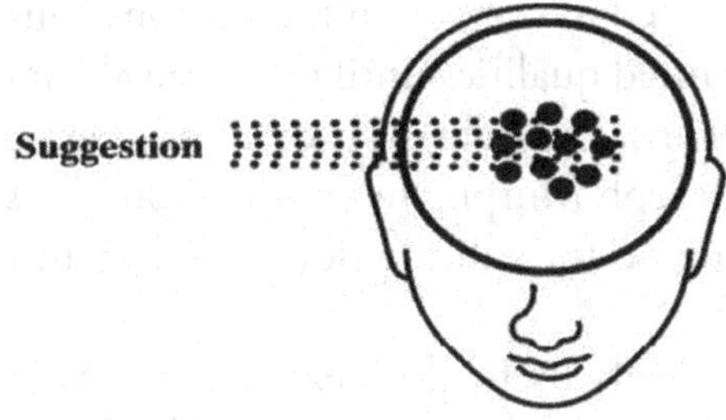

AFTER HYPNOSIS

Scattered again, but now each carries a dose of suggestion.

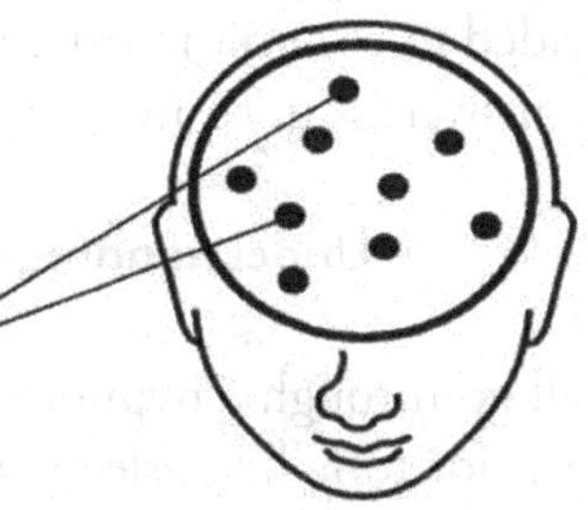

Units of Mind Power
With a dose of suggestion

Figure 2.1 Hypnosis is not sleep or unconsciousness, but a superconcentration of the mind. Suggestion is more potent in hypnosis than in ordinary state. (This diagram is an adaptation of the original published in *Modern Hypnotism* by Dr. S. J. Van Pelt, Associated Booksellers, Westport, Connecticut, 1956. Dr. Van Pelt credits the *British Journal of Medical Hypnotism* as the source for the diagram.)

Can a hypnotized person refuse to carry out an instruction from the hypnotist? Absolutely! A hypnotized person *always maintains free will.* If I could hypnotize people into doing things they don't want to do, I'd have a line outside my office miles long. In reality, it's hard enough to hypnotize people to do the things they *want* to do, such as stopping smoking, letting go of depression, and ending self-punishment, much less attempt to make people do things they *don't want* to do. Coercing people to do things they don't want to do is the exclusive domain of governments and secretive alphabet agencies.

Here's what I'm saying: can a person refuse the "suggestions" of governmental authority? Not without the consequences of fines, confiscation, incarceration, or SWAT!! Can a person refuse my suggestions or those of your garden-variety hypnotist? You better believe it.

Hypnosis can make a person 200 times more suggestible to change than in the waking state, but—and this is a big *but—people have to want to change!* And if the negative feelings and/or beliefs and behaviors are connected to survival in the subconscious, no hypnosis will change the unwanted qualities until the survival connection is changed. That's why subconscious analysis is often needed.

Dr. Joseph Murphy has pointed out, "A suggestion cannot impose something on the subconscious mind against the will of the conscious mind."[21]

That leads us to the next point. Can a person be persuaded to commit murder while in a state of hypnosis? Yes—if he or she could be persuaded to commit murder under ordinary circumstances. If not, then the answer is "unequivocally no."

Understanding the Hypnotic State

We all go through a hypnotic state at least twice a day: the relaxed state just prior to falling asleep and just prior to waking. You are also in a hypnotic state when you experience the dreamy feeling when you take a break from your task and gaze off into the distance. And just about everyone goes into a hypnotic trance within a minute or so of turning on the television (tell-a-vision?).

Suggestions placed in your mind during the hypnotic states before falling asleep and upon waking can affect thought and behavior patterns throughout the day as well as program future goals. These two times are optimal times to program your attitude with positive thoughts. People who, after the alarm sounds, lie in bed telling themselves how much they dread the day's activities will have a difficult day. If, by contrast, during that drowsy state they tell themselves that they are getting better and better at what they do, then that day will be a good day. They will feel better, they will approach their day's activities differently, and they will get positive results.

The Encyclopedia Britannica gives the following definition of hypnosis:

> "Hypnosis is the term applied to a unique, complex form of unusual but normal behavior which can probably be induced in all normal persons under suitable conditions and also in many persons suffering from various types of abnormality. It is primarily a special psychological state with certain physiological attributes, resembling sleep only superficially and marked by a functioning of the individual at a level of awareness other than the ordinary conscious state . . . when hypnotized, or in the hypnotic trance, the subject can think, act and behave in relationship to either ideas or reality objects as adequately as, and *usually better than*, he can in the ordinary state of awareness. In all probability this ability derives from intensity and restriction of attention to the task in hand, and the consequent freedom from the ordinary conscious tendency to orient constantly to distracting, even irrelevant, reality considerations."[22] (Emphasis mine.)

William Jennings Bryan, Jr., M.D., the man who introduced hypnoanalysis to many health practitioners and who was instrumental in gaining acceptance of hypnosis by the American Medical Association in 1958, defined hypnosis simply as "a state of super-concentration of the mind."[23]

Baltimore dentist Bruce Goldberg, who practices both dentistry and hypnotism, defines hypnosis as "a state of increased suggestibility accompanied by a focusing of one's concentration on one thought, idea or person." [24] Goldberg also describes the experience as "simply a way of relaxing and setting aside the conscious mind while at the same time activating the subconscious mind so that suggestions can be made directly to the subconscious, enabling the patient to act on these suggestions with greater ease and efficiency." [25]

Dr. Herbert Spiegel, former Columbia University professor of psychiatry, who is a leading hypnotherapist, describes hypnosis as "a state of aroused intense concentration, *the opposite of sleep*," (emphasis mine). Dr. Spiegel identifies three types of hypnosis:

- spontaneous,
- formal, and
- self-hypnosis.[26]

An example of spontaneous hypnosis happens every time you watch television. Actually, TV produces a visual hallucination in the watcher, one so powerful to completely inveigle the watcher to believe they are watching reality. When you playback a TV show you taped, the camera sees what's on the TV which is lines and blips in uneven but rhythmic ways. Our eyes don't see the blips and lines but fill in the blanks in a hallucinated manner, a manner pleasing to our eyes and senses making the image seem real.

Herbert Benson, M.D., defines hypnosis as "an altered state of consciousness which is artificially induced and characterized by increased receptiveness to suggestions."[27]

The other two types of hypnosis are self-explanatory. Formal hypnosis is generally guided by a hypnotist but it also possible to hypnotize one's self.

Hypnotized subjects are aware of their surroundings at all times. During hypnosis, however, your mind, directs its attention more to the suggestions from the hypnotist than to what is happening in the environment. The hypnotic state is similar to being in a daydream, except that the subject is controlling the daydream, with the hypnoanalyst acting as a guide. It does not mean abdication of personal morals, however. People in hypnosis will do nothing that they would not normally do during any other state of consciousness.

Ernest R. Hilgard, director of Stanford University's Laboratory of Hypnosis Research, shed light on this fact in an interview in the January 1986 issue of *Psychology Today*—"You don't really do anything that's against your basic value system," Hilgard said. "If you're instructed to do such a thing, you simply come out of hypnosis. For example, if you ask a person to strike someone else with a paper dagger, he'll do it. Give him a real dagger, and he'll drop it." So much for the movie cliffhanging candidates!

Hilgard also recounted a nineteenth-century experiment in hypnosis conducted by French psychologist Pierre Janet. A group of medical students hypnotized a nurse and asked her to take off her clothes. Instantly, she came out of hypnosis. One of Hilgard's colleagues tried to recreate the experiment by asking a hypnotized young woman to unbutton her clothes before a group of male students. Much to the colleague's surprise, the woman started to take off her blouse. As it turned out, the woman was a professional stripper. Taking her clothes off in front of an audience was not contrary to her value system; indeed, it was her bread and butter!

In hypnosis, the body can be very relaxed while the mind is super-concentrated and open to acceptable suggestion. The subject remains aware of the environment. Should any major change occur, such as a book dropping or a door slamming, the subject immediately comes out of hypnosis. Barring any dramatic change in the environment, the hypnotized subject focuses attention on the hypnotist's suggestions more than upon other simultaneously occurring phenomena.

However, while in hypnosis, subjects will not reveal secrets or other information that they would not reveal at any other time. Even in trances required for age regressions, people are capable of making choices. They may witness an event in which they were embarrassed, committed an act of which they disapprove, or an occurrence which they prefer not to share with the therapist. Unless they subconsciously want to reveal the information, that event remains sealed.

Another common myth about hypnosis is symptom substitution where another symptom is substituted for the undesirable symptom. Age regression combined with hypnosis is used to identify the cause of a person's problem experienced in early childhood that has caused a now-undesirable behavior. Once the core is discovered, reprogramming suggestions are given to eliminate the problem, not to provide a substitute.

In Chapter Three, I will discuss the complete procedure I follow when I work with a client. In the following abbreviated case history, my aim is only to illustrate briefly the hypnoanalytic method of symptom elimination.

Mary came to me recently saying, "I want to quit smoking." I found that statement interesting. She did not say her problem was smoking; she said she wanted to quit smoking.

Mary told me she had not felt particularly loved or accepted by her mother and had started smoking as a teenager with her girlfriends. When she smoked she felt that she was a part of the gang. The cigarettes made her feel loved and accepted. Obviously, she was mistaking approval of her peers for love. She recalled that she felt insecure about growing up and smoked more when she was out with people. She still smoked more in public than when she was alone, indicating that she still was not completely confident around others.

We talked about all these factors; however, she wasn't sure she was ready to quit. I hypnotized and regressed her back to the first time she smoked. She said:

> *"I'm in my front yard. My best friend and I are there. We're 16 or 17. We're laughing, like we're getting away with something. This fat boy comes by and laughs at us. He tells us how to inhale. We are totally dizzy."*

There was some challenge there, and Mary recognized that a part of her was rebellious at that time and that being connected to her girlfriends was helpful then, but hurtful now.

I gave her suggestions about quitting smoking, stopping her rebellion, feeling alive, and loving herself. She agreed to leave the cigarettes in the past.

After more than a year and a half, she has not resumed smoking. Often, the mere uncovering of the emotional foundation of an undesirable behavior is enough to eliminate it.

Hypnosis Through the Centuries

Although the term "hypnosis" wasn't coined until 1842, there is evidence that people had practiced the art since before recorded history. The oldest written record of hypnotic treatments dates back to about 3000 B.C. In the Ebers Papyrus, the Egyptians described a treatment in which the physician placed his hands on a patient's head. Professing to have incredible therapeutic powers, the physician uttered strange sounds that reportedly healed the patient. The "sleep temples" of Egypt, Greece, Rome, and Asia Minor actually were hypnotic centers of old.

Hippocrates, the Greek physician known as "the father of medicine," discussed what we now know as hypnosis when he said, "The afflictions suffered by the body, the soul sees quite well with shut eyes." Tenth-century physician Avicenna said, "The imagination can fascinate and modify man's body, either making him ill or restoring him to health.

Franz A. Mesmer introduced hypnotism to the medical profession in the late eighteenth century. Mesmer learned the art from a Catholic priest named Father Gassner, who was an exorcist. From Mesmer's well-known practice came the terms "mesmerism" and "mesmerized." Although Mesmer's healing activity became controversial and his popularity waned with leading medical practitioners at the time, some physicians continued to practice the art.

In 1842, James Braid, a British ophthalmologist, replaced the term "mesmerism" with "hypnotism," after the Greek word *hypnos*, meaning sleep. Although the British Medical Association rejected Braid's offer to read a paper on hypnosis at one of its meetings, Braid, unlike Mesmer, remained in excellent standing in the medical community. When Braid realized years later that hypnotism was not true sleep, he tried in vain to change the name to "mono-ideaism." By that time, however, the words "hypnosis" and "hypnotism" were well entrenched in every European language.

Hypnosis in America was widely associated with charlatans and with stage shows as a form of entertainment until Dr. William Jennings Bryan, Jr., founded the American Institute of Hypnosis in 1955. That was the same year the British Medical Association officially endorsed the teaching of hypnosis in medical schools. In Bryan's "A History of Hypnosis", he recounts the following passage from the January 1963 issue of *The Journal of the American Institute of Hypnosis:*

> "Until that time there had been no educational body devoted exclusively to promoting all the phases of hypnosis in medicine and dentistry, and the Institute was founded to fill that gap. (It) has grown . . . to become the world's most respected educational

institution devoted solely to teaching hypnosis . . . to physicians and dentists all over the world."

In 1958, the American Medical Association recognized hypnosis as a legitimate approach to solving certain medical problems, "in the treatment of certain illnesses when employed by qualified medical and dental personnel."[28] Hypnosis is so powerful that in the five decades since, thousands of operations of all kinds—including open-heart surgery—have been performed on patients using no anesthesia other than hypnosis.

Many physicians recognize that the mind and body interact to cause illness. They realize that if the mind can create ill health, it also can heal. The mind and body are integrated parts of a whole being; a change in one part affects the others.

Physicians who agree with this philosophy refer patients to professional hypnoanalysts who are trained in developmental psychology, psychopathology, psychotherapy, and, of course, hypnosis.

Hypnoanalysis Vs. Psychoanalysis

A difference between hypnoanalysis and psychoanalysis persists. While psychoanalysis is the method for discovering and analyzing repressions, drives, and ego states, hypnoanalysis incorporates hypnosis to identify the origin of a problem and to redirect the energy previously used to sustain the problem toward a solution. Hypnosis opens the door to the subconscious, analysis provides insight into the cause of the problem, and the hypnoanalyst offers the patient options toward finding a solution.

During the late nineteenth and early twentieth centuries, the medical world more or less relegated hypnosis to the shelf. Instead, it favored Freudian psychoanalysis. Sigmund Freud was never satisfied with his own results as a hypnotist; he preferred the "free association" technique, or working with responses from fully conscious patients. Maybe Freud was a lousy hypnotist?

As Freud's popularity grew, he denounced hypnosis and the public began to associate the practice solely with direct suggestion. Direct suggestion, however, is only a single aspect of hypnotism. The general public did not understand that the art of hypnotism included analysis as well as suggestion.

The goal of therapy with medical hypnoanalysis is to locate and counteract the negative suggestions received in a person's life relating to symptoms and help the individual drop the defenses that prevent them from maximizing their humanness.

Hypnoanalysis often involves the use of age regression while the patient is in hypnosis to reveal psychologically damaging experiences from earlier in life. Those experiences led to emotional dysfunction that is manifesting in symptomatic behavior. In hypnosis, the patient can relive the damaging experience to produce an emotional release of the suggestion in the subconscious mind. With the origin of the problem uncovered, the hypnoanalyst unties this subconscious knot paving the way to recovery and freeing the patient to live a healthier, more productive life.

In other words, hypnoanalysis is successful because it goes straight to the subconscious root of the problem. It treats the cause, or the underlying reason, for the problem, and not just the symptoms. For example, physical or psychological addiction to anything, be it sugar, drugs, alcohol, tobacco, or whatever, usually have a psychologically based underlying reason(s) for the strong attachment. If unchecked, the passion growing from their addictions can cause physical problems.

Likewise, people suffering from intense phobias nearly always discover through analysis that their fears are the result of earlier emotional shocks. All fears (except fear of loud noises and falling) are learned. People who suffer from various phobias often restrict their activities to avoid the objects or situations of their fears. These avoidances frequently result in emotionally crippling life-styles. Through hypnoanalysis, a person can discover the cause of such fears and overcome them to lead a normal, productive life. In fact, removing fear is one of the easiest uses of hypnoanalysis.

This makes rapid hypnoanalysis a superior method to the tediously slow and often ineffective process of psychoanalysis. While psychoanalysis therapy can last many years, most, though not all, hypnoanalysis cases last from six weeks to three months. Of all medical therapies, hypnosis is the safest it involves no drugs or surgeries, and causes no harmful side effects. Finally, hypnosis feels good; it is beneficial to the body, for relaxation is a precursor to health.

In *The Relaxation Response*, Dr. Benson shows how relaxation is related to good health. Benson first describes the "fight-or-flight" response. This is the body's response to the threat of danger. Notes Benson, "When we are faced with situations that require adjustment of our behavior, an involuntary response increases our blood pressure, heart rate, rate of breathing, blood flow to the muscles, and metabolism, preparing us for conflict or escape."[29]

This response was vital for primitive people contending with physical threats in a wilderness environment. When confronted with a bear or lion, Neanderthals needed the physical energy to swing their clubs effectively or to run for the nearest tree. That kind of behavioral adjustment is rarely called for in modern man; yet our body responds as if our survival depends upon fighting or fleeing.

"When not used appropriately, which is most of the time, the fight-or-flight response repeatedly elicited may ultimately lead to the dire diseases of heart attack and stroke," writes Benson.[30]

Fortunately, animals, including humans, have developed a physiologic response that counteracts the fight-or-flight response. It's what Benson calls the "relaxation response."

This, he says, is "a natural and innate protective mechanism against 'overstress,' which allows us to turn off harmful bodily effects, to counter the effects of the fight-or-flight response."[31] This response decreases the heart rate, lowers metabolism, decreases the rate of breathing, and brings the body back into a healthier balance.

Hypnosis with suggested deep relaxation can evoke the same physiologic changes as the relaxation response, Benson tells us. It results in decreased oxygen consumption, decreased respiratory rate, and decreased heart rate. Hence, hypnosis can be an important ally in the fight against heart disease and stroke.

Going to the Source

Now that you know more about hypnosis and medical hypnoanalysis, you may be wondering how this may apply to you and your problems. Through hypnosis, you have greater access to your subconscious attitudes and feelings that are responsible for your behavior and/or thoughts. Your hypnoanalyst helps you unlock the subconscious origin of your problems and uses gentle suggestions to help you remove limiting beliefs, and replace them with the ability to construct positive, life-affirming attitudes. Through medical hypnoanalytic treatment, you can free yourself to live a healthier, more productive and successful life, whether that success is in an emotional, financial, or spiritual sense.

In later chapters, we will discuss such common problems as smoking, weight control, and various phobias and problems that can be successfully treated through medical hypnosis and subconscious analysis. Turn to the next chapter to learn more information about medical hypnoanalysis and a description of the treatment technique I use.

Code Concepts

- Hollywood melodramas on hypnosis are mostly pure fiction.
- People in hypnosis will do nothing they would not normally do during any other state of consciousness.
- When in hypnosis, one is conscious and more aware of everything that is happening than when one is in the usual state of consciousness.
- Hypnosis is an altered state of consciousness in which the body is very relaxed and the mind is highly focused.
- Everyone goes through hypnosis at least twice a day: The relaxed states we enter just prior to falling asleep and just after waking are hypnotic states. So is the occasional dreamy feeling we experience as we take a break from our tasks and gaze off into the distance. The state we enter when we're creative and states when time becomes distorted are also hypnotic trances.
- Hypnotized subjects are aware of their surroundings at all times. Their minds, however, direct attention more to the suggestions they receive from the hypnotists than to things that are happening in the environment.
- Although the term "hypnosis" wasn't coined until 1842, there is abundant evidence that people have practiced the art since before recorded history.
- Hypnoanalysis is analysis of the subconscious mind, using hypnosis to identify the origin of a problem and to redirect the undiscovered energy used to sustain the problem towards a solution.
- The goal of therapy with medical hypnoanalysis is to counteract the negative suggestions received in a person's life and to help clients drop the useless defenses and guarding that prevent them from maximizing their capabilities.

Expand Your Mind, Change Your Code

1. The next time you watch *Count Dracula* pay attention to the scene where Bella Lugosi "hypnotizes" the beautiful woman he desires. Examine whether or not this seems possible and how popular beliefs about hypnosis may be influenced by images such as this. Have you ever been "hypnotized" like that?
2. Notice times during the day when you get dreamy, when time distorts, when you are being creative or when you are really "into" something. These are examples of natural, spontaneous hypnosis.
3. During your pre-sleep state, while dozing off, ask someone to give you suggestions and notice your responses to a positive suggestion and a negative suggestion. Do you think you can be made to do things you wouldn't normally do?
4. List several areas, qualities, feelings, thoughts, or behaviors you'd like to change in your life.

Chapter Four

Improving Your Reality Through Hypnoanalysis

This is the true joy in life, the being used for a purpose recognized by yourself as a mighty one; the being a force of nature instead of a feverish, selfish little clod of ailments and grievances complaining that the world will not devote itself to making you happy.

I am of the opinion that my life belongs to the whole community, and, as long as I live it is my privilege to do for it whatever I can.

I want to be thoroughly used up when I die, for the harder I work the more I live. I rejoice in life for its own sake. Life is no "brief candle" to me. It is a sort of splendid torch which I have got hold of for the moment, and I want to make it burn as brightly as possible before handing it on to future generations.

George Bernard Shaw

I first became acquainted with the quote from the Irish playwright on the previous page when I was an undergraduate studying theater at Elmhurst College. I saved the quote for nearly twenty years, not knowing why I was saving it. As I was writing this book, I discovered the reason I saved it—it was appropriate for this section. Although I have done my best to adopt Mr. Shaw's attitude in my life, my contributions operate on an individual level rather than on the social level—helping individuals to "thoroughly use up" their lives through improving their reality.

Shaw, an ardent socialist, authored some sixty plays and questioned all manner of social structures from education to government to religion and found them all wanting. He believed reality could be improved upon. Awarded both a Nobel Prize for Literature and an Oscar for his work on "Pygmalion," Shaw stood out as a remarkable human being in the eyes of this twenty year old undergraduate and still does through the glasses of this sixty year old. The concept of the Pygmalion Effect is credited to Shaw. The Pygmalion Effect describes the tendency of individuals who are in unequal power relationships (such as students and their teachers) to perform better when so expected by the more powerful individual.

An Effective Instrument When More Help Is Needed

Frequently people who want their lives to be better feel stuck when traditional therapies do not resolve their problems. Sometimes that is because there is a blockage that prevents a particularly difficult memory from coming to the forefront. Hypnoanalysis, the wedding of the concepts of hypnosis and analysis, has proven to be an effective instrument for helping people move through those blockages when their problems are too difficult to resolve alone, with self-hypnosis, or in talk therapy.

Hypnoanalysis is particularly helpful in achieving permanent positive results for problems such as low self-esteem, depression, guilt, anxieties, and phobias. Hypnoanalysis is effective because it takes a two-prong approach:

1. hypnosis which allows the mind to unlock its secrets, and

2. the analyst who helps the patient identify the subconscious beginnings of these problems guides the client in bringing those secrets to the conscious mind (secrets which usually entail feelings and emotions that have been locked away in the mind's recesses, and then offers guidance to nullify and counteract their interference in the patient's life.

But not all problems of the mind stem from singular events that trigger depression, anxieties, and phobias. Some problems are rooted in personalities disorders molded by pervasive conditions of upbringing. People who are brought up in dysfunctional, alcoholic, or abusive home situations, for instance, may need to undergo constructive personality changes. Such changes require fundamental revamping of basic belief systems. There is no more effective forum in our culture to affect such transformational change than intensive hypnotherapy. It is effective because of the two-pronged approach.

In such instances where a fundamental revamping must take place, I have found that clients' changes are more likely to last when individual therapy is followed up with group sessions before turning the patient loose to work alone with techniques such as relaxation and self-hypnosis. Through this integrated system of hypnoanalysis, psychotherapy, and group therapy, people can grow and mature at their own pace and in their own ways. Unresolved developmental tasks require more than therapist and client to reach satisfactory conclusions. That's where the groups help.

A word of caution: though I encourage self-hypnosis, this technique should not be confused with self-analysis. People sometimes ask, "Why can't I read up on hypnoanalysis and do my own therapy?" Self-help materials often do provide a certain level of knowledge and understanding, but there are limitations to self-analysis. For example, our subconscious throws up roadblocks or defenses against understanding our true motivations. This is doubly true when there are memories of pain, sorrow, hurt, terror, rage, neglect, or child abuse lodged in the subconscious.

In addition, hypnoanalysis and psychotherapy are complex disciplines, and the hypnotic tool is just one component. No matter how clearly an author may describe principles, ideas, and theories, lay readers may misunderstand, or they may read into only the notions that they want. They are apt to miss important points or nuances of self-help ideas and they may unconsciously oversimplify, overlook, or edit the author's ifs, ands, and buts. Many readers of self-help books have entirely misinterpreted the authors' intended results while picking up slogans or buzz words that they misapply, most often to themselves.

So while encouraging and utilizing patient self-hypnosis as support for the hypnoanalysis and group-therapy processes, I discourage solo flights until the problem has been identified and nullified. The client needs the concerned objectivity of a therapist to guide the individual toward resolution of the problem at its root.

Through systematic and periodic checking on a patient, a therapist can determine whether the message is getting through and whether the ideas and principles promulgated are being understood and followed.

What Can You Expect From a Typical Session?

Medical hypnoanalysis is not scary. To eliminate any fears, I will illustrate the process of hypnoanalysis using excerpts from my patients' sessions. Case studies throughout the remaining chapters will provide additional insight into the process. Patient names have been changed to protect their privacy.

As with medical professionals, before embarking on any treatment, it is important to take the patient's history. Before getting into the background though, I typically begin with an initial question: "What's the problem?" Usually, within the first two or three sentences, the patient will reveal information that is related to the basic diagnosis.

The first question is followed by queries such as

- "How long has it been a problem?"
- "What makes it worse?"
- "What makes it better?"
- "What could you do if you are cured of this that you cannot do now?"
- "What will be the result of your treatment?"
- "What do you expect?"

Answering questions during the history-taking period generally allows the patient to let go of defenses. For many patients it is the first time that they ever talked to anyone regarding the issues I ask about. If a patient refuses to answer questions about some areas of his or her past, it may be because the person feels shame about a particular detail of his or her past, and if so, odds of solving the problem decrease.

For example, when I was a graduate student Mrs. X consulted my supervisor because she had trouble breathing necessitating carrying an oxygen apparatus wherever she went. In addition to chemotherapy for a cancerous tumor in her chest, her physician had also recommended hypnoanalysis. My supervisor explained to Mrs. X that a complete history would be necessary before she could begin hypnoanalysis. Mrs. X agreed reluctantly but refused to answer questions concerning her childhood and adolescence and vehemently opposed any discussion of her mental-emotional state, finally discontinuing treatment after only a few visits.

Mrs. X's emotional constriction and subsequent depression and unhappiness were apparent. Her tumor, it seems, was related to her mind-set. Researchers and other clinicians, such as myself, see evidence of the connection between mind-set and illness on a daily basis. It's a good bet, however, that had Mrs. X opened up the hurt, pain, anger, and resentment she had stored inside, she might have been much happier and probably healthier. Cancer is, after all, biological suicide.

I don't know what happened to Mrs. X, but I suspect she died not long after that. The tumor, by the way, was lodged next to her heart and threatened its function. I am convinced that her heart was emotionally dead and her mind was attempting to make the mental image a physical reality. She was probably a victim of the spiritual and physical Walking Zombie Syndrome.

Medically, a syndrome is a number of symptoms occurring together that characterize a specific disease. In hypnoanalysis, we also identify certain conditions by a set of symptoms that characterize them. The Walking Zombie Syndrome, which Mrs. X exhibited, is one where the person feels dead, has made the decision to die (either voluntarily or through coercion in his or her body, mind or spirit) and the body is conforming to the subconscious image.

Hypnoanalysis is a non-threatening procedure. Once I know the patient's reason for seeking hypnoanalysis and what his or her hopes and expectations are, our conversation can turn to his or her early history with questions on marital status, home life, school, and relationships with parents, siblings, and peers.

After obtaining the client's history, during which phase we establish trust and understanding, the patient reclines in a comfortable lounge chair in a private room, wearing a headset and an optional eyeshade while I am in a nearby control room. While watching through closed circuit TV, I gently guide the patient into a state of relaxation.

That essentially is what hypnosis is all about—relaxation. Hypnosis induces a natural state of mind that opens the door to the subconscious. During hypnosis, the patient's conscious awareness retreats and the mind becomes super-concentrated. At this stage, I administer a word-association test, which helps clarify my understanding of the individual's attitudes and feelings. Our word-association tests are based on the work of William Jennings Bryan, Jr., M.D., and are the therapist's version of diagnostic tests such as blood analysis, urinalysis, or X rays. They help to clarify the issues and support the diagnoses.

In subsequent sessions, I discuss with clients their responses to the word-association tests, analyze their dreams, and usually teach them to practice self-hypnosis.

Sessions usually conclude with a suggestion to the patient to dream about his or her problem. Dream analysis is an additional diagnostic tool, usually pinpointing the area needing understanding. Often the dream reveals that a patient's problem originated before memory, at birth, or sometimes even in a past life (or what the patient remembers as a past life). The dream is a direct message from the patient's subconscious mind and, therefore, is essential to the analysis. Additionally, when a patient responds to the suggestion to have a dream, it proves beyond a shadow of a doubt that the treatment is working, as the dream provides a real sign that the subconscious mind is changing from working against the patient to, instead, working for him.

Usually, at that point in the treatment, the patient is ready to age regress, under hypnosis, back to the beginning of the problem when the initial sensitizing event occurred. Age regression uses hypnosis to help the patient's memory return to an earlier period in life such as adolescence and childhood, or to an even earlier time in life such as birth or before birth when the patient's only world was the womb.

The purpose of reverting to an earlier part of life is, ideally, to identify the moment that the experience occurred. By following the memory trail and communicating with the subconscious, the hypnoanalyst is able to uncover the underlying reason behind the patient's problem, addiction, or phobia. Then, in later sessions, we deal with those problems by removing the negative thoughts associated with that occurrence which is causing the problem from the patient's subconscious. Finally, the analyst offers suggestions for positive change. Through this process, each person can improve his or her reality!

Hypnoanalysis is frequently a quick process. To cease smoking usually takes about six sessions over a month's time. Problems such as phobias and depression may take twelve to twenty sessions to resolve. Persons with more serious conditions, such as codependence, sexual abuse, or long-standing personality problems, often choose to follow up in group therapy, supplemented with regular private sessions.

Using Age Regression to Get to the Source of the Problem

I just noted that we often find the roots of patients' problems by following the memory trail through the process of age regression.

Where does the trail of memory begin? One of the most fascinating aspects of hypnosis is its ability to draw memories from an individual's subconscious, some of which seem to emanate from previous lives. Sometimes, these memories expose the roots of problems plaguing the individual in the present life. Whether or not you believe in past lives or that psychological problems could have been carried over from a previous life, the subconscious has a memory of the event. Age regression, through hypnosis, helps uncover that event, regardless of when it happened.

John provides an example of using past-life regression to solve a long-standing problem in the present.

At age 65, John was concerned about his life-long lack of motivation, low energy, and frequent bouts of depression. His wife had died four years earlier. He was interested in past lives and believed in reincarnation. He stated:

"All my life, I've been a loner. I seem content doing nothing. I've had all kinds of businesses and I never really lasted. The problem now is that I am looking at the rest of my life like that. I can't do anything. I sit and watch TV. I can't relate to people, seem to put them off. I've been wondering what makes me tick for some years."

I asked what he thought he could do once he was cured that he could not now do, and he responded, "I think I could start enjoying life just a little bit." His statement exposed his subconscious fear: enjoying life.

In early conversation, John used phrases such as "off-hand" and "never really lasting." He said his depression was better "in cycles, almost monthly" *(like a woman's menstrual cycle)*. People can take advantage of me in nothing flat and I let them." This sounded as if his problem might have sexual overtones.

I asked him how his sex relations were and he said, "They are nowhere. I haven't had sex in a number of years." His history indicated he was reared in the Catholic faith, had married at 22, and had never had sexual relations with anyone other than his wife.

Since his wife's death, he had wanted to establish relationships with other people but had found himself unable to do so. "I don't have any friends. I'm amazed, now that I look at it, how I got through life without any friends," he observed. When the question of guilt came up, he said, "I am not the kind of man I wish I were, for my marriage."

When I asked what he wanted from me, he said, "I want to be able to talk to people, have relationships with them, and not to be putting things off all the time."

Part of the word-association test under hypnosis went this way:

Ryan: Problem . . .
JOHN: *Solving.*
Ryan: Desire . . .
JOHN: *A better life.*
Ryan: There must be . . .
JOHN: *Absolution.* (Indicates he feels guilt for some reason.)
Ryan: Not having sex feels like . . .
JOHN: *It's a pleasant memory.*

We have several terms in the word-association test that are considered slang, curse words, or off color. (As an interesting aside, the origin of shame associated with four-letter words in the Anglo Saxon language dates back to 1066 when the French invaded England. The French brought their Latinate language with them and anyone who was *any*one used French words rather than four-letter Anglo Saxon words. This may be the first instance of political correctness in English history!) The words in themselves mean nothing more than a body part or behavior described in other words. It's the significance put on these words by the hearer or speaker that make the difference. These words give us clues about a person's attitude regarding sexuality, bodily functions, and body parts whether they relate to them from an adult or a child-like perspective or whether shame is involved.

Here is how John responded to those words:

Ryan: Prick . . .
JOHN: *Puncture.*
Ryan: Pussy . . .
JOHN: *Cat.*
Ryan: Fuck . . .
JOHN: *A four-letter word.* (He shook his head.)
Ryan: Cock . . .
JOHN: *Rooster.*
Ryan: Peter . . .
JOHN: *St. Peter.*
Ryan: Come . . .
JOHN: *Escapes me.* (It does escape him, because this is significant.)
Ryan: It all started when . . .
JOHN: *I don't know.*
Ryan: It got worse when . . .
JOHN: *I got married.*

I learned two things from his word associations: 1) John relates to sexuality as a child would and 2) that his problem (reaching out to people) started early in life but worsened when he got married. He related to sexuality as a child would—e.g., giving responses such as "cat," "rooster," etc.

The next step in treatment is to analyze a client's dream. The dream John reported dealt with childhood relationships. "They just made me feel we were poor and there was nothing we could do about it. I was pretty much ignored. I was afraid to relate to people," he said.

That was when the part of John's personality that allowed him to interact with others had died. Under hypnosis, I helped him bring that back to life.

In subsequent sessions, we did a regression to the womb. He had a pretty good experience during that stage, but when advanced to the birth, he said: "I feel strange. I am crying. It is a short time. Somebody is picking me up. It is real strange being washed off. Back with Mom, it feels good. She is smiling."

It was evident that during his initial environmental experience (IEE), his earliest experience with someone other than his mother had made him feel strange. As an infant, he had related feeling strange as the appropriate feeling when relating to people. I helped John understand that this feeling had probably programmed him to feel strange with people. He agreed that his reaction to strangers was inappropriate and was willing to abandon it.

In another regression, I brought him back to a time when he was in his mother's arms, crying. Someone—a stranger—was attempting to take a picture of him in tears, and he felt very bad about it. When I pointed out the connection to John, it helped him to remove his negative feelings concerning those incidents, and for the first time since the beginning of his treatment (about eight sessions), positive change became evident. He came into his next session saying, "Well, I have a tremendous amount of energy. I don't know where to put it." (Think of this in a literal way).

John had become so enthusiastic about hypnosis that he asked to be regressed to a past life from which he had an image of a rape scene. This is how he described the scene:

> *"I am walking through clouds or fog. Above the ground. There is green grass and green trees. A red barn. An open door. Some kind of shoes, leather, ankle high. Black stockings, horse and buggy inside. Nothing in there.*
> *Back on the road again. Concrete, white, dirty. People are there. An old woman. I am about 8 or 10 years old. Inside a building. Climbing up steps. A room or window without glass . . . like I am aimless."*

Then he switched to another scene:

> *"I am riding on a horse. Am male. It is very dark. It is almost like a picture of Rome. There are robes. I seem to be going down a hill, a rocky hill. There is just nothing."*

Though John had wanted to be regressed because of a rape image, what we discovered in these two lifetimes are feelings as related to his present life: feelings of being empty, of being aimless, of not really existing, and of not having any connection to the present physical world.

I worked with John to put those feelings in the past and gave him positive suggestions to become connected to this life. He let go of the negativity he had carried over from those lives and replaced them with positive suggestions about getting involved with people.

An interesting subsequent regression proved to be even more productive. Because he still seemed to experience difficulty in establishing personal relationships, I regressed John to the womb once more. Suddenly, as he was describing typical contented feelings inside the womb, he jumped to a past life, saying he felt as if he had been there long enough, as if he were running. He began reporting what he saw in excited staccato fashion:

> *"I'm on the side of a hill, running away. It is a person . . . the feeling I have had all my life . . . like holding my breath.* (He sounded frightened.) *Somebody is running after me. I seem to be on a shore. There is a sailing ship there. A harbor. I am always so damned curious. I've got to find out what is on the ship. I go up the gangplank of the ship. I am very tense. Visions of a body here and a body there. Looks like foul play. It's somebody's big, long knife. A saber. A pirate. He is very menacing.*
>
> *"I turn tail and take off like a bullet. I am slowed down to a walk and I still have this feeling, this fear."*

John had experienced a spontaneous past life regression. The experience in a past life caused John to feel that his present life was still in danger. While he was under hypnosis, I helped him to leave those fears in the past life, to recognize that his life now was not in danger. After that regression, I saw John only twice more, but two years later he reported that he was doing very well. His early environmental experiences involving others and the past lives he produced spontaneously had programmed his lack of motivation and his inability to develop meaningful relationships. After hypnoanalysis, he had reprogrammed his life, began dating women and having sexual relations.

Whether the past-life information is real or not is immaterial. They could simply be a manifestation—a metaphor—of what is happening in John's subconscious mind. Or these thoughts may be genetic memory. Living in the field of ideas, several explanations for subconscious memories exist. When I work with patients on this level, it is not my job to judge accuracy of what a client presents; my job is to help them understand the underlying emotions relating to the problem in order to help them reach their goals.

Within that framework, as his therapist, I accept what John described and helped him remove the negative suggestions he had locked in his subconscious mind—wherever they came from. John was cured of his problem in about 15 sessions. That is a relatively short treatment time compared to the lengthy periods needed in other therapy approaches. Having practiced many of those approaches, I can personally attest to the relative rapidity with which hypnoanalysis resolves many problems.

Hypnosis Is a Vehicle to Your Subconscious Mind

Hypnosis is a vehicle technique anyone can learn—an astute 10-year-old can learn to be a hypnotist. The hypnoanalytic process, though, is more than just hypnosis. It combines hypnosis with the analysis of the subconscious. The hypnosis part opens up the subconscious, the analysis part helps people pull out the negative suggestions from their subconscious minds, nullifying the negative suggestion, and guiding reeducation and rehabilitation through positive suggestions.

Remember, the patient under hypnosis always remains in control. Hypnosis involves cooperation from the subject; no trance can be imposed on someone against his or her will. The subject who actively resists the hypnotist's suggestions will be about as hypnotizable as a brick. (A joke common in my profession: How many hypnoanalysts does it take to change a light bulb? Only one, but the light bulb must want to change.)

Therein lies a basic truth about hypnotism. Since the subject must cooperate to reach a state of hypnosis, it means that all hypnosis is self-hypnosis. The subject willingly enters the altered state of consciousness. This means each of us can achieve self-hypnosis—without the aid of a hypnotist—and program our minds for improved functioning. We do it all the time and you will see how shortly. Here's a clue: within a minute of starting to watch TV, most people go into a hypnotic trance. That's why Super Bowl Sunday commercial time costs more than a million dollars per minute—because millions of people are watching the messages in a super-suggestive state. Maybe Super Bowl Sunday should be renamed to **Super Suggestive Sunday**.

Through the use of hypnosis, we can develop greater access to subconscious attitudes and feelings that are responsible for our behaviors. While serious problems, addictions, and phobias require help from licensed professionals (and in some cases psychiatrists), through self-hypnosis you can feed yourself gentle suggestions to help remove restrictive, self-confining beliefs and replace them with positive, life-affirming values.

Your Two Brain Hemispheres As They Relate to Hypnosis

Before we go into a deeper discussion of hypnotism, let's take a look at the part of you where hypnosis takes place: your brain. Scientists have known for a long time that the brain is divided into two hemispheres referred to as the left brain (logic and reasoning functions) and the right brain (creativity and emotions).

Most of your conscious activity is done in your left brain. You use your left hemisphere when you talk, read, balance your checkbook, and figure your income tax. The left side of the brain is the logical side. You use it to reason. But reasoning isn't the only aspect of mental activity. Some of mankind's greatest discoveries have come through insight and intuition. Somehow, the brain takes a "short cut" to knowledge and understanding. This "short cut" involves the right hemisphere.

The right brain is the source of your ideas, intuition, imagination, and emotions. It houses your spatial sense, your musical abilities, and your ability to image. Symphonies are composed, poems are written, great paintings are created, and hunches are born in the right brain. When you see a familiar face, your right brain recognizes it but it is your left brain that supplies the name that goes with the face. You are at the peak of your mental powers when your left brain and your right brain are in balance.

Your brain functions at four different frequency (activity) levels. At any given time, your mental functioning is producing a preponderance of one or a combination of the four levels. These levels are defined by the frequency of electrical waves produced by the brain measured on an electroencephalograph (EEG) as hertz (Hz, or cycles per second). The four levels are:

1. Beta level.

During waking hours, you primarily function at the beta level—the level of complete consciousness. Input comes from your five senses: sight, hearing, touch, taste, and smell. At this level, your logical, reasoning, and verbal abilities are at their best. The left side of the brain predominates at this level allowing coping with the world, stress, anxiety, fear, tension, and brain chatter. In this state, the brain's electrical waves are pulsing at a rate of more than 14 Hz, or cycles per second. Most routine activities are completed at the beta level. Both the subconscious and conscious minds are functioning, and concentration efficiency is about 25% at this level.

The Boundary Between the Conscious and Subconscious Begins at the Alpha Level

2. Alpha level.

Alpha wave suggestions tend to represent the highest voltages of all brain waves and are usually measured at 8 to 13 Hz (cycles per second). At this level, the right brain is dominant and alpha waves tend to be produced when an adult person is relaxed and awake, but with eyes closed.[32] At this level, hypnosis occurs. Concentration efficiency is at 95%-100%. Individuals in the alpha state will be relaxed and their limbs will feel heavy, but their bodies' senses will be acute. Typical activities on this level, in addition to hypnosis, are daydreaming, absence of stress, creativity, healing, meditation, going into natural sleep, or awaking. Input at this level is considered intuitive, non-verbal, or paranormal: clairvoyance, clairaudience, and psychic knowing.

3. Theta level.

Deep hypnosis and light sleep are typical of the theta level, when the brain is emitting waves at 4 to 7 Hz (cycles per second) with reduced awareness and creativity. Dr. Barbara Brown of Sepulveda, California, one of the leading researchers in this field, says the theta state seems to be related to "problem-solving, sorting and filing of incoming data, and retrieval of information already deposited in the brain's memory."[33] They appear in the deepest meditation, as do some Zen masters.

4. Delta Level.

The mind is almost totally at rest at the delta or deep-sleep level, when brain waves have slowed to below 4 cycles per second. The average adult achieves this brain-activity level for only 30 minutes to an hour each night. This level may be the sleep-walking, sleep-talking state and/or astral projection.

As we've seen, the slower frequencies are the ones that take us into states of relaxation, deep inward focus, and sleep. Mimicking the brain-wave frequencies with pulsed lights, sounds, and electrical current can induce these states. When brain rhythms follow the rhythms of the stimulation, we call it "entrainment."

Entrainment is the process through which people can be lulled to sleep by the rhythmic crashing of waves against a shore, by the soothing rhythm of a lullaby, and even by the rhythmic clackety-clack of train wheels heard from a Pullman's berth. In my practice, I use a hemispherical synchronization machine to produce entrainment and to help the patient to achieve a hypnotic trance.

During the latter three levels the right brain is ready to receive and remember information, to imagine, and to create. In these states, the mind is most receptive to suggestion through hypnosis.

We Hypnotize Ourselves Daily

Chances are that you've hypnotized yourself many times without even being aware of it. Have you ever gone to bed knowing that it was important for you to awake at a certain time? Were you surprised the next morning when you awoke, precisely at the desired time, either without an alarm clock or perhaps a minute before the alarm activated? Was it magic? No. It was hypnosis—self-hypnosis. You programmed your subconscious, and it did what it does best: It obeyed your command.

Hypnosis is a state of relaxation that opens the subconscious mind to direct suggestion. As previously mentioned, everyone experiences a state of hypnosis at least twice daily—once before awaking and once before falling asleep. At each point, the conscious mind is losing energy, which allows the subconscious to accept the energy and open up to suggestion. That is what happens when you program yourself to wake up at a certain time.

SO—IF YOU CAN SLEEP, YOU CAN BE HYPNOTIZED! And remember, a person who is determined not to be hypnotized will not be. By the same token, anyone who is willing to cooperate with a hypnotist—or to practice seriously the principles of self-hypnosis, which will be discussed later—can achieve a hypnotic state at will. By the way, there's a myth that says only people of low intelligence can be hypnotized. People of above-average intelligence actually make the best subjects. Why? Because for intelligence to function, there has to be imagination, and guess what? Imagination is the key to the subconscious.

The Light Hypnotic Trance

Within the alpha-theta mind-activity level, hypnosis occurs on three different planes called trances: light, medium, or somnambulistic. Hypnosis begins with a light trance or focused attention, similar to the focusing that occurs when you are involved in an interesting project, engaged in a pleasant daydream, watching an entertaining motion picture, or reading a stimulating book. The conscious mind loses track of time and awareness of environment as it focuses totally on the subject or task at hand.

Have you ever driven a car from one city to another, only to realize after reaching your destination that you had little or no memory of the area in between? The reason you didn't remember was that you were lost in thought about another matter unrelated to driving. Your mind was focused, and you were in a light trance—a state of hypnosis. Through repeated experience and conditioning, your subconscious has become conditioned to operate the car with very little conscious thought.

If you are in a light trance while watching an interesting movie, then it is only natural that you are open to suggestion. Documented events back up this fact. During the 1930s, for example, Clark Gable took off his shirt in the motion picture *It Happened One Night*, revealing that he wasn't wearing an undershirt. Instantly, undershirt sales plummeted across the country. What a suggestion!

Sales of Reese's Pieces candy skyrocketed after little Elliot fed them to the extraterrestrial being in the blockbuster motion picture *E.T.* People can be entranced by the screen, and while they're entranced their subconscious minds are receptive to suggestions, including suggestions that they buy certain commercial products over others. Having made that discovery, motion-picture producers charge big bucks to display brand-name products on the screen. It is a subtle form of advertisement that can pay off handsomely.

Make no mistake, though: hypnosis is as powerful as it is simple. As previously mentioned, you can recall popular radio and television commercials years after they ceased to air. The product jingles or slogans have been instilled into your subconscious mind through the power of repetition. It's no coincidence that the best-selling products are usually the ones that are advertised most often. Advertising is a common form of mass hypnosis for which corporations pay dearly. Returns are virtually assured if the product is any good at all. Hence, advertising abounds.

The light-trance level, however, is limited in efficiency for age regression and other purposes of medical hypnoanalysis.

The Optimal Trance Level

Most hypnoanalysts prefer to work at the medium-trance level. On this second plane, an individual is deeply relaxed and more receptive to suggestions. Extraneous noises or activity usually will not break their concentration. The hypnoanalyst has greater access to the client's subconscious mind and the individual is more receptive to replacing existing attitudes and feelings that are responsible for undesired behaviors.

Age regression can be achieved more satisfactorily at this trance level. In a medium trance, people may actually relive events that occurred at earlier times. They will experience the physical or emotional pains associated with the events and will probably even adopt the voice quality and vocabulary they possessed when the events occurred, an experience referred to as a hallucination.

We'll go into greater depth on age regressions in a later chapter, but let me share one of my favorite cases here. I particularly like this case because it demonstrates both age and past-life regression, and demonstrates the profound changes a person can make once the genesis of a problem is exposed.

Case Study: Depression Was the Symptom Here

Alice, a 38-year-old woman, initially consulted me in February complaining of depression. She said she was working a lot but had begun to experience exaggerated feelings of loneliness when she was in her apartment. "I could be dead in my apartment and nobody would know," she claimed. "I'm just feeling alone a lot."

When I asked how long she had had the problem, she reported since around the holidays. I asked, "What makes it worse?" "Well, seeing a family bothers me. I want one of my own. It just doesn't feel like that's open to me."

"What makes it better?" She replied, "Sometimes getting together with people." I asked, "What have you done to help yourself already?" and she responded that she mostly ignored it. "I want to hibernate . . . Pull in some."

Next, "What could you do once you're cured of this feeling that you can't do now?" She answered, "I kind of feel like my life is on hold. I don't know how to answer that." Then she looked upward, as if to heaven, adding, "Having a home feeling, feeling like I belong somewhere most of the time."

With only a page and a half of her history taken, I observed that already this client was saying that she didn't belong. It wasn't just a situational thing; it had to do with her whole feeling about herself belonging in the world.

Asking if she was divorced and whether she was happy, she replied that she was not divorced and not happy. "I want to have a home and family and share my life with somebody."

Next I moved on to age regression questions about her earlier life. I asked about her school life and learned that she went to college for two years. "Were you happy?" Her response: "No. I just didn't seem to fit in socially."

Backing up further: "As a child, were you ever so sick that your parents were really concerned about you?" She answered, "Up to five, I was anemic. I looked like a walking ghost." When I asked her what her childhood was like, she responded, "I'd rather skip it."

I asked her the name of her mother. She told me, so I asked what kind of person her mother was. "I don't know; I never met her." That's when I learned she had been given up for adoption.

I asked a second time what she was like as a kid. This time, she replied, "Quiet—I read a lot and played by myself."

Concluding the history period by asking what she wanted from me, she said, "I want to get myself back on track. I've slipped a little bit, lately—my motivation. That old `I don't care' attitude has been slipping in lately."

Some interesting things came out in her word-association test under light hypnosis. I'll recount it as it occurred, staccato fashion:

Ryan: Complete a sentence beginning with the word "who."
ALICE*:* *Who am I?*
Ryan: Unwanted . . .
ALICE: *Me.*
Ryan: Alice
ALICE: *Me.*
Ryan: The real problem . . .
ALICE: *Me.*
Ryan: Life . . .
ALICE: *Death.*
Ryan: Death . . .
ALICE: *Life.*
Ryan: Sin . . .

ALICE: *Death.*

Being "on hold" was the way that she described her life and it was like death to her.

Ryan: If I ever really let go . . .
ALICE: *I'll die, if I don't get out, I'll die.*
Ryan: Underneath it all . . .
ALICE: *Scared.*
Ryan: I'm afraid when . . .
ALICE: *I'm alone.*
Ryan: All my life . . .
ALICE: *I wanted to be happy.*
Ryan: The one thing I need most is . . .
ALICE: *Love.*
Ryan: It all started when . . .
ALICE: *I was born.*
Ryan: It got worse, when . . .
ALICE: *I was a teen.*

At this point it was clear that she had a very empty feeling about herself, about her identity. She said it had started when she was born.

Ryan: Guilt . . .
ALICE: *Anger.*
Ryan: Punishment . . .
ALICE: *Fine.*
Ryan: I punish myself because . . .
ALICE: *I deserve it.*
Ryan: My punishment is . . .
ALICE: *Hate.*

Obviously, she hated herself. For whatever reason, Alice believed that she needed to hate herself and that she deserved to be punished. This was clearly an identity problem. She was suffering from the spiritual Walking Zombie Syndrome, which is characterized by loss of self-love, adoption of a guilty feeling, and the tendency to punish oneself—the same syndrome as Mrs. X mentioned at the beginning of this chapter.

We reviewed her history and word-association test, I explained the identity problem and the fact that part of her problem was that she felt like a little girl. In addition to the Walking Zombie Syndrome, Alice was also exhibiting classic symptoms of the Ponce de Leon Syndrome which includes immature behavior, not wanting to grow up and not wanting to be self-responsible. She agreed with that assessment.

In a subsequent session, I regressed her to the period when she was being carried in the womb. At two months after conception, she said:

> *"I can't breathe. My chest is heavy. She doesn't want to take care of a baby."*

These were thoughts she had received from her mother while she was in the womb. Then, I regressed her to one week after conception, when her mother was unaware of the pregnancy and had not developed anxiety feelings about having a baby. The patient was then able to feel at peace, happy, as if she belonged in the world.

I led her to remove the negative thoughts that she had taken in from her mother at two months of conception and to bring to her present life the feelings she experienced at one week after conception, feelings of peace, calmness, and tranquility, of being connected with God, the universe, and everybody in it.

After that, we age progressed month-by-month finding out what happened when she was in the womb. At four months, she said:

> *"Something is sitting on my chest. I'm scared."*

Then, she described her mother:

> *"She doesn't like where she is living. She doesn't like my grandparents."*

Suddenly, her breathing became real labored. I asked, "What's happening?" All of a sudden she said excitedly:

> *"I'm in a room. It's dark. I'm by myself. I'm in a bed. I'm a little girl. I'm four years old. I'm sick. I've got pneumonia. I'm hurting. It's hot. I die. There is nobody there."*

Then, she simply described floating through the clouds.

After she had gone through this experience which was very emotional, I asked if the person she saw was herself. She said, "Yes, but I was in a previous life." Viewing herself at four months past conception triggered the spontaneous past-life regression. The feeling of something sitting on her chest at four months gestation was the same feeling she experienced in her chest when she was dying of pneumonia, causing a spontaneous past-life regression, a highly unusual event. Bringing her back to the present, we removed negative thoughts and feelings that she had picked up from her mother prior to birth in this life and the emotions connected to the past-life experiences.

In a later hypnotic session, we returned to the womb again and brought her to the birth experience. She described hurting:

> *"Someone is squeezing me. It doesn't feel good. I want out. I will never get out of here."*

The difficult birth experience had conditioned her to feel like change was negative and that she could not make her life work. Stuck! She tied those feelings to what was happening in her here-and-now life, so I asked her to leave those feelings in the past, and she agreed.

From that point, the patient's attitude began to change. She reported being rid of her loneliness and depression and decided to work on another problem through hypnoanalysis—her weight.

Here's the core of her word-association test on weight:

Ryan: Guilt . . .
ALICE: *Food.*
Ryan: People of the opposite sex consider me . . .
ALICE: *Ugly.*
Ryan: I punish myself because . . .
ALICE: *I'm ugly.*
Ryan: My punishment is . . .
ALICE: *Being fat.*

Ryan: As long as I'm fat, I can avoid . . .
ALICE: *Men.*
Ryan: To me, God is . . .
ALICE: *Life.*
Ryan: To me, food is . . .
ALICE: *Life.*

From this exchange, I concluded that, in her subconscious mind, food and God were connected.[34] One of the things hypnoanalysts stress in treating the spiritually depressed is that God is love. And love was what she really needed.[35] Dr. Daniel Zelling once said, "When the spirit is hungry, the body gets fed."

Under hypnosis I pointed out to Alice that she was afraid of men and that she turned to food when she was scared. We did an age regression back to her early childhood when she was first conditioned to feel that food was love. After the regression, she was able to lose weight, dropping 35 pounds. This case was a complete success. She transformed her reality and is a working professional confronting life without depression or obesity.

Somnambulistic Trances Are Rarely Used

Although the third level of trance, or somnambulistic, happens at a very deep level and individuals are the most open to suggestion in this state, they still will not break their personal moral codes.

Entertainers prefer to work with subjects on this level because a somnambulistic trance usually results in hypnoamnesia. Upon awaking from a trance of this level, individuals may not remember their actions unless they're told to do so. It's in this state also that subjects see objects that are not present (positive hallucinations) or fail to see things that are present (negative hallucinations).

These characteristics make the third level of trance ideal for comedy. Only a small percentage of the population though can truly achieve a somnambulistic trance, so many of the eager audience participants you see in stage shows are hams who want to be part of the show.

Why Use Hypnosis?

A hypnoanalyst uses hypnosis as a tool to age regress a patient to the event in the subconscious at which an emotional problem originated. At that point, the easy part is over; that's when the real work begins! The rest of the process involves analysis and removal of the problem. The hypnosis itself is simple—so simple that, as I pointed out, you have probably hypnotized yourself regularly throughout your life.

As a social worker with traditional social work training, I've practiced traditional client-centered psychotherapy, cognitive/behavioral treatments, and a host of other body-focused treatments as well as light assisted treatment and EMDR. The rapid results achieved by my clients through the use of hypnoanalysis compared to other methods, however, is very impressive! The most intricate of problems can usually be treated in thirty sessions or fewer with medical hypnoanalysis.

The discovery that hypnoanalysis shifted psychotherapy into "high gear," bringing new impetus and creating solutions in the short term, was really exciting. Through hypnoanalysis, many problems are resolved in six to eight weeks.

Although, it's not a 'quick fix' for everything, more intense problems such as PTSD, codependence, personality disorders, and/or active addictions which require longer-term approaches can be resolve fairly easily with this method. The result is that I can help people more quickly, successfully and permanently, and, in this, I am very confident.

To reiterate, hypnoanalysis analyzes the subconscious mind using hypnosis, a natural state of mind, to identify the origin of a problem and to redirect the energy sustaining the problem toward a solution. Hypnosis opens the door to the subconscious; analysis opens understanding to the cause of the problem; and patient and therapist together open up options toward solutions.

As Dr. Bryan pointed out, our purpose is to blast out the negative thought and leave the rest of the mind alone. The goal of the hypnoanalyst is to help patients get over the problems that brought them to us, not to treat every little idea and review everything that has happened in their lives. After all, patients may want to keep some of their hang-ups. That is why, in the initial interview, I require answers to such questions as "What is the problem?", "What do you expect of me?," "What can you do if you are cured of this problem that you cannot do now?"

The subconscious mind does not discriminate against either positively or negatively influenced suggestions. Negative behavior and attitudes are acquired through negative hypnosis or a negative-focused state of attention resulting from anger, worry, guilt, negative self-talk, and especially fear. Fear causes what you're afraid of to come into existence. Positive attitudes and behavior, on the other hand, are the result of positive suggestions or a focused state of attention growing out of productive behavior reinforced by reward, loving attitudes, and positive self-talk.

Medical hypnoanalysis is successful because it accesses the base of a problem and treats the negative suggestion—the underlying reason for the problem—not the symptom or the problem itself. Hypnosis opens greater access to subconscious power, allowing replacement of existing attitudes and feelings that are responsible for undesired behaviors, feelings, or physical conditions. Because the mind becomes more porous under hypnosis, suggestions that might be repelled during full consciousness can be absorbed while in a hypnotic state. The hypnotic state creates two hundred times more suggestibility than is present during the waking state.

We Get What We Expect

As we learn more and more about the power of the subconscious mind, we can begin to see how hypnoanalysis can improve the quality of our lives, both physically and emotionally. Our subconscious controls our lives and our well-being, our health, and our habits. The key is to accept that we are in control of our subconscious and to use that strength to determine our direction. Many people have trouble accepting responsibility for their lives, preferring to abdicate that responsibility to others, to government, or to God.

Smart physicians have known for centuries that good medical practice does not treat the body and ignore the mind. Hypnosis puts the power of the subconscious to work. Dr. Bryan recounted a controlled experiment in which amphetamines were given to members of one group and barbiturates were given to members of another. Participants of each group were told they received the opposite drug. Each group reacted the way they were led to believe they would react, proving that the power of the subconscious is stronger than drugs.[36]

G. Alan Marlatt of the University of Washington and Damaris J. Rohsenow of the V.A. Medical Center in Providence, Rhode Island, substantiated Bryan's finding in more recent research. They divided groups of subjects according to whether they expected to receive a vodka and tonic or simply tonic. The results: Expectations affected behavior more than did the effects or absence of alcohol.

"What the people expected—tonic, or vodka and tonic—determined how aggressively they behaved and how socially anxious and sexually aroused they became," the study found. The drinkers got what they expected, in other words.[37]

Here's a great example from Dr. Eric Imadi, the author of *The Secret Behind the Secret,* of a miraculous cure effected simply by the expectation of the hypnotist:

> "Here's a REAL story documented in the 1952 British Medical Journal . . . In 1951, a 16-year old boy was referred to Dr Albert Mason for treatment. The boy's body was covered with dry, thick, black scaly skin, with oozing bloody serum. Considering the diseases as warts, Dr. Mason decided to use hypnosis to treat the boy. Dr. Mason hypnotized the boy in front of other doctors in a hospital in East Grinstead in Sussex. The thick black skin started falling off within 5 days and after 10 days he had normal skin! BUT that's NOT the most AMAZING thing . . . The most amazing thing is that after talking to the referring doctor, Dr. Mason found out that he had made a medical ERROR!!! The boy did not have warts! He was suffering from a lethal genetic disease called Congenital Icthyosis The boy was born with this INCURABLE disease. To the astonishment of the medical community Dr. Mason (and the boy) had cured a genetic disease with the POWER OF MIND . . ."

What allowed that MIRACLE to happen? The doctor didn't realize he was treating a lethal genetic disease! What if all disease could be treated this way? It's food for thought."

Dr. Deepak Chopra, who wrote *Quantum Healing: Exploring the Frontiers of Mind/Body Medicine*, confirms the influence of mind over body:

> "The mind is not just confined to your brain. It's in every cell of your body . . . our emotions, our feelings, our desires have a very important role to play in how we respond to disease . . . About 80 percent of all the drugs that we use in Western medicine are 'optional' or of marginal benefit, which means that if we didn't use them, it wouldn't make a bit of difference to the person except save money and prevent side effects."[38]

Chopra says that our bodies manufacture their own anticancer drugs, tranquilizers, and antibiotics; but when we are sad, angry, or under stress, we interfere with our internal pharmacy.[39] According to the former chief of staff of New England Memorial Hospital in Stoneham, Massachusetts, the key to most cures is to get to the basic cause of the disease:

> "Technology is very useful and some of the miracles of modern medicine are very remarkable, but we've got to be selective . . . We have the idea in the USA that there is a pill for everything. If you can't believe you ate the whole thing, then have a couple of Alka Seltzers. If you can't go to sleep, take a sleeping pill. If you're feeling anxious, take a tranquilizer. Viagra commercials punctuate other drug commercials on the television. Many of these drugs merely treat the symptoms and not the cause.
>
> "The reason people get ill is something very simple: how they think, how they interact with their environment, how they behave and what they eat . . . Quantum healing simply means understanding the mind-body

> connection at a deep level and recognizing that if we can act at that level, then we can generate the healing response from within the body itself".[40]

As we move into successive chapters, you will learn how to improve your reality using hypnosis to replace bad habits with good ones, strengthen good habits, conquer fears and phobias, succeed in any given endeavor, improve your attitudes, and increase your creativity And what if you could cure any problem, disease or illness that you had? It seems to me the limits of the human mind have not been reached yet. We have much more power than we realize.

Code Concepts

- Medical hypnoanalysis always begins with taking a complete patient history.
- The history taking establishes trust and understanding between patient and hypnoanalyst.
- Within the first two or three sentences of the history, a patient usually reveals information that is related to the basic subconscious diagnosis.
- If a patient refuses to answer questions about an area of his or her past, there is a diminution of hope in solving one's problem.
- By communicating with the subconscious, hypnoanalysts are able to expose the underlying reason behind a patient's problem, addiction, or phobia.
- People of above-average intelligence make the best hypnotic subjects.
- At any given time, we are functioning predominantly with one of four mental-activity levels: beta, alpha, theta, or delta.
- Within the alpha-theta mind-activity level, hypnosis occurs on three different planes or trances: light, medium, or somnambulistic.
- Most hypnoanalysts prefer to work at the medium-trance level.
- The hypnoanalyst's goal is the same as the patient's goal; the goal is not to treat every little idea and review everything that happened in their lives.
- Medical hypnoanalysis is successful because it treats the underlying reason for the problem, and not only symptoms.
- Our bodies manufacture their own anticancer drugs, tranquilizers, and antibiotics; but when we are sad, angry, or under stress, we interfere with our internal pharmacies.
- We subconsciously control our lives and our well-being, our health, and our habits. The key is to accept that we are in control and to use that strength to determine our direction.

Grow Your Mind, Decode Your Subconscious

1. In three sentences or less, state your problem. If more than one problem, use three sentences for each. Meditate on these three sentences because the cause of your problem is indicated in them. Since subconscious analysis requires training and experience, a cause may not seem readily apparent. This is natural. However, it is possible for your subconscious mind to give you clues and understanding by asking for clarification and help.
2. Be honest with yourself: if questioned about your history, are there areas you'd prefer not to divulge? If so, write down the feelings associated with those areas. Pay attention to guilt, shame, fear, hate, anger, or grief.
3. Are those areas related to your problems as far as you know?
4. Experiment and learn to identify your brain-wave levels. Your most suggestible times of the day are just before going to sleep and just prior to waking up in the morning. During these times, ask your subconscious mind for solutions, clues, direction, etc., to whatever problem is facing you.
5. Be patient, keep asking, and learn to recognize the signs coming from your subconscious mind in terms of coincidences, synchronicities, strong feelings, hunches, flashes of brilliance or insight from out of nowhere.
6. Think about your relationships with teachers, bosses, therapists, or others to whom you show respect or look up to. Do they or did they expect you to do well or not? How did it feel and did you perform to their expectations?

Chapter Five

Habits Make Life Heaven or Hell

The chains of habit are generally too small to be felt till they are too strong to be broken.

Samuel Johnson

Your Habits Are Your Choice

Samuel Johnson was not entirely correct. Neither was Horace Mann when he said, "Habit is a cable. We weave a thread of it every day until we cannot break it." Habits are learned behavior. We do establish them by repeated action, but they can be broken.

A habit is an act repeated so often that it has become automatic. As we discussed previously, when you do something automatically without consciously thinking about it, you are in a trance like state. And trances are hypnosis; hence habits stem from hypnosis, self-hypnosis, or self-suggestion.

Habits, both good and bad, are products of mental conditioning—they result when your subconscious mind accepts suggestions. These suggestions, lodged in your subconscious mind, are there because you decided (whether actively or passively) to accept them. You can also make a conscious decision to dislodge those suggestions, which can be done in an active, thoughtful manner.

Self-suggestion, or autohypnosis, can result in either positive or negative purposes. An example of autohypnosis for negative purposes is smoking. Smokers, whether or not consciously decided, have hypnotized themselves to believe that cigarettes help them cope with life. On the other hand, reformed smokers have used self-suggestion for a positive purpose—to dehypnotize themselves (remove the negative suggestion) and to associate cigarettes with the reality of poor health and eventual death.

Along the same vein, chronic overeaters have hypnotized themselves to associate food with love, security, and contentment. Breaking the pattern calls for a new trance, but with a different type of self-suggestion.

Hypnosis in and of itself is neutral, as is the subconscious mind. The way you program your mind is what makes your life heaven or hell. The philosophy among hypnoanalysts is that the key that *locked* the mind must be the same key used to *unlock* it. In other words, to be cured of the negative habit, the individual must take several actions: first, the emotional incident(s) that caused the problem or symptom to become part of the subconscious mind must be removed from the mind; then he or she must understand the negative reinforcing behavior and thoughts that perpetuated that behavior; and, finally, to accept positive suggestions to replace the unwanted habits.

Medical hypnoanalysis accomplishes this task incredibly well. Once again, keep in mind that the individual must *want* to make that change for hypnoanalysis to be effective. Before we look at how we can dislodge unwanted habits, let's consider how we get them in the first place.

Whether Or Not You Develop a Habit Is Up To You

Developing a habit is a matter of attitude. Unless physical dependency is involved, most behaviors do not become ingrained overnight. Once a person either accepts or rejects a particular behavior, the seeds are sown. The seeds grow into full-blown habits through continued cultivation and repetition.

Charles Reade, a nineteenth-century philosopher, said, "Sow an act, and you reap a habit. Sow a habit, and you reap a character. Sow a character, and you reap a destiny." To paraphrase Mr. Reade: the path most of us take in developing our character passes three-mile posts: Attitudes lead to actions, actions lead to habits, and habits lead to life-styles. Let's look at those steps individually:

1. Attitudes lead to actions.

Your thoughts are products of your feelings and attitudes. When you feel good about yourself, you tend to function within a positive cycle. You think constructive, productive, healthy thoughts, and your behavior reflects your positive attitude. Conversely, negative feelings, especially shame, guilt, hate, anger, or despair lead to destructive, unproductive, unhealthy thoughts and behavior—a negative, self-limiting cycle. Your actions (how you respond to events, circumstances and events in your life) will be influenced by your attitudes.

2. Repetition of actions leads to habits.

Most of your behavior is based on one of two motivations: what makes you feel good or is pleasurable or, alternatively, avoiding painful feelings, thoughts, or memories in the attempt to feel good. When the action is repeated often enough, it becomes a habit—an act that is performed unconsciously. Fumbling with coins in your pocket, making clucking noises, or tapping fingers on your desk are all habits performed unconsciously as a result of repetitively performing that act.

If the objective is to feel good, why so many people adopt self-destructive actions, you may ask. Regardless of how you view other people's destructive behaviors, realize that they are getting some kind of positive reward from the destructive act or they would not be doing it. The positive reward may be the avoidance of pain.

Nonsmokers may wonder why their smoking friends persist in their habits in spite of the hacking coughs and other resultant health consequences. Smokers may explain that they like to smoke and that it gives them something to do with their hands in social settings. Nondrinkers may wonder why alcohol abusers continue to drink when the practice makes them foolish, dangerous, and hung over. Drinkers will reason that a cocktail (or several) helps them relax. People who shun drugs may wonder why marijuana users persist in assaulting their lungs and numbing their brains. Pot smokers may say that a joint helps them to understand "the real meaning of life."

Frequently, the subconscious reasons for the various destructive habits are hidden from the individual and connected to the person's survival hierarchy. That's where hypnoanalysis and age regression can help. More on those topics later.

3. Habits lead to life-styles.

We are a composite of our habits. *Webster's New Collegiate Dictionary* defines a habit as "the prevailing disposition or character of a person's thoughts and feelings: mental makeup."[41]

- Through *internal communication within your conscious mind,* your attitudes dictate your actions.
- Through communication *from your conscious to your subconscious* mind, your actions dictate your habits.
- And through reverse communication *from your subconscious to your conscious* mind, your habits dictate your life-style.

For thousands of years, habits—both forming them and kicking them—have been a matter of concern for philosophers, teachers, parents, politicians, and professionals involved with human well-being or human manipulation.

Contrary to what Reade said, however, our destiny does not have to depend on a pattern of ingrained, unconscious, personal habits. Medical hypnoanalysis offers a method to breaking those patterns and has come of age in helping us conquer unwanted or destructive behavior. One goal of hypnoanalysis is to assist individuals in understanding the basis of their behavior so that they can recognize and deal with their mysterious compulsions. Once you understand that you didn't set up the rules and values for your life, that those rules and values can be changed, and you take responsibility for changing the ones that don't work in your life, then happiness is within your reach.

Hypnosis gives us greater access to the subconscious attitudes, memories, and feelings that are responsible for behavior. Hypnoanalysis then helps in unlocking the origin of a habit, a thought pattern, or an area of concern because it allows access to regions of the mind that are not consciously accessible. A hypnoanalyst can guide a person toward improving behavior and correcting weaknesses by using gentle suggestions to help remove limiting beliefs and to construct positive, life-affirming ones. The process is successful because it goes to the basis of the problem. It treats the underlying reason for the condition, not simply the symptom.

If you bite your nails, it's not because of a physical addiction you cannot overcome. You bite your nails because of an emotional attachment, a release of tension or some other reason. If you are a smoker, the real reason for your habit is buried within your subconscious mind, and a successful way to uncover that reason is to communicate with your subconscious. Through hypnosis, you can pull out the reason behind the habit and then deal with it permanently. Once that is done, you will no longer feel the need to smoke and you will need only to concern yourself with the physical dependence, which pales in comparison with the emotional dependence.

The key to success, however, is the patient's desire to change. Hypnoanalysis, as with other forms of treatment, will work only if an individual wants it to work.

Triple Allergenic Theory

Dr. Bryan used the "triple allergenic theory," borrowed from medicine, to help identify and understand the development of habits and psychological problems. Bryan theorized that psychological injuries parallel the development of physical allergies. "You can't be allergic to strawberries without eating a strawberry," he pointed out. "You've got to come into contact with a foreign-body protein—the **antigen**—before the body builds up **antibodies** (to fight off the foreign body) . . . The antibodies sit and wait for the antigen to come back. The next antigen-antibody contact then sets into motion actions that cause the nose to swell or the skin to break out in a rash. The next time you eat strawberries, there are so many antibodies that you get a real big reaction."[42]

The same thing occurs psychologically, Bryan contends. People are born with only two fears: the fear of falling and the fear of loud noises. Think about it. You don't develop a fear of dogs unless you are told to be afraid or unless you personally have a negative experience such as a dog biting you. A kid would pick up a worm and eat it unless the mother said, "Ugh! That's a worm! Dirty!" The kid learns "Worm! Ugh!" and the next time reacts the same way. A young child may see a grandparent's house burn down and develop an intense fear of fire, even of a lighted match.

The event causing the psychological condition may not be related in any way to the actual problem. For instance, a teenager's parent may die unexpectedly while the young person is attending a school basketball game which may develop into a dislike for the sport because of the psychological association with the parent's death.

Many psychological problems are manifested by sexual symptoms. If a young man, for example, has an automobile accident following his first intercourse experience, he might become impotent. Remember that the middle-aged female smoker we talked about earlier was a lonely teenager who felt accepted by her peers when she smoked that first cigarette on the front lawn. By the time she sought treatment, she no longer needed acceptance by a group of young people, yet she still smoked because the habit had become ingrained into her lifestyle.

Bryan defined three clearly recognizable developmental stages of habits or emotional problems:[43]

1. The Initial Sensitizing Event (ISE).

The initial sensitizing event, ISE,—the first time that a person experiences a negative emotion associated with an event—may be either a single traumatic occurrence or a conditioning process that happens to a person and is forgotten. The ISE usually occurs at a young age, is not recallable by the conscious mind, and produces no symptoms, but it is stored in the subconscious mind and can become the basis for what will later manifest as the problem.

For instance, the first time a particular food is eaten, an individual may find the taste, the texture, or something about the food unpleasant, but may not experience a physical reaction. Tomatoes, for example, are a food to which many people are "allergic." The taste of a tomato is unique and is not a food that would be readily eaten by a child. The first time a small child is fed a bite of tomato, he might spit it out. Although the ISE is not consciously recallable later, the child subconsciously recognizes that he does not like tomatoes. He may, in fact, transfer the dislike to any red, juicy fruit.

Some psychological injuries remain hidden from the conscious mind, and often no symptoms appear. But the subconscious mind stores up psychological "antibodies", and when the subconscious perceives a repetition of the "antigen" (the injury), these antibodies pounce to prevent "re-injury."

2. The Symptom-Producing Event (SPE).

SPE occurs when a symptom becomes associated with a triggering event, regardless of whether there is a direct connection. (An SPE is the time when a client first remembers having a specific symptom.) The symptom-producing event can trigger either an emotional or physical reaction, which is usually remembered. A war ensues between the psychological antigen and the antibodies that were built up by the original ISE.

In our previous tomato example, let's say that a subsequent eating of tomatoes occurs concurrently with another unpleasant experience. Several children are playing near some tomato plants and they see the attractive fruit. They decide to pick and taste one. The event deteriorates into a "hey-these-would-make-good-grenades" behavior in which the youngsters strip the plants of the tomatoes and have a mock battle. The child whose parents were custodians of the tomatoes is punished in front of his friends for being the "ringleader" in the destructive behavior, and they all are sent to wash up. When the little fellow (whose grandfather had established the tomato plants), washes away the smelly tomato residue, he discovers a rash and runs to his mother for sympathy. The angry parent comments, "It's the acid in those tomatoes. That'll teach you to destroy Grandpop's garden!" In this incident, the child has now come to associate tomatoes with punishment, lack of affection and a physical reaction, all of which may pop up later in life when he is again exposed to tomatoes.

3. The Symptom-Intensifying Event (SIE).

Continuing on with the previous example, when the child attends a community social three years later and his mother hands him a plate and commands him to eat every bite if he wants dessert, he finds himself facing a slice of that offending fruit. He holds his breath, swallows the tomato, and almost immediately breaks out in a rash all over his body. The doctor checks him for various childhood diseases and says lay off the tomatoes. The child is happy. He hates tomatoes anyway.

The truth may be that this child is not physically allergic to tomatoes. His reaction is psychosomatic, meaning that he subconsciously connected tomatoes to the punishment he got in front of his friends at age six.

Symptom-intensifying events are always recallable and such an event may, in fact, be the one that motivates the visit to the doctor or the hypnoanalyst.

Needless to say, I don't see many patients who are worried because they get a rash when they eat tomatoes, but I do see patients whose conditions are caused by a similar progression of events. Hypnoanalysts are daily faced with solving such questions as: "Why do I have this unreasonable fear of open spaces? I know they are harmless." "Why do I get nauseated every time I go to a basketball game?" "I love my wife; why am I impotent?" "Why can't I get rid of this smoking habit?" "Why do I masturbate every time I see a pretty girl?"

Among the techniques in which I have been trained is reductionism which is designed to help clarify patients' awareness of their problems and alleviate their symptoms. That approach makes for an expensive, drawn-out treatment and, while the patient has symptomatic relief, he or she may still carry around the original problem.

Bryan described the hypnoanalytic process as "removing the voltage"[44] of the incident by letting the patient relive it. Once that is cleared up, the patient is usually well. The Bryan hypnoanalytic method is a rapid voltage regulator.

The following multifaceted case is a good example of how a sequence of events and an event unrelated to the presenting symptoms developed.

Dom Had a Strange Combination of Symptoms

Dom, a 34-year-old-engineering manager, had an odd combination of complaints: absent-mindedness, difficulty remembering things, inability to spell correctly, easily distracted on the job, and procrastination.

I asked how long the problems had existed, and he said, "I've always had them, it's just gotten worse in the last two or three years. I've even been to a neurologist about it since it started getting worse."

I asked what makes it worse, and he said, "I can't say that I can think of anything."

When I asked what makes it better, he said, "Nothing."

I inquired what he had done to help himself, and he repeated that he went to a neurologist who performed a CAT scan and blood tests that turned out negative.

"What do you think you could do after you're cured that you can't do now?" I asked him.

"I think I could be a much-improved contributor to my job and my life, a more effective manager."

Dom did not say that he was having any specific trouble, either with co-workers or with his job. However, when he said that he could be an improved contributor to his job and his life and a more effective manager, he was telling me something: He was experiencing a lack of motivation and was unable to get promoted on the job.

I asked him what traumas had occurred in his life. He recounted that his father had died when he was nineteen years old and that he had a few car accidents. He seemed to put special emphasis on an accident at work four years earlier.

I asked what he wanted from me. He said he wanted to be able to spell words with confidence, routinely remember things, be better organized, and read with improved comprehension.

Now, this was a man who was already fairly successful. His primary motivation in consulting me was to improve his memory. He did mention that he had not had a very tough life.

Using the triple allergenic theory, I summarized his initial sensitizing, symptom-producing, and symptom-intensifying events:

1. His father's death occurred when he was still a teenager. The event was significant, leaving him without the kind of support and nurturing he needed to become an adult. His father's death, therefore, was a symptom-producing event (SPE)
2. Coinciding with an accident at work four years earlier, Dom had married and his first boss had died. Those were symptom-intensifying events (SIE).

I still had not identified the initial sensitizing event, ISE, so I implemented a word-association test.

Ryan: Fear . . .
DOM: *Success.*
Ryan: Success . . .
DOM: *Remembering.*

This indicated that there was a both a fear of success and a fear of remembering. Then this question came to mind: "What might he be afraid of remembering?" That was something we needed to determine, so I took this approach:

Ryan: It all started when . . .
DOM: *I couldn't remember.*
Ryan: It got worse when . . .
DOM: *I tried harder.*
Ryan: I'm just like . . .
DOM: *My dad.*

Since his dad was dead, that could have meant that he was feeling dead in some way. Indeed, a part of his mind *was* dead. He had said that the one thing he needed most was to be able to remember. So for Dom, remembering equaled both fear and success. The one thing he wanted most? Success.

Ryan: Complete a sentence with the word "why."
DOM: *Why can't I relax?*
Ryan: I'm afraid when . . .
DOM: *I don't remember.*
Ryan: Sometimes, I feel like I am stuck at age . . .
DOM: *20.*

The major event (ISE) that affected his life was his father's death when he was 19. He's been unable to psychologically move beyond age 20.

I returned to the area of guilt in the word associations.

Ryan: Guilt . . .
DOM: *Not being able to spell.*
Ryan: Punishment . . .
DOM: *Not being able to remember.*
Ryan: My punishment is . . .
DOM: *Not being able to remember.*

From Dom's responses, I reasoned that the major issue here was a death suggestion. A part of the client's mind was killed off when his father died. I suspected a secondary problem was the Ponce de Leon Syndrome, (mentioned in Chapter Three)where he was psychologically stuck being younger than his physical age. I verified that condition with more word associations:

Ryan: When fire breaks out . . .
DOM: *Run.*

That is more like what a little kid would say. Most adults don't run when fires break out.

Ryan: Come . . .
DOM: *Go.*
Ryan: Screw . . .
DOM: *Nut.*
Ryan: Peter . . .
DOM: *Pan.*
Ryan: Prick . . .
DOM: *Pee pee.*

These words with sexual connotations are used because they can help diagnose a Ponce de Leon Syndrome. As mentioned in a previous case example, persons with delayed emotional maturity will make childlike responses. Dom's responses suggested he was experiencing this syndrome.

It was evident that we had several unrelated symptoms to work on. We began working on his tendency to criticize himself for not remembering or behaving as he thought he should. The criticism problem was fairly easy to deal with under hypnosis. He understood the significance of the behavior and agreed to stop self-criticism.

In a later session, I regressed him to the symptom-producing event, his father's death when Dom was 19 years old the point at which his mind had stopped developing. Utilizing hypnosis, we wiped out Dom's negative experience and brought back to life the parts of him that had died with his dad. I coached him and taught him to be his own father now that he was an adult and to learn to give himself the things he needed. Despite several sessions, though, we were unsuccessful in correcting his self-criticism, bad memory, and failure to allow himself to be better.

We did another regression—this time back to when he was in school participating in a spelling bee with letters and numbers on the blackboard. He described a situation in which he was embarrassed because he couldn't spell and felt very inadequate. The experience had apparently caused Dom to decide that he was not going to spell again—ever. After he recognized in therapy that his current weak spelling behavior was founded on some erroneous information picked up when as a child, Dom made a conscious decision as an adult that he did not want to continue living his life based on something that happened when he was nine years old. Dom decided that he could and would spell correctly.

When Dom came to a subsequent session and I asked him how he was doing, he said, "Okay, good. Pretty confidant. Still disappointed. I didn't get the promotion."

He had been looking for a promotion. "He was my mentor and champion," he continued. "He's been out since April. I'm sad and mad. He was a replacement for my father." Often when someone loses a parent prematurely, he or she will relate to work superiors as a substitute for the lost parent.

Suddenly, we had a broader scenario. Through further questions, I learned that the Dom's boss had just died and Dom was feeling really bad about it. You may recall that he was still dealing with his father's death, which had occurred more than 10 years earlier, and now he had lost another father figure. This was a real blow to him.

We worked on his grief and the loss of his mentor. He continued bringing up the death of his father though. Finally, Dom agreed to be his own father and not look to other people for fathering. He pledged to give himself the love, caring and direction he needed.

As we worked out those problems he said he was doing better, that his memory was better, but he still needed to work on his self-confidence and his ability to speak up. We went back to the spelling bee. As a fourth grader, he had been unable to spell the word "available" and was one of the first to "sit down". We discovered that Dom drew a significant correlation between his feelings during that spelling bee and being asked in his current business environment to "stand up" and give presentations.

After we identified and expelled that problem, Dom improved steadily and soon was not only giving presentations before groups, he was also enjoying giving them. His memory improved and he stopped procrastinating. He was promoted several times during the course of his treatment and his salary increased by 100 percent. He went on to replace the boss who died.

The memory problem was merely a symptom relating to the underlying problem of the need for a father. The initial sensitizing event, ISE, was the spelling bee. His father's death was the first symptom-producing event, SPE; and the other events were symptom-intensifying events, SIE.

Let's interpret the case: *Dom was willing to give up, to sacrifice, something of lesser importance to maintain something of greater importance.* He sacrificed his memory skills in order to maintain feelings of love and connectedness to people from the past. The real issue, the underlying diagnosis, had to do with his feelings of love for himself, of love for his father, and the way those feelings died when his father died, reinforced when his boss (whom he had viewed as a father figure and mentor) died.

An interesting sidelight about this case is that his boss was sick and out of work before Dom even came to me for treatment. He did not mention this until his boss' death. That is when the picture finally came into focus: his boss's illness and impending death was the symptom-intensifying event that caused Dom to seek therapy.

This case was fairly involved, with several concurrent issues stimulating his subconscious mind. I enjoyed working with Dom, who has become very successful since he gave himself permission to grow up.

Healing Clients Using Past Life Regression

Advances in the treatment of psychoneurotic and psychosomatic conditions through hypnoanalysis have been well documented. Dr. Bryan claims to have treated 20,000 cases.[45] Hypnoanalysis practitioners are not miracle workers. However if we ignore the sensationalism from hypnosis' early days and look at the progress being made today (when the practice is used therapeutically), the conclusion becomes evident: Hypnoanalysis is an important and useful vehicle in health care and an effective tool to solve problems when other approaches have been unsuccessful. The roots of depression, anxiety, psychosomatic problems, and phobias can be uncovered through careful hypnoanalytic procedures, history taking, word-association tests, dream analysis, and age regression.

Past-life regression can carry the process one step further. One case involved a man with a colon condition who worked for years on the psychological and emotional components of his problem as well as the medical aspects—with no success. After being regressed to a past life in which he was stabbed to death in the exact spot where the colon was inflamed, he was able to release the feelings and negativity connected to that killing and his irritated bowel cleared up. It seems that this man carried the results of this previous life trauma into his current life. Sound incredible? Yes, but there are numerous case histories of an even more dramatic nature.

Garrett Oppenheim, Ph.D., recounted for the magazine *Contemporary Sexuality* the case of a woman who was having major sexual problems in her relationship with her husband. Under hypnosis, her subconscious produced a memory from a previous life. The woman remembered being a farm girl in the seventeenth century. One day, as she was feeding the pigs, four strangers beat her, raped her, and pushed her into the muck and mud of the pigsty, where she was left to die. Once that memory was exposed to her conscious mind, she was able to overcome her sexual problems with her husband.

Dr. Bryan has also recounted a number of fascinating case studies involving past-life regressions. One involved a 33-year-old Australian man who had been impotent his entire life. His therapist was an Ukrainian-born hypnotist who had immigrated to Australia, who knew little about the United States and who spoke English with difficulty.[46]

Under hypnosis, the patient remembered being with General Custer at the Battle of the Little Big Horn. Although this uneducated Australian patient knew little about American history, he described the battle and how he had hidden in a hollow log to escape death. This patient regarded his behavior as an act of cowardice and carried the guilt with him to his grave. After his death, he remembered, his spirit crossed the Pacific trying to escape the scene of his cowardice. He told of being reborn as an Australian. This patient's account of the historical event was startlingly accurate in some respects, erroneous in other respects. Dr. Bryan said the historical inaccuracies are no greater than one would expect from someone retelling an event from conscious memory.

Once the Australian had been assured that his act was not born of cowardice but rather from good sense, his subconscious stopped "punishing" him, and his impotence went away.

One of Dr. Bryan's most poignant accounts involved a 22-year-old woman who had once been a bright college student. She sought help after her grades dropped precipitously and her energy and motivation were drowned in a sea of melancholia. Dr. Bryan recognized the Walking-Zombie Syndrome: something had happened to make her believe she had actually died. Having accepted the death suggestion, she was living out her life as if actually dead.[47] Her symptoms seemed to correlate in time with a visit to the dentist. The Muzak system in the dentist's office was playing "The Merry Widow Waltz" as she was administered the gas anesthesia. She felt that if she could be put under gas anesthesia again she might remember what caused her horror.

Administering hypnosis and trilene gas as an anesthetic, the patient initially associated the awful incident with a concrete ceiling and a room from which she could not exit. After repeated efforts to discover the initial sensitizing event, the horrible episode came to light during a past-life regression: Her subconscious remembered when she was a 14-year-old Jewish girl in Germany. She was sent to Auschwitz and, as she arrived at the train station, a band was playing "The Merry Widow Waltz." She was directed into a room with a concrete ceiling along with many other Jewish prisoners. They thought they were there for a shower. Then, from the showerheads, out came the gas. Her subconscious remembered the horror of dying in the infamous gas chamber.

Once the memory was expunged from her subconscious the woman—an Irish Catholic born in 1950—was able to return to college and become a good student once more. Dr. Bryan reserved judgment, as I do, on the reality of the past-life experience. But there was no question that in the woman's memory it was a reality, and by treating it as a reality, Bryan was able to help the patient overcome her problems.

I once had a male patient who always felt a strong aversion toward rape, an aversion he told me about only after he had regressed spontaneously to a previous life. In the prior life, he remembered being a woman in India who was raped repeatedly by her husband's relatives on their wedding night. During the regression, he cried and looked quite upset. Afterward, he told me he couldn't understand how any man could force himself on a woman. He said he didn't believe he had it in him, and now he understood why.

Removing Habits That Make Life Hell

People act on their emotions, not on their intellect. Hypnoanalysts work to reveal the emotion behind a habit or a behavior. They find the initial sensitizing event (the negative suggestion) in the subconscious mind and take the energy out of it. Whatever the problem is—whether it is depression, overweight, smoking or some other symptom—somewhere in the subconscious mind a negative suggestion has been accepted. This negative suggestion then becomes associated with survival, and the patient engages in harmful behavior, thoughts, or feelings to avoid the pain of losing something more important.

In Dom's case, the negative suggestion he accepted unconsciously was that he died when his father died. He felt that he was not grown up and that he couldn't perform as well as his peers. That was true in fourth grade, when he could not spell the word "available," and it was true as an engineering manager who could not remember important things, could not handle the routine expected of him, and could not stand up and give presentations. Bringing to consciousness the initial sensitizing event neutralizes the emotional trigger and relieves the patient's anxiety, helping him realize he did not need approval and support from his father or a substitute.

Understanding the reason behind a habit is not always necessary in order to deal with it, however. As we will discuss later, depending on the strength of unwanted habits, they can sometimes be changed through using self-hypnosis. The inflexible habits, though, must be treated by a specialist. Either way, an individual can remove the habits that make life hell and replace them with habits that make life more like heaven!

Code Concepts

- Habits are learned behavior. We establish them by repeated action, but contrary to popular option, habits can be broken.
- Both good habits and bad habits are the products of mental conditioning, the result of your subconscious mind having accepted either positive or negative suggestions.
- To be cured of an inflexible, unwanted habit, an individual must relive the emotional incident from which the problem triggered, reject the negative input associated with the event that is lodged in the subconscious mind, and accept positive suggestions to replace it.
- The paths most of us take in developing our character passes three mileposts: attitudes (beliefs and values) that lead to actions, actions that leads to habits, and habits that lead to lifestyles.
- Our attitudes dictate our actions. Through communication from our conscious to our subconscious minds, our actions dictate our habits. And through communication from our subconscious to our conscious minds, our habits dictate our lifestyles.
- People are born with only two fears: the fear of falling and the fear of loud noises. All other fears are learned.
- William Jennings Bryan, Jr., M.D., the father of medical hypnoanalysis, defines three clearly recognizable developmental stages of habits or emotional problems: the initial sensitizing event, the symptom-producing event, and the symptom-intensifying event.
- In hypnoanalysis and age regression, we leave all the positive input alone and seek out only the incidents that caused the problem.
- People act on their emotions, not on their intellects. Hypnoanalysts work to reveal the emotion behind a habit or a behavior.
- Bringing to consciousness the initial sensitizing event disarms the emotional trigger.

Understand Your Code Exercise

1. List three habits you want to change that are related to the problem(s) that you listed in the exercise at the end of Chapter Three.
2. Make a list of 3 new habits you'd like to initiate in your life.
3. List the attitudes and actions in your habits that contribute to negativity in your lifestyle.
4. Identify where each of the attitudes and actions from the previous question fits into the order of importance listed below.

- Spiritual survival
- Analytical or Psychological survival
- Physical survival/air, water, food
- Territorial survival
- Sexual survival

5. What you are sacrificing to maintain something more important?

Chapter Six

Stress: When Reality Riots

Any man can be
just about as happy
as he makes up his mind
to be.

Abraham Lincoln

What Is Stress?

Our bodies were designed to deal with threats in a fight-or-flight mode. When our ancestors saw a bear or a lion, they had to make up their minds whether to fight or run for their lives. In either case, their bodies needed an extra charge of energy to get them through the emergency. This resulted in our bodies being designed to provide that extra voltage when challenges are perceived, a design that the human body still incorporates. Our ancestors also needed a mechanism to turn off the extra energy when the threat had passed. Our autonomic nervous system is composed of three parts: the sympathetic nervous system, the part that gears us up to deal with threats; the parasympathetic nervous system, the part that allows us to rest and relax; and the enteric nervous system, the part enervating with the viscera. It's when our sympathetic nervous system stays "on" or becomes over-stimulated that the trouble begins.

In modern society, however, the challenge rarely comes in the form of a physical threat that requires us either to fight or to run. The "threat" tends to be more on a psychological level, such as a handful of bills you can't pay, divorce, surfacing of ancient emotionally-laden memories, an audit notice from the IRS, moving, deaths, a tanking economy negatively affecting your lifestyle, or the anxiety of job loss.

In such cases, we feel the stress, but fighting, fleeing, or freezing will not remove the threat. So we find ourselves in situations in which we are energized for action but have no means of discharging that extra energy. When this happens, we experience "distress," caused by the excessive accumulation of pent-up emotional and physical responses.

Stress is "the nonspecific response of the body to any demand placed upon it."[48] Said another way, stress is a demand upon an organism for change. The change can be perceived as either negative or positive. For most people, change is stressful, and since our lives are a succession of changes, stress will always be with us.

Not all stress is negative. Some stress is good. It keeps us alert, interested in life, and motivated to grow. In fact, without stress, we tend to become complacent and might get little accomplished. The minor emergencies of daily life place demands on our bodies for action. Reacting positively to these situations is stressful but manageable.

Thus, normal stress provides the stimuli that keep us going in everyday living.

Negative stress, on the other hand, can adversely affect your health and well-being. Over the last few years, you have probably heard the theories of the effect of stress on your mental and physical health so let's examine exactly what constitutes stress, the warning signs of its presence, and how we can cope with it.

There Are Limits To How Much Stress You Can Handle

Our ability to cope with stress changes from time to time throughout life. Depending largely on the type, amount, duration, and intensity of stress each of us experiences, we may reach a critical limit, a personal point that differs for each individual. How that stress is dealt with also varies from person to person.

As an example: Leah became my patient when her parents were concerned over her behavioral problems and her astral projection powers—her ability to separate her spiritual from her physical being and leave her body at will. Leah, on the other hand, indicated her chief problem was not her out-of-body experiences, but rather complained of headaches and that her parents blamed her for her sister's problems using Leah as a go-between—a "telephone operator," she called it. The 15-year-old girl described family relations with typical teenage frustration and anger. Her conversation was splattered with four-letter words, posturing, and impulsive statements.

The parental pressure had started three years earlier, when Leah's sister began dating a boy the parents disliked. Leah tried to solve the conflict between her parents and her sister by discussing the matter with them. When that failed, Leah unconsciously began altering her own behavior so as to worry her parents even more and to take the pressure off of her sister. Leah said:

> *"I talked to them and stopped bringing home nice boys and tried bringing home some assholes. And I want to kill them . . . It stops me from going out with nice guys, and I won't go out with anybody."*

In other words, Leah was sacrificing herself, sacrificing her dating life to maintain something more important to her—stability in her family. This was the stressor in Leah's life.

Two facets of this case were particularly interesting. I asked Leah to describe herself, and she said she was a brat, "I don't really get into it *[her objectionable behavior]*. I just do it to do it."

Secondly, Leah said she was born with cranial stenosis (the absence of the normal soft spot in her head). She had two operations for the condition, first at 6 months, and again at 18 months.

Then she revealed the clincher, again with typical teenage lack of focus. I asked what she wanted from me and she replied:

> *"I want to find out what my past lives were. A lot of things freak me out. I have this power. I came up like a light and turned into 5,000 lights. I want to learn to control it. I want to lose weight and I want to get better in school so they [her parents] quit coming down on me."*

How's that for an assignment?

Leah went on to talk about her out-of-body experiences, saying that her spirit leaves her body many, many times at night and travels around. I knew I could do nothing about her parents "coming down on her," as she called it, but I could help her learn to deal with the astral projections and to stop sacrificing herself to maintain the family telephone-operator position.

I regressed her to the first time she left her body. She was in the hospital at about six months of age recovering from surgery to her head.

> *"It hurts across the top of my head. It's painful. I am thinking, 'Why is this happening?' I am waking up from it. It hurts a lot."*

We discussed the fact that her headaches were a kind of subconscious proof that she was alive and that her out-of-body experiences originally were attempts to escape physical pain. Later in life, the out-of-body experiences continued as a way to escape emotional pain. Under hypnosis, we removed the pain she had felt as a baby and helped her to understand that she no longer had to be the family go-between.

In a surprising development, Leah ended up mad at *me.* By understanding the unconscious reasons why she practiced astral projection, Leah lost the ability to leave her body. She was angry with me because she had only wanted to control it, not lose it all together.

Despite being "mad" at me, Leah reported 18 months later that she was doing very well after changing schools, was obtaining good grades, and was dating appropriate types of persons. "I've got the little kid out of me," she said.

Even though Leah was curious about her previous lives, I did not use past-life regression with her simply because it wasn't necessary to complete her treatment. I will use past life regression only if the treatment warrants it or if the patient requests it after the initial problems have been solved since most problems can be resolved without using that technique. It's important that the hypnoanalyst know when and how to initiate the regression.

Stress Manifests Itself In Many Ways

Many conditions that we call diseases are actually psychosomatic illnesses caused by stress. Psychosomatic illness results when a part of the body fails to function properly—not because of infection or disease, but because of tension or distress. When your stress reaches the saturation point, your body sends you warning signals. Those signals include tension, sore muscles, irritability, backache, fatigue, depression, listlessness, disinterest in what is happening around you, overeating, drinking too much, anxiety-related symptoms of heart palpitations, or digestive problems such as cramps, gas, and diarrhea or constipation. You may fail to recognize those stress signals until a crisis confronts you, forcing you to admit to and possibly deal with an over stressed condition.

Medical research has shown that stress is a major factor in about 75 percent of all illnesses. From Dr. Hans Eysenck at the University of London, studies have proven that chronic unmanaged emotional stress is about 6 times more predictive of cancer and heart disease than smoking, cholesterol, or blood pressure (*Science of the Heart* p. 9). Knowing how much pressure and tension you can cope with and when and how to reduce it will help you avoid health-threatening or even life-threatening situations. The correlation between stress and heart disease, for example, has caused many heart specialists to recommend relaxation therapy to patients who are at high risk for coronary problems.

Most people are unaware that many common life situations create high stress. T. H. Holmes and R. H. Rahe developed a stress-evaluation test called the "Social Readjustment Rating Scale," which assigns a numerical value to life situations which create stress. The numerical values are called "life-change units", or LCU.[49] The Holmes-Rahe scale is a good tool for predicting the effects of stress, perhaps even "distress".

For example, the life event that is the most stressful is the death of a spouse (100 points). Some events, such as a minor violation of the law, are scored low at 11 points. Everything in between—from pregnancy, change in financial state, loss of job, and change in sleeping habits to the beginning and ending of school—are assigned numerical values depending upon the level of stress a person might experience.

Totaling the LCU point values of the stressors in your life provides a good predictor of your physical health. A score of 300 or more usually equates to an 80 percent chance of illness! Any time you score more than 150 on the test, you are probably experiencing distress that could result in an associated health change. The test can be used to develop your "Stress Quotient." Everyone is unique and will have different quotients.

The Holmes-Rahe scale is reproduced in its entirety in Figure 5.1. Use the scale to calculate your stress level. Each person's tolerance for stress is different so I encourage you to use this scale to figure out what your stress limit is, and when you find yourself approaching your limit, take action to reduce the stress you are experiencing.

The following case is an excellent example of how the severe stress following the death of a spouse (the highest stressor on the scale) leaves the survivor more than twice as vulnerable to illness or accidents as the average person.

James' Stress Was So Great, It Eventually Killed Him

James and Lucille had been married more than 50 years and had reared six children when she developed a heart problem. Following bypass surgery, Lucille returned to her home and James nursed her.

Then Lucille had a stroke causing her to spend several weeks in a hospital and therapy center before returning home in a wheelchair. Again James nursed her, assisted by a housekeeper through the week and daughters who traveled more than 100 miles to help out on weekends.

When Lucille died, James was at loose ends. He played lots of golf, attended to business investments, and visited his children. James suggested to one of his daughters, a single professional with more than 20 years at her position, that she give up her job and move back home to live with him. When his daughter refused, James married Estelle.

Estelle's husband had died about a month after Lucille's death. The two couples had known each other in church and community functions and both needed companionship. It seemed like a good idea. Estelle rented out her house and moved into James' home, the one he had shared with Lucille.

Upon returning from their honeymoon, Estelle, who was unfamiliar with James' home, opened a door and tumbled down a set of stairs. She suffered multiple wrist fractures and several bad bruises, confining her to bed for several weeks. Repeating his history, James nursed his wife.

Shortly after Estelle was up on her feet again, James suffered a mild heart attack. "Nothing serious," the doctor said. "He'll be up and about soon." In the meantime, James missed the annual family reunion held by Lucille's family on Labor Day, an event he had always enjoyed and his one opportunity to visit with his former long-time in-laws. "That was probably best," he reasoned. "Lucille's sisters might resent Estelle's presence and I would hate to leave her alone for the day."

Three months later, James experienced a massive heart attack and died. "He's had a hard time of it," his children said.

Add up James's life-change score using the Holmes-Rahe scale. James was piling change on top of change. Is it any wonder he succumbed?

Social Readjustment Rating Scale

Rank	Life Event	Mean Value
1	Death of a spouse	100
2	Divorce	73
3	Marital Separation	65
4	Jail term	63
5	Death of a close family member	63
6	Personal injury or illness	53
7	Marriage	50
8	Fired at work	47
9	Marital reconciliation	45
10	Retirement	45
11	Change in health of family member	44
12	Pregnancy	40
13	Sex difficulties	39
14	Gain of new family member	39
15	Business readjustment	39
16	Change in financial state	38
17	Death of a close friend	37
18	Change to different line of work	36
19	Change in number of arguments with spouse	35
20	Mortgage over $10,000 *	31
21	Foreclosure of mortgage or loan	30
22	Change in responsibilities at work	29
23	Son or daughter leaving home	29
24	Trouble with in-laws	29
25	Outstanding personal achievement	28
26	Wife begins or stops work **	26
27	Begin or end school	26
28	Change in living conditions	25
29	Revision of personal habits	24
30	Trouble with boss	23
31	Change in work hours or conditions	20
32	Change in residence	20
33	Change in schools	20

34	Change in recreation	19
35	Change in church activities	19
36	Change in social activities	18
37	Mortgage or lien less than $10,000 *	17
38	Change in sleeping habits	16
39	Change in number of family get-togethers	15
40	Change in eating habits	15
41	Vacation	13
42	Christmas	12
43	Minor violation of the law	11

* This scale was originally developed decades ago. Adjusted for inflation, the current figure would be about $300,000.
** When this scale was originally developed, most wives did not work outside the home. An updated scale would read "Spouse begins or stops work."

Figure 5.1

How Can You Eliminate or Reduce Your Stress?

All right, now that we know what stress is and what its symptoms are, how do you cope? You can avoid stress in many ways. It should not be a surprise that the easiest route to controlling minor stress is to talk to someone. The simple act of sharing your problems with a sympathetic ear helps to reduce stress. Also, discuss with others ways how they handle stress to obtain a better understanding of how others cope and look for ideas you can incorporate to reduce your stress.

Hypnosis is another safe method of stress reduction because it relaxes the mind. It does not utilize drugs and is often the quickest way to teach people to relax and manage their stress. Many good hypnosis programs exist on the market in CD or Mpg 3 form. One that I produced is called "Relax the Worry and Tension Away." You can also make your own or have me create one for you, as we will discuss later.

In addition to seeking out a sympathetic listener or utilizing hypnosis, other ways to cope with stress include . . .

- Avoid making too many changes at once, especially those with high LCU values.
- Think of options to eliminate or reduce the source of your stress (break routines by using your creative problem-solving ability).
- Schedule fun times into your normal activities.
- Take up an aerobic activity such as dancing, walking, running, swimming and engage in that activity for 30 minutes three times per week. Studies show exercise reduces anxiety and causes the brain to release endorphins, the brain chemicals that create a sense of well-being.
- Practice deep breathing exercises combined with visual imagery or yoga.
- Listen to Baroque music (Vivaldi, Correlli, and others); Baroque music has a 60-cycle beat, which is calming.
- Soak in a hot tub or use a sauna.
- Follow a balanced diet and avoid (or at the very least) minimize intake of junk foods, refined carbohydrates, and sugar.

- Get your mind off yourself and your problems by doing something for others, such as volunteering with a local non-profit.
- Practice meditation or prayer.
- Engage in nonverbal expression through art, clay, dance, or mime.
- Set priorities.
- Learn how to become more flexible and how to avoid rigidity.
- Take regular naps.
- Let go of the idea of trying to be perfect.
- Escape through books, movies, or plays.
- Get or give massages, share nurturing and hugs.
- Use the Emwave Technology developed by The Institute of HeartMath. (www.heartmath.org)

I particularly encourage hugs—it is one of the most potent methods for healing emotional wounds, relieving stress, and building self-esteem. Studies show that the person who receives an abundance of warm hugs during childhood grows up with more confidence and poise, more self-esteem, and greater ability to cope with life's challenges. The person starved for hugs grows up with a constant need for outside stimulation to maintain morale and self-esteem. The hug is a powerful generator of beta-endorphins, substances manufactured in various parts of the body which have a soothing effect on certain receptors in the brain. Endorphins are also produced by strenuous exercise and are the source of the "jogger's high."

The Power of the Hug

Greg Risberg, M.S.W., a therapist, consultant and speaker, is an authority on hugs. At his seminars, he identifies seven types of hugs.[50]

Risberg calls the first type of hug the "A-frame". In this type of hug, the shoulders of the hugger and the huggee barely touch and if you were to view their bodies from the side, they would form an "A-frame". Trying to activate the beta-endorphin pump through this type of hug is like trying to activate your automobile's starter when there is no battery connection.

Next is the one-side hug which is slightly better. In this type of clinch, the two partners touch closely at one shoulder, but the hugger is still held at a distance.

The two-sided hug is an improvement. Both shoulders touch, but the lower torsos are still apart.

The shoulder-to-waist hug begins to establish a better connection. In this embrace, the partners stand closer, and the huggee no longer holds the hugger away, though the lower halves of their bodies still don't touch.

Next comes the shoulder-to-pelvis hug. This type of hug is more powerful because the endorphins are flowing freely, and before they are aware of it, the partners may be into the shoulder-to-knees hug.

The observer can barely distinguish the sixth type from the seventh type which is the biggest endorphin-pumper of them all—the "shoulder to the tips of the toes and everywhere in between" hug. Do it with someone you love, or who needs your love, and see if you both don't feel a lot better for having shared such a powerful hug.

Stress Can Be Experienced Even As An Infant

Much of my work as a hypnoanalyst is in treating people who are suffering from stress and anxiety. Though not all of my clients are adults, most are. Yet, I often discover that the event that triggered their current stress occurred in childhood, sometimes in infancy, at birth, or even in intrauterine life. In his newsletter, Dr. Louis K. Boswell reports that researchers at the University of Wisconsin have documented reduced immune responses (lasting for several weeks) in baby monkeys that were separated from their mothers. When they were isolated, the young primates experienced altered white blood cell counts, making them more susceptible to illness. "Study of this particular stress response in monkeys has revealed the probability of long-term effects of early-life stress," Boswell concludes. "Infant isolation due to divorce, hospitalization, or the death or prolonged absence of either parent could yield unhealthy consequences in later life."[51]

It would be reasonable to expect that human infants would also have long term effects of early life stress. Diane's case is one example.

Diane's Symptom Was Fatigue

Diane, an attorney by profession, complained of chronic fatigue, lack of motivation, and difficulty getting up in the morning. A young mother, she had not worked outside the home for four or five years, which time frame corresponded to the duration of her fatigue and other symptoms. She believed that things she *should* do took precedence over creative activities that she enjoyed, yet she procrastinated about the things she felt she should be doing.

This resulted not only in guilt over responsibilities she did not perform, but it also created frustration because she did not allow herself to engage in activities she enjoyed precisely because those obligations had not been completed.

According to Diane, her life was almost perfect. She had everything she had wanted and worked for. She loved her husband and her children, was happy with her religion, and had a perfect house in a perfect community. She just didn't know why she was so tired and lacked motivation, why she couldn't structure a fulfilling day for herself when her life was so great.

Diane's history, though, involved a number of troubling experiences. A bout with cancer had resulted in several mastectomies. When she was still a child living at home, her sister had suffered a mental breakdown. Her mother died when Diane was twenty-six, and her brother died when she was thirty.

I asked whether there were any problems when her mother was carrying her. She told me that right after she was born, Diane's mother had undergone both a mastectomy and a hysterectomy. For three to six weeks during that family crisis, the infant Diane had been cared for in the home of her aunt Maye.

Her feelings of guilt, she told me, were associated with the things she didn't do. Her expectation from hypnoanalysis was that she would feel more energy and would stop procrastinating.

I age regressed Diane and learned that her birth trauma and her separation from her mother were the initial sensitizing events (ISEs) out of which her current problem had grown. The deaths of her mother and brother and her own mastectomies were symptom-producing events (SPE). Giving birth to her children and giving up her professional life-style to stay home were the symptom-intensifying events (SIE).

As is often the case, Diane's symptoms were due to both physical and emotional disorders contributing to each other. She had unconsciously chosen a "flight" response to her situation. The fight-or-flight response, you will recall, is a built-in survival mechanism that helps you either defend yourself or escape from threatening situations. If you do not constructively deal with the challenge, the challenge will deal with you destructively. This is what had happened with Diane.

From her therapy, Diane realized that, although she had freely decided on motherhood over career, her self-esteem was suffering and she responded by neglecting creative activities in favor of doing everyday household chores.

Diane's symptoms disappeared with the initial therapy sessions, but eventually reappeared. At her request, I did a past-life regression to help us determine what events caused retriggering of her symptoms. The past life regressions uncovered memories of breast torture and neglect, stressors from those lives that she carried into this lifetime.

Here are the young attorney's responses to her treatment and her description of the hypnoanalytic process:

> *"At the time I came in for treatment, I felt [my fatigue and low motivation] was at 10 on a 1-10 scale . . . I didn't understand why I couldn't handle it. For about a month after treatment, I didn't feel the problem existed at all, then I noticed it creeping in a little [2 on a scale of 10]. I felt [the resurgence] had to do with a past life, what I saw, how I died in a war situation. I felt that I carried self-pity into this life, but I think I've worked it out with self-hypnosis. I found the [hypnosis] process fascinating. Two of the weeks when I learned I had a death wish and negative feelings about women were anxious and difficult. My conscious mind didn't want to believe this about myself. . . I found all the positive reinforcement was relaxing and peaceful."*

The death wish she spoke of was the Walking-Zombie Syndrome which she had been exhibiting.

Asked if she experienced any unusual events, side effects, or circumstances during treatment, Diane said:

"Seeing a past life, pregnancy, labor, and delivery was unusual for me.

"Hypnosis has to be the single most important thing I've done for myself in my lifetime.

"Though I felt something was holding me back, I didn't think I was crazy or mentally ill, and I didn't think my situation warranted traditional treatment. [Hypnoanalysis] clarified what the problem was and took care of it. Prior to [hypnoanalysis], I had been walking around feeling dead inside, but not realizing it, since this was all I had known.

"After hypnoanalysis, I feel energetic and alive. It eliminated my feelings of self-doubt and I became more creative. Good things started happening to me at the same time. Once, I had a dream and its theme was that I was afraid to live and afraid to die. I'm not afraid of either anymore. Life is more fulfilling now, and I'm sure death will be also."

Age regression under hypnosis can help both patient and therapist define events that contribute to psychosomatic disorders, such as Diane's extreme fatigue, occurring in adulthood. Because these symptoms are so often present among the young professional population, this particular syndrome is often referred to as the "Yuppie" disease or Chronic Fatigue Syndrome.

Post Traumatic Stress Disorder Is More Common Than You Realize

Certain types of stress are so traumatic that they manifest in psychosomatic illnesses. Another familiar manifestation of psychosomatic illness is Post Traumatic Stress Disorder (PTSD), frequently exhibited by people who have been in combat but PTSD is not limited to that group. PTSD has been around under different names for generations. It is most often exhibited by victims and witnesses of manmade and natural disasters, such as hurricanes and earthquakes, criminal assault, rape, burglary, torture, war, hostage situations, acts of terrorism; accidents, storms, fires, floods, animal attacks, car, sea, rail, and air disasters and other violence not normally within a person's experience.

Though called by different names, PSTD has been observed by the medical profession for at least the last century and a half. During the U.S. Civil War, a problem was diagnosed which was called "Soldiers Heart", which symptoms resemble contemporary Post Traumatic Stress Disorder. Following World War II, returning vets were said to be suffering from "shell shock." Work with Vietnam veterans produced the PTSD classification. More recently, high numbers of soldiers returning from Iraq and Afghanistan have reportedly sought mental health treatment for adjustment problems associated with PTSD symptoms. According to an article appearing in *USA Today*, over 12,000 veterans have sought treatment for this disorder.

PTSD is not limited to people in the military, however. Other groups of people, such as those claiming to have been abducted by aliens, forced into Satanic Ritual Abuse or secret mind control experiments, also tend to exhibit similar symptoms.

The Trauma Model[52] developed by Colin Ross, M.D. seems to work very well in helping clients who have lived through abuse in their past. This model helps clients shift the locus of control (the belief that the abused person caused or deserved the abuse), allows clients to recognize their ambivalent relationship toward the perpetrator(s) (that is, understanding the love/hate feelings towards their abusers), and then grieving the loss they experienced as well as bringing the body back to life, thus moving the client toward health and wellness.

Sean Blamed Himself for His Buddy's Death

Sean, 40, entered my office in a wheelchair. He had lost his legs in Vietnam. When I asked what the problem was, he said:

> *"Two things: About two weeks ago, I really flew off the handle. I grabbed my wife and son."*

Then he added:

> *"I just wanted to get to the bottom of it. Things I had let build up and didn't tell anybody about."*

He hesitated, then went on:

> *"Intense rage. I had headaches for about 10 years. The last two days I haven't had them. I've felt more relaxed ever since I started smoking."*

I asked how long his temper had been a problem, and he said in an emotional voice:

> *"It wasn't temper—rage. It was real different. It just came up. Boom. A combination of things that just built."*

He said that nothing made it worse, but cigarettes made it better. When I asked what he had done to help himself, he responded:

> *"Looking inward. Putting myself back on track. Meditation."*

I asked what he thought he would be able to do once he was cured that he could not do now, and he thoughtfully replied: "Not always be putting myself out on a limb and carrying the rest of the world's problems." He paused, then added: "I want to find the cause [for the rage] and then I will know for sure that it will not happen again." Another pause.

"It doesn't bother me any more." He looked toward heaven. "It's 21 years. I was hit in Vietnam in 1966. A fencepost. Two others died. I was the most severely wounded. I heard my buddy screaming, 'God, don't let me die.'"

Though an experienced therapist, I found myself unprepared for a war-ravaged 40-year-old paraplegic's response to my query about traumatic events in his life. I had expected the loss of his legs to be the chief issue, but when I asked what hurt him most, he again looked upward and said:

> *"The divorce was a bummer, a heavy one. The death of my father, a real heavy one. I miss him. When I was 11."*

I waited without comment and he picked back up:

> *"I wouldn't call Vietnam traumatic. I saved a little girl from drowning. That first 12 hours was real rough."*

Notice that among Sean's first words to me was "two": he said that two things were problems. The number "two" kept showing up all over the place during the history taking. And it got even more interesting!

I asked him about drugs and he said, "No, I was on morphine every two hours for two weeks when I was in the hospital."

I asked him about eating. He reported that he "tries to eat two meals a day."

Children? "I have two."

He told me he spent 30 months in the hospital after Vietnam, losing 100 pounds. That, he said, was traumatic. He also reported that he was born two months prematurely, nearly drowned when he was 6 or 7 years old, had kidney stones when he was 13, and yellow jaundice at some time. Despite those events, he felt that his childhood had been fantastic.

He could not recall any early memories of his mother, who was in a nursing home at the time he was consulting me. "She hugged me only once, after my dad's death," he offered, but added that he had been close to his grandparents, who died when he was 12 or 13.

When asked about any guilt feelings, he listed only his friend's death in Vietnam. "I wasn't able to help him," he said.

When I asked what he wanted from me, he said simply, "resolution of why the rage was there."

So, in the word-association test, we were looking for an ISE in Sean's past that caused a lot of rage to develop.

Ryan: The real problem . . .
SEAN: *Not being able to relax.*
Ryan: One thing I need most is . . .
SEAN: *To relax.*
Ryan: Birth . . . *[Note Sean's response.]*
SEAN: *Hanging.*
Ryan: What I don't want you to know is . . .
SEAN: *There are men killed.*

Ryan: Because I couldn't help him . . .
SEAN: *He died.*
Ryan: It all started when . . .
SEAN: *Childhood.*

From his responses, it appeared that his birth felt like death and was probably the initial sensitizing event. It also appears that he experiences guilt over having killed in Vietnam.

While he was under hypnosis, I explained my sense of his problem and regressed him back to the womb. Sean's was the most emotional experience I have ever seen while working with a person under hypnosis. Although he was reclined in the chair, he kept rising, screaming, and writhing while reliving the experience.

At six or seven months inside the womb, he said:

> *"It's warm. I am in breech position. My head under the sternum. Uncomfortable. (He was evidently in pain.)*
>
> *"It must be time for me to be born. My chest hurts. It's hard to breathe. I am stopped in the canal. It's pressure on my lungs. A lot of pain. I'm scared, need help. I'm coming out. I'm out, but I passed out. They're turning me over, cleaning me off. It's cold, it's cold. They're wrapping me up. (Sean starts shaking all over and making a lot of noise.)*
>
> *"They're not getting the ice, the ice off me. They lay me down on my back, Mom's left side. Warm, but hard to catch my breath. I can't see, it's dark and scary."*

At that point, I had Sean leave his traumatic feelings from birth in the past, along with any association with them that was connected in his here and now.

In the next session, Sean reported feeling good, not getting easily upset.

During another visit, I regressed Sean to the time when he was drowning around age 6 or 7. He recalled:

> *"We were swimming in a natural reservoir. I slipped through an inner tube. It didn't bother me, though I couldn't breathe. My brother pulled me up, then I got scared. He was coughing up water.*

I removed this death suggestion from his subconscious. However, here was the ISE for Sean's feeling of responsibility for other people—that his brother was coughing because of Sean. Then we focused on his case of survivor guilt stemming from the Vietnam war. During his regression, I asked him to stop blaming and punishing himself for the deaths of his two friends. At this point, he let go of his spiritual death wish.

Once these situations were reviewed and the effect on the subconscious nullified, Sean was freed up enough to stop treatment. My preference was to give him a few more reinforcements, but, as my mother used to say, "The proof is in the pudding." Two years later, Sean continues to do well and has not re-experienced the rage toward his family that so frightened him.

The number two that kept coming up seemed to refer to the two deaths in Vietnam. Had he continued in treatment, I would have known for sure. Frequently, but not always, numbers that show up repeatedly are significant.

When Sean relived the Vietnam scene, I wept from the pain of hearing it. Here was a man who was nearly blown to pieces himself—a man so gravely injured that he would never again walk on his own legs. Yet his thoughts were on his buddies, and his concern for them haunted his subconscious for years afterward.

Though the number two had significance in Sean's life since it kept showing up, the significance itself was never identified.

Symptoms And Treatment Of PTSD

War veterans are not the only persons experiencing posttraumatic conditioning, of course. Young survivors of Israeli-Palestinian conflicts, terrorist bomb blasts in Afghanistan, or the genocide in Rawanda, whom you see on the evening news scurrying amid the rubble are candidates for PTSD, aren't they? How about victims of the Persian Gulf Wars, the devastating earthquakes killing thousands, Hurricane

Katrina, or the Japanese tsunami sweeping away people like rag dolls? Each of those young survivors will probably exhibit PTSD at some point in their lives.

The Holmes-Rahe scale provides a long list of other traumatic events that many or all of us will face in our lifetime. While such occurrences as death of a spouse or family member, divorce, or changing jobs are not life threatening and are not considered to cause PTSD, they are, nonetheless, traumatic.

Dr. Boswell lists the following symptoms routinely experienced by PTSD sufferers:

- They persistently re-experience the traumatic event in nightmares and flashbacks and experience marked distress at exposure to symbolic events. They are invaded by thoughts of the past event.
- Because their nervous systems are conditioned to respond to particular stimuli, they are plagued by persistent, increased arousal, making it difficult for them to sleep, concentrate, or control anger. They may also have an exaggerated startle response.
- They avoid any place, person, or thing that would arouse memory of the traumatic event, thus limiting their ability to have a successful career, marriage, or future plans. [53]
- In addition, PTSD sufferers may experience chronic pain, anger and rage, suicidal tendencies, depression, substance abuse, and self harm impulses.

When working patients suffering from PTSD I guide them back to the ISE (Initial Sensitizing Event) and work with them in recognizing and leaving the effects of the trauma there in the past. This opens their minds to dealing with the major traumatic event in their lives. I then offer gentle suggestions to help them reshape their lives. Hypnoanalysis in particular helps PTSD victims to cope with present and future problems in a positive, effective manner.

If we fail to remove the source of the problem-causing stress, many PTSD sufferers resort to alcohol, drugs, or other antisocial behavior, which provide short-term relief. Eventually, though, the behavior will translate into more long-term problems.

Code Concepts

- Stress, as defined by Hans Selye, is "the nonspecific response of the body to any demand" placed upon it.
- Not all stress is negative. Without stress, we might get little accomplished. Normal stress is the challenge of everyday living.
- Our bodies were designed to deal with stress in a fight-or-flight mode. When reacting to normal stress appropriately, a charge and discharge mechanism operates and relieves the stress.
- Distress is the excessive accumulation of pent-up emotional and physical responses to routine anxieties, tension or traumatic events.
- Our ability to cope with stress changes from time to time throughout life. Depending largely on the type, amount, duration and intensity of stress experienced, we may reach a critical limit, a personal point that differs for each individual.
- Psychosomatic illness results when tension or distress interferes with the proper functioning of some part of our bodies.
- Medical research has shown that stress is a major factor in about 90 percent of all illness.[54]
- The easiest route to minor stress control is to talk to someone.
- Hypnosis is another safe method of stress reduction.
- Events from childhood, infancy, the prenatal period and birth, or even from a previous life, are factors affecting stress in adulthood.
- The isolation of an infant resulting from divorce, hospitalization, or the death or prolonged absence of either parent can cause unhealthy consequences in later life.
- Age regression under hypnosis can help both patient and therapist locate events that contribute to psychosomatic disorders.
- Posttraumatic Stress Disorder (PTSD) is often suffered by victims of criminal assault, sexual assault, ritual abuse, incest, accidents, war, and other violence, and by victims and witnesses of such natural disasters as hurricanes and earthquakes. Dr. Colin Ross,

M.D., proposes the Trauma Model for helping people heal their lives. www.rossinst.com

- The United States Department of Veteran Affairs provides resources for vets at: www.ptsd.va.gov

Growth Exercise

- Take the stress test and write down your score. ___________
- The following are symptoms of too much stress. Circle those that apply to you.

feeling harried	hurrying around
driving, talking, or eating faster than usual	feeling bored, apathetic, depressed, listless, or having no energy
disturbances in sleeping or eating patterns	chronic dissatisfaction or agitation
having no fun	a lack of interest in sex
feeling withdrawn	perfectionism
perfidiousness	work-aholicism
developing nervous	habits accident proneness
memory problems	showing poor judgment
feeling victimized by your life, decisions.	autoimmune diseases
aches and pains	nausea
general malaise	digestive disorders
chest pains	rapid heart beat
skin conditions	using alcohol using drugs, or other substances to relax

Chapter Seven

Relaxation: Turnpike To Subconscious Healing

We now have scientific proof the mind can heal the body.

Dr. Herbert Benson
"The Relaxation Revolution"

The empires of the future are the empires of the mind.

Winston Churchill

Mastering Your Mind is Really Very Easy

Most of this book's content up till now has been centered on the hypnoanalyst's use of hypnosis to uncover "codes" locked away in the subconscious. Hypnosis however can serve a multitude of purposes outside of the therapy arena with numerous benefits, benefits that can be unlocked without the need of a therapist through self-hypnosis.

Sometimes complicated concepts are actually quite simple. That is the case with self-hypnosis—you really can master your mind utilizing this very simple process. You can use self-hypnosis to program your mind for whatever you want in your life. In my practice, I encourage it for reinforcement and I teach patients to use it for continued growth following hypnoanalysis.

Self-hypnosis will not enable you to perform magic or display talents that you do not already possess; but you can use it to develop new skills, create life situations, and deal creatively with stress. It will also help you overcome blocks and self-imposed limitations that prevent you from making the best use of your abilities and talents. Self-hypnosis can also help you develop your latent potential as well as serving as a tool for relaxation, stress relief and "sleep learning", the focus of this chapter.

As we saw in a prior chapter, stress can have a major impact on your body. One of the best and most natural methods for stress relief is hypnosis—including self-hypnosis—because it induces a relaxed state and research has shown relaxation to be a natural stress reliever. More on that shortly.

Self-hypnosis is a natural exercise that most of us practice regularly. As previously discussed, we develop habits through self-hypnosis or mental conditioning. Because of past programming, we function on automatic pilot more than we realize. If you did something a certain way 10 years ago, it's a safe bet you do it the same way today, unless a crisis forced you to change or you consciously decided to change.

Through subconscious mental conditioning, you move through rooms in your home without consciously telling your arms and hands to reach out and turn knobs. Your feet hit the brake automatically when driving in touchy traffic. You awake at your preferred time daily . . . So how do you master self-hypnosis?

Easy Does It

Relaxation is the key to self-hypnosis, the key that opens the door to taking control of and reprogramming your attitudes, your behavior, and the stress in your life. Relaxation is a normal state. Being tense requires energy. The choice of whether you are relaxed or tense is yours. Self-hypnosis, however, does have to be a total body-mind experience. You cannot be physically relaxed while mentally tense, or vice versa.

Achieving a relaxed state is a skill that we all knew as babies but that most of us have forgotten by adulthood, so let's explore the process. Simple deep breathing is the easiest road to relaxation. Deep breathing is a natural stress reliever as it counteracts the sympathetic nervous system's fight-or-flight response and restores the body to its normal functioning by activating the parasympathetic nervous system. Typically, shallow breathing actually contributes to a distressed state, while deep breathing helps ward off distress before it begins by keeping the body and mind relaxed.

Let's look at the process of self-hypnosis as a way to program your mind. After you have practiced these simple steps a few times, you will be able to achieve a relaxed state at will:

1. Deep breathing.

Deep breathing is the first step to total body/mind relaxation and is an asset if you want to be able to reprogram your mind. Most people breathe shallowly, from their chests rather than from their diaphragms. Your diaphragm separates the chest from the abdomen and is below your rib cage. Hyperventilation, the opposite of relaxation, results from rapid, shallow breathing. Shallow breathing cuts down on oxygen intake and encourages muscle tension. Follow these steps to become adept at deep breathing:

a. Choose a very quiet location, lie down, and get comfortable.
b. Place your hands just below your rib cage and inhale deeply through your nose.
c. Exhale, through your mouth, as completely as you inhale. Concentrate on emptying your lungs. Practice inhaling through your nose and exhaling through your mouth until you

are comfortable with the pattern. Your hands should move up and down rhythmically as you breathe in and breathe out.

2. Relaxing.

Relaxation is a progressive event throughout the body. While you are in your quiet spot, follow these steps to achieve total body relaxation:

a. Lie down, or sit in a straight-backed chair, and tense your entire body.
b. Relax your body, one part at a time, starting with your feet. Concentrate on relaxing your feet, then move up and concentrate on relaxing your ankles, then your calves. Follow the procedure up through your knees, thighs, abdomen, trunk, hands, arms, shoulders, neck, and face, relaxing only one body area at a time.
c. You can condition yourself to go into a deep-breathing, relaxed state by adopting a cue and repeating it as you achieve relaxation. Keep saying over and over "I'm relaxed and calm," or any other phrase that is comfortable for you. "I'm cool and awesome or chilled" is acceptable, for example. Eventually, you can rapidly achieve a relaxed state by simply using the cue. That's self-hypnosis in action!

3. Imaging.

After your body is relaxed, you can relax your mind through daydreaming. Let your thoughts wander to pleasant environs, quiet places, settings that create feelings of comfort and tranquility. Perhaps it is a favorite spot by a quiet stream; maybe the scene is in front of a warm fire.

Daydreaming is a natural fit for the suggestive relaxation pattern. It makes you feel good about yourself and conditions your subconscious for reprogramming. Recall that when you are completely absorbed in something, you are unaware of time or what is occurring around you. Your mind cannot concentrate on two things at once. Thus, if it is focused on a pleasant, positive image, it cannot be preoccupied with negative thoughts. In this state, your subconscious is freed and receptive to creative activity.

4. Visualizing.

Mental programming can take place at this stage. The conscious mind must be in a passive state for the subconscious to accept programming. A focused state of attention (sometimes called a trance) creates the best conditions for accepting self-suggestions. This state is in the alpha level of awareness.

In this state, while you are fully cognizant of what is happening around you, by choice you are concentrating on a matter of importance and creating mental images of what you want to happen. Visualize the situation you want.

Be sure to use the present tense. If you want to lose weight, "see" a slim you in a smashing new swimsuit, strolling on the beach, being ogled by members of the opposite sex, or at a party being complimented on your appearance. If you want to stop smoking, imagine yourself facing the urge to smoke but overcoming the desire while experiencing breathing deeply and freely without coughing. To rid yourself of fear of water, visualize yourself swimming confidently in cool, clear water, enjoying the refreshing sense one gets from a mountain pool. If you want to overcome illness, visualize yourself strong and healthy, participating in your favorite physical activity.

For more details on the techniques of self-hypnosis, turn to Appendix A at the back of this book.

Believe Your Visualizations

Remember the old expression, "seeing is believing"? Because of my experience with hypnosis, I think it is the other way around: *Believing is seeing.* Then add feeling and the statement reads: *Believing with feeling is seeing on steroids!* When visualizing, see what you believe you are going to see. You bring to a situation what you expect you are going to experience.

Visualization activates the subconscious mind. It puts you in charge of your life. The subconscious does not recognize the difference between fantasy and reality. You will be what you visualize that you will be and feeling is the engine behind subconscious power. There's an old saying: "Whatever the mind can conceive and believe, it can achieve."

What you actually see merely validates your belief system. Take for example a salesperson who believes that winter months are slow and verbalizes, "It doesn't make any difference what I do this time of year, people don't buy my product around the Christmas season . . . all the other salespeople are slow too this time of year." The salesperson will subconsciously look for—and consciously see—only the evidence that supports the belief as true. He will see only indications that business is down during the winter months and is unlikely to think of ways to increase business. Thus, the belief is validated and continues to strengthen. In reality, it may be that his competitors *prefer* a slow Christmas season because they welcome the opportunity to go duck hunting on Chesapeake Bay or spend time with their families. Consequently, both parties create self-fulfilling prophecies.

Based on the concept that "believing is seeing," you can consciously *choose* what will show up in your life, regardless of your chosen profession. The game of life is not a game of chance, but a game of choice—and the choice is yours.

Different Types of Imagery

The use of imagery enables you to "create" memories. Most of us indulge in spontaneous imagination when we turn our minds loose to roam at will. The daydreams that thus occur are similar to night dreams: We do not plan them or direct them. It is like the involuntary recalling of a memory.

When you use your conscious mind to create the scenes or circumstances you would like to exist, it is called "willed imagination." You construct your own daydream, imagining things as you would like them to be. The image created as a result becomes fixed in your memory as firmly as if you had actually lived through it. Your subconscious accepts this memory as reality and directs your responses accordingly.

For most people, a daydream is like an image projected on a movie screen, observing but not participants in the scene. In his book *Imagineering for Health*, author Serge King calls this "picture imagination." Another form of imagery is what King calls "mime imagination." Utilizing these techniques, you become a participant in the image rather than just an observer.[55]

To illustrate: picture a dashing new sports car parked beneath the palm trees on a sunny beach. Let it be the make and model of your choice. You get into the car. As you turn the ignition, the engine roars to life. You snap it into first gear, engage the clutch, give it gas, and feel the seat press against your back as the car accelerates. You've just experienced "picture imagination."

Now physically step out onto your driveway. Picture that same sports car sitting in front of you. Imagine your real hands opening that door. Imagine yourself sliding into that seat and driving the car down the familiar streets of your neighborhood. You have now brought your image out of never-never land and into your present—your "here and now". This process is referred to as "mime imagination."

As King points out, picture imagination is good for memory recall, for developing new ideas, for planning projects, and for various types of meditation. Mime imagination is a better technique for improving personality and relationship skills, your environment, and your health. Many athletes use mime imagination to prepare for competition by polishing their techniques and instilling self-confidence.

Imagery can involve your other senses as well as mental pictures. You can imagine tastes, smells, sounds, and feelings in addition to visual images.

When you imagine the smell of coffee brewing in the morning, of roses perfuming a country lane, or of salt air and suntan lotion on a sunny beach, you are using olfactory (the sense of smell) imagery. When you imagine the taste of a banana split, of saltwater taffy, or of a filet mignon topped with béarnaise, you are using gustatory (the sense of taste) imagery. These forms of imagery can be used to "create" pleasant experiences.

Auditory (hearing) and kinesthetic (touch) imagery are also powerful ways of visualizing what you want. Auditory imagery involves the sense of hearing so perhaps your imaging includes the sound of surf crashing against a beach, of birds singing in a garden, of rain pattering on the rooftop.

Kinesthetic energy, involving the sense of touch, might include "images" such as feeling the coolness of the water as you first dive into a pool, the bracing warmth of a hot shower at the end of a weary day, the feel of the wind and the snow as you ski down a spectacular slope, and the solid feel of bat meeting ball as you swing for the fence.

Individuals vary as to which sense they respond to and this tends to affect the type of imagery they prefer. The hypnoanalyst's task is to determine which sensory type predominates in a particular patient, then use this knowledge to communicate more effectively with the patient.

The therapist can determine the patient's preferred mode of imagery by listening carefully to the verbs the patient uses. A person who uses words such as "look," "see," "bright," and "dark" is saying, "I prefer visual imagery." The patient who uses words such as "feel," "heavy," "light," "pressure," "grasp," or "hold," is saying, "I prefer kinesthetic imagery." People who use words such as "hear," "say to myself," "talking," "sounds like," and "tune in" are signaling that they prefer auditory imagery.

When the therapist communicates by using similar words, the patient understands the therapist better and knows, intuitively, that the understanding is mutual.[56]

Tips for Boosting Visualization Effectiveness

Keep these tips in mind to boost your visualization effectiveness:

- *Repeat your visualizations.* Repetition etches the image into your subconscious mind.
- *Practice often.* Frequent practice leads to improvement. By choosing the same time daily, you can make a habit of self-hypnosis.
- *Maintain control over your imagery.* Say no to undesired images and feelings.
- *Breathe from your diaphragm* during your visualization periods to maintain your relaxed state.
- Be sure to *create the exact feeling* that your goal will produce in you, thereby associating the image with the feeling. Keep in mind that the intensity of the subconscious program depends on your feelings.

If you have trouble with imagination, such as unable to imagine yourself lithe and slender in a new swimsuit or managing a thriving, demanding business, it could mean you have a self-esteem problem. Through age regression, hypnoanalysis can help you discover and deal with the event or relationship that resulted in your present lack of self-esteem. You may have lost confidence in yourself because your subconscious is harboring memories of earlier experiences, relationships or events that battered your self-esteem. This was the case with Lindsay, who came to my office searching for "inner peace, for an end to the war that was going on inside me."

Lindsay's Self-Esteem Was in the Gutter

Here's how Lindsay told it:

> *"My self-esteem was in the gutter from a newly broken relationship. I had failed at my business. My children had been admitted to an adolescent psychiatric ward for emotional disturbance. I was 50 pounds overweight. My life was a mess!*

When she started treatment, Lindsay ranked her problems at 10 on a severity scale of 1 to 10. As I worked with her, I determined that Lindsay was in a spiritual depression. She approached just about every aspect of her life from a negative perspective. As her therapy was approaching a successful conclusion, Lindsay made the following comments.

> *"The war inside me is slowly coming to a close; my self-esteem is no longer at the bottom of the barrel all the time—maybe 25 percent of the time. I have a very good job with tremendous potential. My oldest daughter is doing much better, but the younger one is still struggling.*
>
> *"My hypnoanalytic process has been a truly rewarding experience. I gave a part of me in the history and word-association tests that no one ever knew. In fact the history and word tests were revealing to me as well.*

"After the initial, face-to-face history, my journey into hypnosis began. We regressed back to being in the womb, allowing me to let go of certain issues associated with my birth. The death suggestion I had carried around most of my life was incredible.

"Little by little, Ryan has helped me peel away layers of problems. As issues came up, his awareness and intuitiveness allowed me to deal with them and let them go.

"My therapy has helped, changed, and affected me in many very positive ways. My overall disposition is better. I am able to work through problems as they arise. I've lost 40 pounds. I've increased my income and continue to receive good performance reviews with offers of other jobs within my company. My relationship with my daughters has improved. I'm able to talk with my former husband. And, my opinion of myself has gone from 0 to a 9, with 10 being the highest.

"I now look forward to all the endless possibilities that my life has in store for me—I should say, 'for the new me.'"

Re-imaging Can Help Solve Problems

To help Lindsay deal with her issues, under hypnosis I gave Lindsay suggestions to assist her with re-imaging. As I did so, I discovered that Lindsey was having trouble with positive imagery. Her self-esteem had ebbed below the point necessary for personal respect, and having lost respect for herself, she could not image herself with value. She was in a self-defeating cycle.

In such situations, I recommend the following suggestions to clients to help in re-imaging and used them with Lindsay:

1. Vanquish negative images

What is stopping you from succeeding? Any limit other than lack of knowledge or experience is a self-imposed limitation. Learning is available, and so is experience. *Assuming that you do not have the skills or characteristics to be attractive, bright, talented, organized, energized, or succeed is an act of self-sabotage.* Identify your negative self-images and put them aside.

2. Re-image

See and feel yourself in situations opposite to your current situation. Think of this as a game that requires you to see your future desired life-style. Assume that you will face no obstacles in achieving your desired situation. Simply expect that you will be able to devote your full attention to reaching your goals. See yourself, as you want to be. Your route to the goal will be easier if your imagery is not fraught with self-doubts and "what-ifs."

You have the opportunity, through the process of personal renewal and re-imaging, to discover limitless adventure. Some people are afraid of new experiences, even when their old ones are destructive or create bad feelings while others recognize they are alive only when they feel bad.[57]

The key to that adventure is within you, but you can only open the door if you are willing to accept new challenges and peer into unexplored horizons of change and growth.

Keep Imagery Statements Positive

The power of visualization lies in the quality of your images. Your programming statements must be positive to achieve positive results. If you cannot imagine a situation, you *will* have difficulty achieving it. By the same token, the stronger the feelings attached to the imagery of something you desire, the better your chances of reaching it. Think of your strongest positive feelings and attach them to your visualizations.

Use mime imagination, as described in the previous section, to bring your images into the here and now. When you put yourself into a scene, take all your senses with you. Let your imagination create for you the sights, sounds, feelings, tastes and smells of the reality you desire.

Self-affirmation statements are the core of conscious activity in reprogramming your subconscious. Keep the following rules in mind when planning your reprogramming:

1. Self-affirmations must be in the present tense

Since the subconscious deals only with the present, keep your affirmations in the present tense. For example, don't pledge, "I *will* get up early tomorrow." Affirm instead, "I enjoy getting up early."

2. Keep self-affirmations in the first person

Your subconscious has no control over anyone or anything except you and your actions. Say, "I enjoy being productive at work and my efforts reward me more and more" or something similar, not "I *will* get a raise at work" or "My boss will give me a raise." Your subconscious does not have the power to guarantee someone else's actions or that you actually receive a raise. It can only be used to improve your productivity, thereby, leading to a raise and can draw circumstances to you to improve your situation.

3. Brief self-affirmations are more effective

The subconscious can accept short (seven words or less) affirmations easier than it can accept lengthy, verbose intellectualizations.

4. Repeat self-affirmations frequently

To assure that self-affirmations become rooted in the subconscious, repeat them at least seven times consecutively, pausing briefly between each repetition.

5. Visualize success while programming your mind

Visualization without emotional backing is less powerful than when it is propelled by powerful feelings (love, sex, admiration, etc.).

6. Image success from two perspectives

"See" your images both as a spectator and as a participant. Visualize yourself receiving the award as "best whatever" of the year and see yourself from the view of someone in the audience. Use all your senses, including auditory and kinesthetic imagination. Hear the applause as you step up to receive the award. Feel the solid weight of the plaque or the smooth curvature of the loving cup as you take it into your hands.

7. Never visualize failure

Unsuccessful people tend to focus on negative results such as "What if I don't win?" The subconscious is attracted to its images—whether positive or negative—and does not discern between the two. Fear produces that which one is afraid of resulting in a negative outcome. Visualizing success is necessary for a positive outcome in any endeavor. Say no to fear—after all, FEAR is nothing more than **F**alse **E**xpectations **A**ppearing **R**eal.

Sleep Learning (Hypnopaedia[58]) Also Effects Change

As previously mentioned, effective visualizing occurs when your brain is in the alpha state. The alpha state can also be a doorway to learning. As you slip from the wakeful state into light sleep, you enter a state in which the *conscious* mind is relaxed and the *subconscious* mind is ready to absorb new information and ideas. Thomas Budzynski, Ph.D., calls this the "twilight zone."

Budzynski and his colleagues at the Biofeedback Institute of Denver conducted research into sleep learning during the 1970s. They found that as individuals fall asleep they go from "a relaxed alpha brain-wave pattern, accompanied by slow, rolling eye movements, to the disappearance of alpha and its replacement by slower, small-amplitude theta waves . . . within roughly five to 10 minutes."[59] During this brief period in which the mind drifts from the alpha state into the theta state, "people may not only have creative insights but may also be more in touch with the unconscious in general. They are hyper-suggestible and capable of learning certain things more efficiently and painlessly than during the day when logical and analytical factors are in control."[60]

Arthur Koestler explained it this way:

> "The temporary relinquishing of conscious controls liberates the mind from certain constraints which are necessary to maintain the disciplined routines of thought but may become an impediment to the creative leap. At the same time, other ideas of ideation on more primitive levels of mental organization are brought into activity."[61]

Adds Budzynski:

> "The twilight state, I believe, opens a kind of pipeline to the unconscious, to the non-rational half of our brain that we usually ignore. If we learn to open the pipeline at will, rather than by chance, perhaps we can resolve some of the conflicts between the conscious and unconscious mind—conflicts that create problems in many areas of our lives."[62]

Budzynski's "twilight state" and Koestler's "temporary relinquishing of conscious controls" are both characteristics of hypnosis. Hence, a person can be taught, through self-hypnosis, to achieve at will the state of consciousness in which sleep-learning can take place.

In recent decades, sleep-learning has become a popular method of assimilating information or influencing behavior. Athletes use it before performances. Students use it to learn course material. Doctors use it to assist patients in overcoming illness. Parents use it to direct positive results in their children.

Dr. Leo Martello gathered the following well-known examples of successful sleep-learning for his article in *The New Journal of Hypnotism*:[63]

- Through sleep-learning, entertainer Art Linkletter picked up enough of the Mandarin Chinese language in 10 days to carry on a televised conversation with the vice-consul of Nationalist China.

- A reporter for *Mechanics Illustrated* studied Spanish in her sleep for seven nights. After the experience, she was able to read books and carry on conversation in the language.
- A high-school graduate passed the examinations for a four-year college course following nine months of sleep-learning.
- Branches of the U.S. armed forces taught servicemen Morse Code using sleep-learning methods.

"The subconscious mind itself never sleeps and has a perfect memory," writes Martello. "In our competitive society, tensions are part of our everyday living; yet sleep learning has been a boon to people suffering from frustrations, tensions, inability to relax or sleep well, and other complaints which prevent one from making the most of his inner resources."[64]

The Prehypnotic Suggestion

There's an easy and simple way to program positive attitudes into your subconscious. I call it the "prehypnotic suggestion". You can do it with a simple exercise just before you go to sleep and just after waking, when your subconscious is most open to suggestion in (or moving into) a hypnotic state.

Take a blank sheet of paper and write a positive suggestion on it. For example, you might write, "I am the best salesperson on the staff. I am going to prove it during this sales campaign by winning that trip to the Bahamas."

Having written down the suggestion, fold the paper in half, covering what you have written. Keep it by your bed. When you first wake up in the morning, open it and read it three times in succession. Do the same thing just before you fall asleep at night. Repeat this for 30 days and see what happens.[65] (You may want to write one suggestion for morning and one for evening. You can do that by writing on both sides of the paper.)

The more sensory data you give the subconscious mind through the suggestion, the more effective the suggestion. See yourself impeccably groomed, wearing your most potent power suit, giving a flawless presentation to a major client. Visualize the lines on the sales chart climbing steadily upward. See yourself on the deck of the cruise ship, inhaling the ocean air, or sipping a tropical drink beneath gently swaying palm trees, or dancing to marimba music with someone you love. Hear the music of the marimba band or the drone of the surf massaging the shore. Feel the warm tropic breeze against your face. Taste the tangy sweetness of the drink and feel the lazy, warm glow from the rum.

Another technique involves a partner in the suggestion process. Make a deal with your spouse or someone close to you. Have your partner repeat the suggestion to you just before you go to sleep and again in the morning after you wake up. Your partner could whisper the suggestion into your ear as you're drifting off to sleep, "I love you. You are on your way to winning that sales contest and we're going to the Caribbean."[66]

If you do not want to ask someone to repeat the same message to you every morning and every night for 30 days, there's a simple alternative: Get the suggestion on tape. Have your partner record it so that you can play it each night upon retiring and each morning before arising. Or ask a friend or relative to record the same or related suggestion on an audiotape and finish the recording with as many positive affirmations and suggestions as you would like.

As you can see, self-hypnosis is not some supernatural state in which you walk around like a robot. Self-hypnosis is as natural as falling asleep and waking up. When you are in this state, your subconscious has its ears open, awaiting suggestions from you. You can take advantage of this openness by making sure that your subconscious hears only positive suggestions, for the suggestions it hears are the suggestions your subconscious will act upon. Keep them positive!

Many books exist on relaxation and self-hypnosis. Here are a few suggestions to get you started:

You Can't Afford the Luxury of a Negative Thought: A book for people with any life-threatening illness—including life. John Roger & Peter McWilliams (Prelude Press, 1995).

Peace, Love, & Healing Body-Mind Communication and the Path to Self-healing: An Exploration. Bernie S. Siegel, M.D. (Walker & Co., 1998).

You Can Heal Your Life. Louis L. Hay (Hay House, Inc., 1999).

Self-Hypnosis: Easy Ways to Hypnotize Your Problems Away with CDROM. Dr. Bruce Goldberg (Career Press, 2006).

Secrets of Self Hypnosis: Making It Work for You. Dr. Bruce Goldberg (Career Press 2005).

Code Concepts

- Relaxation is the key to self-hypnosis and reprogramming your mind, the key that opens the door to taking control of your attitudes, your behavior, and the stress in your life.
- You can utilize the processes of relaxation, self-hypnosis, imagery, and sleep learning to program into your mind whatever you want and to boost your self-esteem.
- You can condition yourself to go into a deep-breathing, relaxed state by adopting a cue and repeating it as you achieve relaxation.
- The subconscious does not recognize the difference between fantasy and reality. You can be what you imagine, believe, and feel to be true.
- Self-affirmation statements are the core of conscious activity in reprogramming your subconscious.
- The power of imagery lies in the emotional quality of your images.

Code Changing Exercise

1. You have 100% of your energy. Recognize that your subconscious can heal your life. Answer the following question intuitively, quickly and without calculation: What percentage of your energy is used up in problems? ____________
2. List three positive suggestions using your imaging power that will be very powerful in your life from this time on.

   a.
   b.
   c.

3. "Y.E.S." (You Expect Success) For the remainder of your life, maintain an attitude of YES. Say 'yes' to health, wealth, and happiness.
4. Consider adopting the following affirmation as yours for all time: "I am willing to release the pattern within me that has caused this condition or experience—I accept responsibility and build only great things in my life" (contributed by Roy Johnson, M.D.).
5. Next time there is anything uncomfortable in your life, regardless of its origin, say this to yourself, **"I'm sorry this is in my life. I love myself. Forgive me. Thank you!"** This technique comes from Joe Vitale's book *Zero Limits*. It's called Ho'oponopono, a very powerful way to condition your subconscious mind.
6. Read "The Relaxation Revolution" by Herbert Benson, M.D. or go to his web site: www.massgeneral.org/bhi and order the CD "Bring Relaxation to Your Life" by Olivia Hoblitzelle. Benson's revolution indicates genes can be activated for healing through relaxation. Consider Dr. Benson saying this,

   "You have the innate ability to self-heal diseases, prevent life-threatening conditions and supplement established drug and surgical procedures with mind body techniques that can improve your physiology, biochemistry, brain functioning, and genetic activity."[67]

Chapter Eight

Surviving Without Smoking

A bad habit is at first a caller,
then a guest,
and at last a master.

Anonymous

Smoking: Uncontrolled Substance Abuse

Mark Twain said: "Stopping smoking is easy. I have done it a thousand times." It's a lament heard far too often. According to Dr. Ahmedin Jemal, director of the American Cancer Society's Cancer Occurrence Office, "At last count, 43 million Americans smoke, and that's unacceptable. Smoking is the single most preventable cause of cancer. A third of all cancers are due to smoking." This figure represents a large percentage of the adult population and of this population, nearly one million smokers quit every year.[68]

Tobacco, alcohol, and coffee are the three most abused chemical substances in our society. A large percentage of America's health-care dollars is spent treating lung cancer, stroke, heart disease, and other conditions caused by use of these substances. Research shows that smoking permanently destroys air sacs in the lungs. Every drag on a cigarette irritates and changes cells and lung tissue.

The American Cancer Society publishes a list of more than 80 reasons to stop smoking, including the dangers from cancer, heart attack, stroke, emphysema, bronchitis, poor circulation, poor coordination and vision, coughing, clogged and black lungs, slowed reflexes, reduced endurance, more frequent colds, influenza and pneumonia, miscarriages, wrinkles, and asthmatic attacks. As each year passes, research links smoking with more and more physical problems.

The late chest surgeon Dr. Harold Levin added to the case against smoking. Levin reported that a one-pack-a-day smoker destroys 1 percent of his lungs each year. Lung cancer is not reversible. Most lung-cancer victims will be dead within six to nine months; 1 out of 5 will survive one year, and 1 out of 10 will be dead within five years. All end up with lung disability.

Smoking is more than a physical addiction and bad habit, however. Just as importantly, smoking involves an emotional attachment and an addictive relationship that can be very disquieting to release. Pointing to the effects of nicotine, former U.S. Surgeon General C. Everett Koop contended that cigarettes were as addictive as cocaine or heroin.

My experience with addicted persons supports Koop's conclusion, though my work deals more with the subconscious psychological or emotional addiction than from a strictly physical dependence on nicotine. What the connection to smoking means for the smoker's emotions and his or her subconscious is what really counts. Falling in love is a powerful stimulant on many levels. Similarly, smoking is also a powerful stimulant, except that the smoker may "fall in love" with the grim reaper so to speak.

Knowledge and Awareness Have Increased

After the surgeon general's statement became public, I began receiving more calls from smoking-cessation seekers. As a result of that influx of calls, I collected a fair amount of data describing the love affair people have with cigarettes. "They're my only friend," one lonely widow said. "I don't know what I'd do with my hands if I quit," quipped a celibate smoker. "I'm mad at myself for being controlled by a long, thin, white thing," fumed another.

These examples illustrate my point that an emotional bonding takes place between cigarette and smoker. Why else would anybody continue a slow-motion suicidal behavior with so many harmful side effects, unless the person is crazy (which is usually not the case with smokers)?

Smoking Is Not Love, But Hate

Smoking is like getting mad at yourself. How is that? Well, smoking is a logical choice for someone who believes he or she is guilty of something and needs punishment.

During my treatment of smokers, I read to the client words and phrases such as . . . "Punishment," "The reason I smoke is . . ." and "My punishment is . . ."

Roughly 40-50% of my patients respond under hypnosis to the word punishment" with: "self," "guilt," "necessary," "hate," or "unavoidable." People rarely, if ever, respond positively to the phrase "the reason I smoke is . . ." The responses to this phrase usually are: "terrible," "no good reason," "nervousness," and "anxiety." Almost invariably, clients respond with "smoking" to the phrase "my punishment is . . ."

Smoking Was Sally's Security Blanket

We punish ourselves for the strangest reasons. I had a client named Sally who used smoking as punishment for herself because she was adopted. Once she realized what she was doing, Sally gave up smoking easily and has remained cigarette-free for more than four years (as of this writing). Sally came to my office saying she "guessed" she was finally ready to give up smoking. She told me:

> *"I've been battling it for a long time. I just think I need emotional reinforcement. I quit once for a whole year after I had surgery, but I began again after I broke up with somebody about 15 years ago."*

Both her parents and several other people in her family smoked. Sally originally started smoking at 16 (thought she looked "cool" smoking and everyone was doing it), gave it up at 40, resumed the habit at 41, and was 56 years old when she came to me. Recognizing that taking up smoking at 16 because she thought she "looked 'cool' and everyone was doing it" was a symptom-producing event, I asked why she considered smoking a problem.

> *"It's just an emotional crutch with me. I use them as oral gratification. Whenever I get emotionally upset, I reach for a cigarette. I want to be healthier again. I smoke a good pack a day."*

I asked her about traumatic events in her life.

> *"A friend died recently—a heart attack in his sleep. He was 68. We had broken up the previous year, but there was still a lot of anger."*

The friend's death turned out to be a symptom-intensifying event. Searching in her background for other traumatic events, we uncovered that Sally's parents had died 22 years earlier—within four days of each other. This event created a huge death suggestion in her subconscious. As I plowed further into her history, I found additional death suggestions:

> *"My surgery 15 years ago, chest and breast. There was a possibility of cancer, but I came out clean. I had pneumonia and nearly died at six years old . . . Oh God, I don't remember . . . whooping cough as a child, a baby. I had my tonsils out [she looked to heaven] in second grade. My nose had to be operated on twice to breathe. The second time they straightened it out, I was about 18. Somebody held me under water at 12 or 13. I had a D&C about 10 years ago. I never got married."*

Then came the information we'd been searching for: the initial sensitizing event.

> *"I was adopted. I didn't know about it 'til I was 16 years old. My parents never intended to tell me."*

That was the key. Her adoption was the *initial* sensitizing event; learning about it was a *symptom-producing* event. Sally started smoking when she found out she was adopted, in addition to having all those death suggestions: the pneumonia, the tonsils, the whooping cough, the nose jobs, and the near-drowning.

During her word-association test, in response to my phrase "If I were happy . . ." Sally said, "I would stop smoking." When I said, "I punish myself . . ." she said, "Because I don't think I am good enough because I am adopted." She also said she started smoking because she thought it would be "sexy."

Once we reviewed her history and word-association test, Sally made a conscious choice to leave smoking in the past. She realized she was filling in empty emotional space. She was suffering from both spiritual and physical Walking-Zombie Syndromes.

In Sally's subconscious mind, smoking proved that she was indeed alive spiritually and emotionally. She filled in the empty spaces inside her by smoking, too. As a result of this awareness and agreeing that what she needed was not smoke, or self-punishment, but love, caring and the companionship of other people. Sally stopped smoking, stopped punishing herself, and sought out the particular gratifications that she needed, namely to bring her self-love back to life.

Sally left cigarettes in the past, not even coming back for her sixth session. She felt so good about her progress that she called me a year later to thank me again for helping her understand her problem.

Reasons For Smoking Are Usually Locked in the Subconscious Mind

A person who smokes has a lot more going on within than merely the development of a physical addiction or a bad habit. Frequently the serious underlying reasons for this behavior are enclosed within the subconscious mind. Those reasons are what we search for and uncover during hypnoanalysis.

The key to successful therapy is enabling clients to understand how their misinterpretations of reality caused them to smoke as a way of surviving a particular event. By smoking, Sally punished herself for her "unworthiness" resulting from having been adopted. And following all those scrapes with death when she felt she could not breathe, Sally proved she was alive by seeing the smoke (breath) coming from her lungs.

The Marine Was a Chain Smoker

Philip M. Bonelli shared a classic survival example in the *Journal of Medical Hypnoanalysis*.[69]

> "My favorite case is a 55-year-old ex-Marine who had been smoking four packs of cigarettes a day. When he came into therapy, after taking a detailed history, it became apparent that this individual did not begin smoking until he was on a Pacific island during the Second World War.
>
> "One day enemy aircraft were strafing the island. He was crouching in a foxhole with another Marine, frightened for his life. At that point the other Marine offered him a cigarette saying, in effect, that if he

> smoked the cigarette, he would feel better, that is, he would be safe. In a moment of high emotional energy (trauma) my patient smoked the cigarette, making the subconscious survival association that if he did smoke he would feel better, or in other words, he would survive. He smoked the cigarette and he survived that particular attack.
>
> "Thereafter, each time there was an enemy attack he lit a cigarette believing, subconsciously, that by smoking the cigarette he would be ok. The result was that he did survive. [But his survival had nothing to do with his smoking.] This, of course, reinforced his whole subconscious concept that if he smoked he would live. Subsequently, he got out of the war without a scratch, but smoking four packs of cigarettes a day."

Truth Or Myth?

It's important to separate the truth from myths about smoking. Smoking is much more than a simple addiction to nicotine. Smoking is not something one does for pleasure, though people claim so; it is a very dangerous habit. Smoking is an emotional attachment, an investment of energy in a deadly behavior. The physical dependence on nicotine is not what prevents smokers from quitting. What prevents smokers from successfully quitting is what smoking represents in the subconscious.

Smokers get what they expect. If they expect relaxation, they get relaxation; if they expect to be energized, they get a spurt of energy; if they expect sexual stimulation, they experience stimulation. (Nicotine, however, is a stimulant not a relaxant, and smoking can actually inhibit sexual performance and endurance due to decreased blood flow.)

Dr. Ellen Langer substantiated the mind-body theory in recent research at Harvard University. In work that won her the Distinguished Contributors to Psychology in the Public Interest Award from the American Psychological Association, Langer compared the mindful and mindless approaches to dealing with addictions such as smoking or alcohol abuse.

Langer found that smokers in nonsmoking environments did not experience strong cravings for cigarettes. They could forgo their habits in a movie theater, at work, or during religious holidays (Orthodox Jews are not permitted to smoke on the Sabbath). When the same individuals returned to settings where smoking was allowed, however, they experienced withdrawal symptoms if they could not smoke. On smoke breaks at work, for instance, the craving returned.

Admitting that this phenomenon occurred mindlessly, Langer and her students then designed an experiment to determine whether the same effect could be achieved mindfully—in other words, whether people could control the experience of temptation. She reports:

> "In designing a second experiment to answer this question, we assumed that a mindful person would look at addiction from more than one perspective. For instance, it is clear that there are actually advantages as well as disadvantages to addictions. But this is not the usual point of view of someone trying to break a habit.
>
> "People who want to stop smoking usually remind themselves of the health risks, the bad smell, the cost, others' reactions to their smoking—the drawbacks of smoking. But these effects are not the reasons they smoke, so trying to quit for those reasons alone often leads to failure. The problem is that all of the positive aspects of smoking are still there and still have strong appeal—the relaxation, the concentration, the taste, the sociable quality of smoking.
>
> "A more mindful approach would be to look carefully at these pleasures and find other, less harmful, ways of obtaining them. If the needs served by an addiction or habit can be satisfied in different ways, it should be easier to shake."[70]

As we saw in the earlier case study, Sally agreed to find ways other than smoking to fill her personal acceptance and survival needs.

Quitting Is Different For Each Person

We know from experience that stress builds up when someone tries to quit smoking. In dealing with "the crazies," the American Cancer Society recommends: "Learn to relax quickly and deeply. Make yourself limp, visualize a soothing, pleasing situation, and get away from it all for a moment. Concentrate on that peaceful image and nothing else." Relaxation and visualization—sound familiar? That was discussed in a prior chapter and it is what happens during the first session for patients seeking therapy to stop smoking.

The process is essentially the same as with the other cases presented where the first step is an initial consultation and taking of history. Then, as the patient—wearing headsets and a blindfold—reclines in a comfortable lounge chair in a private room, I am in a nearby control room where I gently guide the patient into a state of relaxation. And as we already know, relaxation encourages hypnosis, a very natural state of mind which opens the door to the subconscious.

During hypnosis, the conscious mind retreats and the subconscious mind becomes super concentrated. By communicating with the subconscious, we uncover the underlying reasons for smoking. Then, in subsequent sessions, we deal with those reasons and resolve them. Once the causes are removed, patients no longer feel the need to continue smoking.

The "Europes" Both Quit

One of my most interesting experiences involved a retired couple who both desired to quit smoking. I'll call them Mr. and Mrs. Europe. Mrs. Europe was a 55-year-old retired woman, born in Germany.

I walked in and said, "Are you ready to quit smoking?" and she said, "Yeah!"

I asked, "What's the problem?"

She responded, "I enjoy it; that's the big problem. I really enjoy it, but you come to the point where you wake up hacking. My chest is tight. I don't get over colds. I've tried three times to quit smoking."

I inquired, "Why do you consider smoking to be a problem?" and she said, "It takes a lot of time away from my precious time."

Now, that was interesting—she was older and considered her remaining time precious, but that was my suspicion and I had to investigate deeper to find out exactly what she meant. She said she'd been smoking about 30 years and usually had two packs a day, so I asked when she had started.

> *"I was a waitress, about 19 years old. I came over to the United States in 1949. I thought it was cool. I was just learning the language and I was young and dumb."*

> I asked about traumatic incidences in her life.

> *"The war. Children dying from typhoid fever and malnutrition. I couldn't stomach the shooting of guns. When I was nine years old, in Germany, both my aunt and uncle were killed and my father was taken to Siberia for a year and a half."*

> Then she continued with a host of traumatic events.

> *"I lived with the Russian officers and saw rapes at [age] eight or nine. I had diphtheria at seven. The thing to do then was to send people sick with diphtheria to a camp. I was in that hospital for seven weeks. My father was sort of an alcoholic and beat my mom, but that was nothing new. It was standard behavior in Old Europe."*

She also reported that she had had a hysterectomy at age 34. Then we uncovered an interesting point. I asked her when she got married. She had married Mr. Europe at 19—just before she began smoking.

I then asked her what she could do when she quit smoking that she could not do now. She said, "Oh, I'll have more time." Subconsciously, she was probably talking about more time to be alive, more time on the planet.

The remarkable thing about Mrs. Europe's case was that her smoking revolved around her coming to the United States—leaving her family, going through the traumatic events in World War II, and getting married. All those things happened within a few years. She started smoking while she was learning the language. It was a way of being connected, a way of proving that she was accepted in America.

In her word-association test, I said, "I'm just like . . ." She answered, "My dad." Her father, of course, had been dead for many years. Under hypnosis, I lined up all the traumatic events she had experienced as death suggestions: She had seen people die and others raped. She had left her home and given up her family. She had been alone. Her homeland had died so far as she was concerned.

She met and married her husband and smoking had seemed the natural thing to do. However, as is typical with people experiencing the Walking-Zombie Syndrome, smoking was proof to her subconscious mind that she was really alive.

Once I explained all that to her, she agreed with it and also agreed to stop smoking. Her sessions concluded with positive suggestions for her.

In a subsequent session, she came in saying, "I'm doing terrific. Not a one. So far, this has been so easy. I found two in the medicine cabinet and broke them up. How could people smoke!" After smoking for 30 years, Mrs. Europe did not even experience withdrawal symptoms.

A year later, she called, reiterating how helpful the positive suggestions had been and how easy it had been for her to quit after she understood the reasons she smoked.

Mr. Europe's Case Was Quite Different

Retired, 63-year-old Mr. Europe had been born in Poland and had come to the U.S. when he was six or seven years old. At his initial session with me, I asked him if he was ready to quit smoking and he said, "Yeah, I think it's time to give it up." I asked, "What's the problem?" and he responded:

> *"It seems like you are rewarding yourself for anything you do. You get nervous; anxious; you want to light up a cigarette. It's a reward. You are rewarding yourself and it makes you feel good."*

So, I asked, "Why do you consider smoking to be a problem?" His reply was very revealing:

"You think you are going to die if you don't have one. You've always got to have that pack hidden somewhere."

Within the first few sentences, this man had told me that cigarettes were proving he was alive. His reason for smoking was similar to his wife's in some respects—both had Walking-Zombie Syndrome. Mrs. Europe had had many death suggestions and smoking cigarettes was proof that she was alive, but her problems were more generalized. Her death suggestions were directed to her spirit, her body, her mind, and her country, among other things.

Mr. Europe started smoking in high school for reasons very different from his wife. "The other kids were smoking," he said. "We used to sneak one."

Mr. Europe said that he rewarded himself with cigarettes, that when he was 16 he would sneak them. He was still sneaking cigarettes as an adult, providing proof that he was alive. I asked Mr. Europe why he wanted to give up smoking, and he said, "I don't want to die from it, that's for sure." Let's pursue his subconscious thinking further under hypnosis through the word-association test:

Ryan: Because you think you're going to die if you don't . . .
MR. EUROPE: *Quit smoking.*
Ryan: When I started smoking . . .
MR. EUROPE: *I felt big.*

The last statement subconsciously signified his maleness. Now, that was a sign that in his mind he was proving that he was alive. His psychological "like" was connected to his smoking and being grown up. At age 16, there was another element to this man's story.

In the word-association test, many different factors will show up that would not normally be revealed if I were simply to trust the history and what a person says. For example:

Ryan: Anxiety, feels like . . .
MR. EUROPE: *Excitement.* (I had asked earlier what conditions influenced his smoking and he said that anxiety brought it on.)
Ryan: Smoking serves as a defense against . . .

MR. EUROPE: *Tension.*
Ryan: Tension feels like . . .
MR. EUROPE: *Anxiety.*
Ryan: Excitement feels like . . .
MR. EUROPE: *To be aroused.*
Ryan: Stimulate?
MR. EUROPE: *Arouse.*

Already, I was beginning to get a sense that smoking for him was a sexual substitute as well as proof that he was alive. One way he kept his sexuality alive when he was growing up was to smoke. He felt big when he smoked. All his responses were connected.

Under hypnosis, I explained to Mr. Europe that his smoking was about keeping himself alive, being big, and the connection to sexuality, he understood it and agreed with it. He said that he was definitely more interested in sexual activity than his wife was, and that he could understand how smoking could be a sexual substitute. After all, the mouth is used not only for smoking, eating, and talking, but also in sex; and teenage boys are normally very sexual.

I typically suggest to the client to have a dream about the problem he or she is trying to solve and did so with Mr. Europe. He dreamed he was installing and connecting waterproof boxes, under water, waist deep. Installing and connecting are both words that reflect sexual imagery. Also the dream's setting—waist deep, under water—suggests sexuality. We discussed the threads of a sexual component running through his history and his word-association test, and the meaning of the dream was clear to him. When the threads were woven together in his subconscious mind, Mr. Europe's dream confirmed the sexual connection to his smoking.

While Mrs. Europe's subconscious reason for smoking had been to prove that she was alive, the reason was different for her husband. Her case was spiritual—loss of love in several areas. His was clearly a case of sexual substitution that had begun when he was a teenager trying to prove that he was a man. Once we talked it over, Mr. Europe was able to let go of his smoking and, I assume, took a deeper interest in his sexuality, as I had suggested.

These are only two of the many different themes or variables that we often identify as causes for someone smoking. The reasons are unique to each person because of their experiences. Individuals react to and interpret their experiences in unique ways corresponding to their private logic.

My job is to help people come to terms with their streams of connectedness, with the order of survival within their subconscious minds. Smoking is almost always tied to a person's survival. Although a smoker's behavior does not usually make conscious sense, smoking can have a very deep subconscious connection to survival of one's mind, body, spirit, sexuality, or territory (see the earlier section on the order of importance of survival).

For Smokers, Hypnosis Provides Access to the Subconscious

Through hypnosis, greater access to subconscious attitudes and feelings that are responsible for behavior becomes available. It is possible to improve behavior and turn weaknesses into strengths by using gentle suggestions to remove limiting beliefs and to construct positive, life-affirming ones. However, the client must want to change. Hypnosis will not work unless it is accepted and wanted.

As with other behavioral issues, the underlying subconscious root causes of the emotional need for smoking are identified, analyzed, resolved, and removed. Then, when a person is free to give up the need for smoking, hypnosis techniques are used to remove the unwanted smoking habit pattern. This is the treatment of choice for the heavy smoker who has been unable to stop smoking with other methods due to strong emotional need and attachment.

In addition, self-hypnosis is taught for easy, natural, and effective withdrawal to safeguard against substitution of other unwanted habits and to develop the ability to relax with mental imagery, improve health, breathe easier, and to achieve more successful results, in general.

The success rate in my simple, six-visit smoking cessation plan is up to 90 percent. No shots or drugs are used. Using the hypnoanalytic technique, I simply remove the subconscious motivation to smoke and create habit reformation. The best part of hypnosis is that it feels good. And as an ex-smoker myself who quit cold turkey 40 years ago after going through a year of hell, I feel good that I can help someone else avoid the hell I went through. Nobody has to feel withdrawal symptoms. I wish I had known of a hypnoanalyst at the time I decided to quit.

Benefits of Quitting Smoking

Most people are aware of the adverse health consequences of smoking. Most smokers, however, are unaware of the positive changes you can expect as early as 20 minutes after you put out your last cigarette. Consider these facts. Within 20 minutes after your last cigarette:

- Your blood pressure will decrease to your normal reading.
- Your pulse rate (heart beat) will decrease to your normal reading.
- The temperature of your hands and feet will increase to your normal level.

It is never too late to stop. According to a Yale University study that examined 2,674 smokers and former smokers between ages 65 and 74 with years of addiction, the risk of coronary heart disease is reduced once they stop. Research indicates that ex-smokers had 52 percent less risk of heart disease than those who continued smoking.[71]

The following list describes other physical changes you can expect after you quit smoking:

- Your body begins the healing process almost immediately!
- Within eight hours after your last cigarette, your blood's carbon-monoxide level will decrease to the normal amount and your blood will carry the normal amount of oxygen.
- Twenty-four hours after you quit smoking, your chances of a heart attack will decrease.
- 48 hours after your last cigarette, your sense of taste and smell will return to near normal.
- Within 72 hours, the bronchial cilia will start to grow back and you'll begin to smell and taste things better.
- Three days after you stop smoking completely, your bronchial tubes will start to relax. You will begin to breathe better, air will come in easier, and your lung capacity will increase.

Within 5 days, you can expect to experience the following:

- You will stop coughing.
- You will feel and sleep better.
- Your endurance will be increased.
- You will have more energy.
- You will digest food better.
- Your circulation will improve.
- Your coordination will be better.
- Your lungs will start to clear up.
- Your irritability level will decrease.
- You will enjoy life more and be proud of yourself.

Within one year of smoking your last cigarette:

- You will cough less; have fewer times of breath shortness, sinus congestion and tiredness.
- Your risk of coronary heart disease will be cut in half.

Between 5 and 15 years after your last smoke, you will:

- Reduce your chance of dying from lung cancer to nearly half.
- Your risk of stroke is reduced to nearly the same as someone who never smoked.
- Your risk of lung cancer goes down to that of someone who never smoked.[72]

Some additional good news here as more people overcome their dependence on cigarettes: Overall incidence rates of cancer for all racial and ethnic populations combined decreased by 0.8% per year from 1999 through 2005 in both sexes combined.[73]

Code Concepts

- Tobacco is one of the three most-abused chemical substances in our society.
- Smoking one pack a day destroys 1 percent of your lung capacity each year.
- A lot more is going on in smokers' subconscious minds than merely the development of a physical addiction or a bad habit. Serious self-destructive, underlying reasons exist for smoking cigarettes or using tobacco.
- Smoking is not only a physical addiction and a bad habit; it is also an emotional attachment, an investment of your energy in a deadly behavior.
- Smoking is nearly always enmeshed with and confused with a person's survival levels.
- My job in hypnoanalysis is to help smokers come to terms with their streams of connectedness and with the survival of the subconscious.
- Positive changes will begin to occur in you body as soon as 20 minutes after you have stopped smoking.

Trust Your Imagination

Imagine you could trade smoking for something dear to you, something physical. What if the smoking gods could magically make smoking benign and remove all the harmful effects in exchange for you simply giving up a leg, arm, your nose, or some other body part. What would you be willing to exchange to the smoking gods in return for "healthy" smoking?

What are you giving up now to the smoking gods?

Chapter Nine

The Trouble With Food: A Full Body Ignores A Hungry Spirit

We are what we repeatedly do.
Excellence then is not an act but a habit.

Aristotle

Security is mostly a superstition.
It does not exist in nature . . .
Life is either a daring adventure or nothing.

Helen Keller

Over-eating, Obesity, & Eating Disorders, Though Common, Are *Not* Normal Human Conditions

Food is fuel for the body so when a person uses food in ways other than to nourish the body, it is a pretty sure bet that that person is using food to kill pain, to comfort self with food, to fill empty emotional space, and may have an eating disorder. Eating disorders are not normal and, unless there is a physical reason, almost always related to psychological and/or emotional reasons. As the title of this chapter suggests, overindulging in food becomes a substitute for what the spirit needs: a full body ignores the hungry spirit.

Depriving yourself of food (anorexia), bingeing (overeating, then under eating, then overeating again) or bulimia (the vicious cycle of forcing yourself to vomit so that you can eat some more) are also food disorders stemming from emotional issues. Food disorders frequently are the physical manifestation of poor self-esteem or the unconscious need to punish one's self. The cases shared in this chapter provide excellent illustrations of how events in early life lead to eating disorders.

Based on current research, childhood obesity is an epidemic in our country. According to the CDC, approximately 37% of all adults are obese. Over the last 20 years, U.S. obesity rates for both adults and children have skyrocketed. You can check the figures yourself at www.cdc.gov/obesity. Something is radically wrong here.

Certain kinds of fat, sugar, sugar substitutes, and additives contribute to obesity. My focus in this chapter though, is not on specific foods, except for one that is a frequent issue: bread. Many overweight people seem to have addictive eating patterns for wheat and wheat products which supply a never ending source of empty calories. When working with clients with food issues, I ask the client about his/her food intake. In about 90% of those cases, discontinuing wheat and dairy products helps considerably with altering negative habit patterns.

For purpose of our discussion, I am using the CDC's definitions. "Overweight" and "obesity" are labels for weight ranges that are greater than what is considered healthy for a given height. The terms also identify weight ranges that are linked to increased likelihood of certain diseases and other health problems.

Why Does the Weight Come Back?

Whether overweight or grossly obese, expressed as BMI or Body Mass Index[74], eating disorders are complex involving psychological, physiological, and social components. Eating too much is a symptom and only one part of the larger problem. Attempts to treat the symptoms alone usually result in failure and abandoned diets.

Any magazine will reveal what most people know intuitively: diets don't work. If diets were effective, there would not be the current glut of miraculous, doctor-sponsored, revolutionary, high-fiber, low-sodium, ad nauseum diets. If there really was a diet that worked, it would catch on and the market would dry up. Oprah can vouch for this personally. Anyone familiar with Oprahs's history knows how difficult losing weight has been for her.

Diets fail because they do not address the real problem. People overeat for subconscious, emotional reasons, not necessarily because they like the taste of food. This fact—that being overweight is a symptom of a psychological problem—is very difficult for overeaters to accept. Obesity, once it becomes entrenched, takes a considerable amount of effort to nullify because if the emotional attachment to overeating is not relieved, a repetitive cycle of weight gain, guilt, dieting, and more weight gain begins.

Along with the emotional and psychological component, the body gets accustomed to more weight and its set point (the weight at which the body feels comfortable) begins to rise, making weight loss more difficult. Add to this a slower metabolism, decreased activity, and the stimulation of the physical survival instinct by dieting[75] and you get obesity, depression, and hopelessness.

Recently, a weight-loss client came into my office with her eight-year-old daughter. The little girl sat down and announced: "My mom eats too much." This outspoken child, in her attempt to be helpful, thought she had identified the reason for her mother's problem. In her mind, her mother's overeating seemed straightforward enough. Like the child, many adults believe that weight problems stem simply from eating too much. The quantity of food a person eats doesn't begin to touch the complexity of eating disorders.

Being Overweight Is A Hard Life

Nearly all people with eating disturbances are negative thinkers. As a result of trying repeatedly and unsuccessfully to lose weight, or losing then regaining weight, their self-esteem plummets. They begin to think that, no matter how much they starve themselves and how hard they try, they cannot win the battle of the bulge. They are right. Even if dieters succeed in taking off excess pounds, they usually regain the weight when they resume their normal eating and activity habits. Often, they end up weighing more than they did before they started dieting.

Although it is a step in the right direction, jumping into a busy exercise program is not the answer either. Exercise alone is neither efficient nor effective in reducing weight. Without changing eating habits, exercise is at best a temporary method of getting rid of excess fat. Regardless of how much you exercise, you will not lose weight if your body continues to take in more calories than it burns. To successfully maintain an appropriate weight, individuals with weight problems must adopt and practice eating healthy as well as exercise routines that support them.

An emotional attachment to food is usually the primary motivator for people with overweight issues, obesity, and eating disorders. It is not just a case of too little information or not enough motivation. Therefore, it is absolutely essential that weight control be attacked on at least three fronts:

- psychological/emotional issues;
- eating habits; and,
- activity levels.

It has been my experience that some people will accept eating and activity modifications but will resist all efforts at psychological or emotional interpretation. Attempting to avoid the emotional pain and preferring to experiment with every fad diet that comes along, many end up in despair and grow increasingly despondent and fat. This is unfortunate because help is very much available.

The reason for failure, in part, has to do with the nature of psychological/emotional treatment coupled with an innate sense of wanting to be right about and in control of yourself. Richard, one of my weight-loss clients, had been the victim of a very controlling parent. As he grew up, Richard learned that among the very few things he could control was what he ate, as well as his bodily functions. Therefore, as a rebellious act, overeating became identified with his self-esteem. This case took a great deal of therapy, but his eating disorder was eventually resolved.

Psychological issues revolve around your beliefs and attitudes about yourself, others and the world in general. Woven inside the fabric of your beliefs lies your basic instinct: survival. Surviving is most important—your #1 concern! To be a human being means the need to survive. The survival instinct operates in three dimensions: mind, body and spirit.

People deal with perceived threats to their survival by overeating, resulting in obesity; by refusing to eat, resulting in anorexia; or by such behavior as going on eating binges, purging (bulimia), or other self-destructive actions. Unless the underlying negative suggestion to the person's survival is removed, all dieting and food management will be counteracted by the will to survive. If, in the subconscious minds of overweight people, staying alive is associated with overeating, then what happens when they diet? Right, they feel like they are going to "die".

The following case is an interesting example of a client whose weight problems stemmed from pre-birth threats to her survival.

She Saw the Connection Clearly

When my secretary asked Barbara her name, she responded with her real name but immediately amended it to "Fred Flintstone." Actually, she did look a little like Fred. She was short and chubby.

I greeted her with my usual, "What's the problem?" and she said right off:

> *"Don't you know by now? I don't know. I have an idea. I think I'm afraid of being rejected."*

Then she repeated herself before going on.

> *"I think I'm afraid of being rejected. I think the weight is a defense mechanism and a way not to deal with either. I feel like so many other things are gone, I can honestly say I feel content [except for concern about] the weight right now. And the weight comes down to a larger issue."*

Barbara did not identify the "larger issue," so I asked how long her weight had been a problem.

> *"I've always dabbled with the weight since I was a kid. It really hit about eight years ago. I met this guy, Alex [fictitious name]. I was truly in love with him. Then, one day he trailed off into the distance."*
>
> I asked, "What do you want from me?" and she responded:
>
> *"I want [pause] to feel more comfortable in relationships. I don't want to be terrified, to cling and to be walked on."*

I asked if there had been problems during her birth or when her mother was carrying her. Barbara revealed that her mother had been told that she could never have children and that she, Barbara, had been born more than six weeks prematurely.

Frequently, the premature baby emerges into a traumatic emotional context. The context can be the result of the baby's wanting to get out of the womb quickly or from the perception that the mother wishes to eject (read "reject") the fetus. In either case, the baby experiences trauma associated with being in the womb. So Barbara had hit on the cause when she said that her weight came down to a larger issue.

When I regressed her to the prenatal experience, Barbara did, in fact, feel that her mother did not want her. It was a mutual consent that her mother wanted her out and that she, Barbara, would leave earlier than normal. As a result of that experience, Barbara concluded that she was not really wanted.

Her problem was spiritual. Twice in the initial interview, Barbara had said she "was afraid of being." As a result of that fear, she *was not being*; she had become a spiritual walking zombie. Barbara had an identity problem stemming from the death suggestion to her spiritual component before birth. She felt as if she didn't belong in the world. If her own mother had not wanted her, then who would? That's the way the private subconscious logic goes.

Under hypnosis, I helped Barbara understand that her mother was having problems with the pregnancy that were not related directly to her. Her mother would have felt uncomfortable regardless of who was in her womb. Barbara was, therefore, able to let go of her feeling of rejection and stop overeating to "keep herself alive." This addictive behavior, however, didn't solve her existential emptiness. The only time she felt "filled up" was when she was stuffed with food.

In this case, the initial sensitizing event was her prenatal experience. The loss of her boyfriend was a symptom-intensifying event. All of her life, she had tried to fill up her emotional void and, upon taking her lover, felt complete at last. Once he rejected her, the pain became aggravated, and it was then she sought out therapy.

This particular client demonstrated several features in her personality that hypnoanalysts call a Ponce de Leon Syndrome (emotional and psychological immaturity). For example, believing that another person can fill one's emptiness is a childlike fantasy. Unfortunately, this client stopped treatment before I could help her with those illusions, even though she claimed victory over her eating disorder.

Pam Felt Possessed by Food

Pam, a single, 43-year-old research analyst with a major insurance company, came into my office saying she was having trouble maintaining weight loss. At 5'4" and 150 pounds, she had already regained 10 of the 30 pounds she had managed to lose and felt she was heading back to obesity.

Pam reported being overweight since age seven, a year during which her family had moved and she had had a tonsillectomy. I knew from past experience that tonsillectomies frequently result in death suggestions. People who have had tonsillectomies with ether as an anesthetic never forget that experience. A common statement is that we put a sick or injured animal "to sleep." Ether anesthesia—being put to sleep—is often subconsciously felt as being put to death. The individual goes into the hospital and is gassed. All too often, victims of ether—induced anesthesia tonsillectomies smoke cigarettes to prove they are alive, or overeat to fill up the empty space that was created by the death suggestion of the anesthesia. Smoking and overeating are only symptom-producing events, however. As the therapist, it is the initial sensitizing event that I seek to identify.

So I asked Pam what she wanted from me and she said, "I want to get to a reasonable weight and stay there. I don't want to be possessed by food. I'm addicted to eating."

Analyzing history, dreams, and word-association responses is a Sherlock Holmesian search for clues for the initial event, symptom-producing events, and, of course, the symptom-intensifying events. Mainly, I am searching for the initial event, then the conditioning events that caused the person to stall with the problem.

On the word-association test, Pam answered, "I don't know" to—

"The reason I am overweight . . ."
"If I knew, I would never be punished . . ." and
"My punishment is . . ."

So all those responses equal each other, and being overweight has to do with something about punishment. Earlier, I had said the word "problem" and she had responded "none," a response typical of adolescent problem denial. I took this direction in the word-association test:

Ryan: I reward myself . . .
PAM: *Often.*
Ryan: When I'm thin . . .
PAM: *I feel sexy.*

Evidently, Pam was avoiding being sexy by being overweight. I had to look deeper to find the reason for it.

Ryan: The one thing I need most is . . .
PAM: *Love.*
Ryan: The love stopped when . . .
PAM: *My mother died.*

This was a hint that some of Pam's emptiness resulted from her relationship with her mother, and that she felt love had died along with her mother. Her mother also had a weight problem and died at 65 when Pam was in her early twenties.

Ryan: Instead of food, I'd really rather . . .
PAM: *Make love.*
Ryan: Because of the emptiness . . .
PAM: *Feels horrible inside.*

When I reviewed all my observations and explained to Pam that she had a spiritual Walking-Zombie Syndrome, that her self-love had died, and that she was punishing herself, it made sense to her and she was eager to continue.

Throughout the weight-reduction program, which runs about 30 sessions, I gave Pam many suggestions about developing a strong self-image. I encouraged her to not be possessed by food and to use food for fuel—not as filler or a defense against other negative elements in her life.

The analysis of her assigned dream was helpful also. Reporting her dream, Pam wrote:

> *"It was very dark. I was confined in something very close to me, like a box. I was in an upright position and there was beating and scratching at the box. I made sounds, but I wasn't screaming. I had the feeling of suffocating. There was no one else in the dream. I woke up highly agitated, hot and sweating."*

When I reviewed this dream with her—indicative of birth imagery or prenatal experience, Pam said:

> *"I was terrified I was dying. There was a part of me that wanted to get out, but I put a brick wall around myself."*

Concluding that her overweight condition was a substitute for that safe, womblike experience, I decided to regress her to the time she was three months old intrauterine. In that session, Pam talked about being confused about her father and that her mother was very upset that her father would never be a good provider.

Pam reported that she had never wanted to be in the way in her family and had always worked hard to gain her parents' approval, even to the point of sacrificing herself. Here she was at 43. Never married. Although she was very attractive and had had several affairs, Pam had never been able to grow past a childlike dependency on her parents. This was the Ponce de Leon Syndrome in action.

In another session, I regressed her back to the womb and to birth. She said:

> *"It feels painful, awkward and I recognize it is going to be a change from security. I am afraid. It is different. It's wide open. I am insecure. Nothing close and secure to me.*
>
> *"They wrapped me in a blanket to take me to the nursery. It feels like there is so much space, it's overwhelming. All these babies."*

When she recognized that feeling of needing to be wrapped up, of needing to have something close to her, of security that was threatened by her birth, she was able to let go of the negative suggestions she had received from the birth event, suggestions that caused her to feel protected by excess weight.

In this case, I dispensed with the other symptom-intensifying events and symptom-producing events since, once she discovered that feeling in the womb, Pam recognized how she was using food to achieve a sense of security. Pam eliminated elements of punishment and immaturity on her own and was no longer tied to the memories of her parents. After these sessions, she reported an increased ability to form secure and loving relationships with both men and women.

Weight cases are frequently very involved, with numerous elements contributing to the problem. Pam's case was fairly simple and straightforward. She has kept in touch with me over the years after completing her therapy and continually reports that she is doing very well, though she still has to come to terms with the ups and downs of normal life.

Problems are not Always as They Appear

From the preceding examples, you can understand how weight problems originate from an emotional-psychological-spiritual time warp and how obesity is only a symptom. What looks like the problem at face value is in reality not the problem at all, but a solution to an earlier problem.

Some weight-control programs urge people to associate something unpleasant with the foods they crave. For example, they are told to see chocolate bars as riddled with worms. Those suggestions may be effective for a while but if the root cause of overeating is not ferreted out and dealt with, if the self-image is not changed, some other food will just be substituted for the "wormy" chocolate bars, and the "dieters" will go right on maintaining their "survival" behavior.

Hypnoanalysis Discovers the Cause Behind the Cause

Beliefs hidden in the subconscious, which have no basis in current fact, can control a person's eating patterns and behavior, resulting in the individual's being overweight or underweight. In my work as a hypnoanalyst, I have helped many people come to terms with the real reason behind their overeating—to discover the cause behind the problem. The comprehensive hypnoanalysis weight-loss program I use first identifies, then analyzes, resolves, and removes the underlying subconscious emotional and psychological causes for the need to overeat. Then, a medically managed weight-reduction food program is individually designed and prescribed, using hypnosis techniques to remove the undesirable faulty eating habits and related behavior problems.

Using this program, excess fat and inches come off easily and naturally, allowing for a permanent return to normal, lean weight levels through healthy, practical, positively controlled, sensible eating patterns, without the use of will power, medications, or starvation diets. My program emphasizes developing a positive mental attitude, an improved self-image, increased activity and energy levels, and a feeling of health and well-being—physically, mentally, emotionally, and spiritually.

The Case of Mrs. Processor

"What's the problem?" I asked the patient.

"Too much," replied Mrs. Processor.

Obviously, she had "too much." The lady was overweight.

"I'm dieting forever," she told me. Her kids would tell her she was fat. She had lost weight several times, but each time she regained it. Her older brother also was "very large."

She told me she was suffering from depression. She had sold her house. Her parents had moved to Florida. She had lost a relative to death in the past year. She said she had a lot of "death suggestions" coming at her.

"What makes you feel better?" I asked.

"Spending money makes me feel better, and then I feel guilty. I feel good when I'm eating, and I feel guilty afterwards."

I asked what she would be able to do after being cured of these problems that she couldn't do before the cure.

She answered that she would like to get over the feeling of being ugly and "probably just feel better and be myself."

"What do you want from me?" I inquired.

"To get rid of all this. Basically, I'd like to lose weight and feel good about myself."

After taking her counseling history and working with her in many sessions, we seemed to be getting nowhere. Mrs. P. wanted to be put on the weight program, so I obliged.

I asked her what the problem was with her weight, and she said it was probably from not taking time to eat properly. Finally, toward the end of the tenth weight session, the truth came out: "Maybe I'm afraid of men."

I explored that comment with her.

"Back when I first got married, I didn't really date any men."

We went to the word-association test, and it went like this:

Ryan: My relationship to food reminds me of . . .
MRS. P: *Sex.*
Ryan: I really desire . . .
MRS. P: *Food.*

So in her subconscious mind, Mrs. Processor equated food with sex. Subconsciously, it was sex that she really desired.

We continued the word-association test.

Ryan: My fat serves me as a defense against . . .
MRS. P: *Sex.*
Ryan: Sex . . .
MRS. P: *In bed.*
Ryan: What I'm afraid of . . .
MRS. P: *Being attractive. When I'm thin I'm afraid.*
Ryan: Affair . . .
MRS. P: *Scary.*
Ryan: If I were thin, I'd be . . .
MRS. P: *Sexy.*
Ryan: I'm afraid when . . .
MRS. P: *I'm alone.*

It didn't require a clairvoyant to see that Mrs. Processor's underlying issue was her desire for more sex.

How often did she have sex with her husband?

"Maybe three times a month."

How often would she like to have it?

"None. It's not the main thing in my life."

Was sex satisfying?

"To me, yeah, but not to him," she laughed.

When I explained to Mrs. Processor the relationship between her desire for sex and her problem with weight, she terminated the treatment.

"I don't think we're dealing with the right things," she said.

We were, in fact, dealing with the right things. Though I had done birth regressions and regressions to events in her past, we never seemed to make any progress because Mrs. P. was unwilling to deal with the core issue.

Her case demonstrates how people will sacrifice themselves to maintain something that's more important. (Remember the order of importance). Mrs. Processor was married and did not want to leave her husband, even though their sex life was unsatisfactory. She was afraid that if she became thin and attractive she would want to have an affair which would threaten something that was much more important to her—her connection to love, to her husband, and to her family. Needless to say, she didn't have to do that. All she really had to do was to deal with the fear and with the fact that she wanted to have more sex. She could have *dealt* with her feelings and without having to *act* on them.

It would be inaccurate to characterize Mrs. Processor's problem as a sexual issue. While it looked like a sexual issue, it was really a spiritual issue. She was sacrificing her body to obesity in order to maintain her spiritual connection, which had to do with love and her husband. She was willing to stifle her sexual impulses and to forgo sexual gratification while sacrificing her body to keep something more important—her relationship to her husband and family. How tragic that she could not be brought to realize that the sacrifices were not necessary.

Mrs. Processor's story is not all tragedy, though. She did undertake a number of changes in her life. I recently received a letter from her in which she told me how she was doing. She wrote:

> *"I've grown in several ways. One: I think more, which means I look at the situation first, think about it, and then my reaction is either helpful or meaningful. I don't react and then think about what I should have done or said or not eaten.*
>
> *"I take more time for myself. I sew more, read, take walks, etc. I really try to think why I want to eat. Is it anger, hunger, or necessity?*
>
> *"I've learned that I can't change what my parents do. I may not like it when they drink, but it's not my problem.*
>
> *"[It] still is very difficult for me to determine why I eat. I really feel I'm trying to eat good things, but I haven't lost weight. I know I should write down what I'm eating during the day and that would help, but I don't do it. Some day I will.*

> *"My relationship with my husband is better because we are talking more. I can tell him what's bothering me, and he's starting to tell me things that bother him. I feel we're getting better."*

So all wasn't lost in this case. Mrs. Processor developed significant insight, and the quote from Dr. Bryan seems to the point: "Leave something to God."

Eating Disorders Do Threaten Survival

Bulimia and anorexia nervosa are eating disorders that are life-threatening. Obesity, often presents a threat to a person's overall health but is not life threatening unless the obesity is severe. If overall health is at risk, more than medical attention is needed because medical attention alone (or in conjunction with dieting or exercise) works only on the symptoms, not on the problem.

Through hypnosis, I regress eating-disorder patients to their childhood or prebirth experiences to discover the initial sensitizing event that set them up for destructive eating patterns. Through hypnoanalysis, patients receive immediate relief from their life-threatening symptoms as well as a permanent resolution of the problem. As simple as this sounds, Herculean effort is often required of both the patient and the hypnoanalyst to effect a cure. The patient in these cases is really the hero or heroine because they stick with the treatment even when it is frustrating and at times feels that it is "two steps forward and one back."

Janice Was Searching Everywhere

Janice was seeing four other therapists and was suicidal when she sought my help for anorexia, depression, and low self-esteem. Rather than overeating, Janice was depriving herself of food. I greeted her with, "What's the problem?" and she laid out a list that would overwhelm the most astute professional:

> *"Not liking myself. I feel beneath everybody. Making decisions. I can't make a decision. I think everything has*

to be perfect in what I do, or it makes me mad. Jealousy. I think that has to do with not liking myself. Growing up in an alcoholic environment, 'cause I was always made fun of a lot. My dad would make fun of me, then abuse me. The basic problem right now, though, is not liking myself."

I asked how long it had been a problem, and she said as far back as she could remember. When I asked what she would be able to do once she was cured that she could not do now, she said:

"Be alone. I don't like being alone because then I feel lost. Every once in a while I get an anxiety attack."

So, I asked about past traumas: accidents? deaths? illnesses? operations? problems in her sex life? She groaned, "Oh, God!" From this response, I concluded that her relationship with God was the most traumatic problem. God translates into love, for God is love. Then she went on with another overpowering list of negative events in her life:

"When I was a little girl, I watched this friend [who was] forced to take her clothes off in a stream, and I didn't do anything to help.

"My dad's drunkenness. My brother went away to school and left me alone at 12.

"My Aunt Emily died, and I was made to go up to her casket at age eight.

"Then my dad tried to drown my mother in a pool when I was a teenager."

Notice that all these traumatic things had to do with losses of love. Janice was an incest victim, so the first loss was the love of herself. She cried when telling me about it. I asked about premarital intercourse and she said:

> *"All I remember was that I was real scared. My brother was going away to school and he wouldn't protect me any more. I was probably around 12 years old. It started at eight years old."*

I asked if there was anything she hadn't told me that she thought I really should know and she responded:

> *"Just the fact that I'm not a very nice person. I'm jealous."*

When I asked what she wanted from me, she said simply, "I guess that I'll like myself a lot better."

Janice was experiencing a spiritual problem. She felt self-loathing conditioned by her loss of love, experiences in the womb, and living in an alcoholic/abusive house.

Janice's womb regression revealed that her mother felt totally overwhelmed and that her father was actively drinking while abusing her mother, who questioned whether she could handle another child. The pregnancy was fraught with turmoil. Janice, being totally dependent on her mother, incorporated the negativity and, hence, was born with the feeling of being unwanted.

But there was more to her case. People who experience sexual abuse carry a lot of guilt and shame and Janice had been conditioned to feel as she did by the things that happened to her.

Janice's first sexual experience was at eight years of age, with her drunken father. Her words: "With Dad in my bedroom. All I remember was that I was real scared. My brother was going away to school and he wouldn't protect me any more."

She complained of feeling seven years old frequently, and in a dream analysis identified the feeling that she stopped growing at eight and wished to get no older.

Janice's food disturbance was related to a time she recalled in regression. When she was 16, her father didn't want to have sex with her any more because of her weight. She decided that "food's bad for you." Consequently, when she felt rejected, her symptom was abstinence from food. In Janice's subconscious, the idea of getting approval was linked to being sexually desirable.

This is an oversimplification of this case. It took a lot of courage for Janice and a lot of work on the part of both of us, but it was well worth it. She is functioning today and continues to grow.

With her anorexia under control more than two years after concluding her therapy, Janice evaluated her treatment:

> *"Well, I still will judge myself too harshly and think myself beneath others at times, but I have a much higher regard for myself now. I am kinder to me, more loving to me, able to take a compliment and voice my opinion. One very important thing I learned and now notice with others is that if you take time for yourself, you are able to give more to others—be more loving and therefore more loveable. Positive does attract positive."*

Most Eating Disorders Require Professional Attention

Dr. Louis K. Boswell points out that the chief nutritional problem of poor people in the U.S. is obesity. He calls the situation here a matter of quality not quantity, and reveals causes for the problem discovered through hypnosis:[76]

> "Under hypnosis, one of the most common self-images that overweight people struggle with is of feeling poor, poor in intelligence, poor in material and spiritual possessions, even though they may have all they need and want. Many of my patients who are successful in losing weight attribute their success to shedding a false belief that they are impoverished and poor. New attitudes and a success-oriented outlook on life help them develop better eating habits and a healthy body image."

Rarely are people able to recall, on a conscious level, the initial sensitizing event that causes their eating disorders. Under hypnosis, however, an analyst can examine occurrences in early life that cause people to consider food as more than simply fuel for the body. When those sensitizing events are discovered, analyzed, and brought to the patient's consciousness, the patient can let go of the habit and is able to accept positive input, namely that food is only fuel. Only then can permanent weight control occur. People who ride the diet see-saw without changing their self-images have difficulty kicking their weight problem.

Past-life Regression in Treating a Ponce de Leon Syndrome

With permission from the *Medical Hypnoanalysis Journal,* I include here my article on treating an interesting case of the eating disorder bulimia [overeating, forcing oneself to vomit, then continuing to overeat]:[77]

> "Past-life regression is used by some therapists as a tool in treatment. It can be very effective as part of the regressive work in hypnoanalysis. In the example that follows, a past-life regression experience was the pivotal point that seemed to help this client through an impasse.
>
> "Helga (fictitious name) appeared in my office two years ago with numerous complaints: depression, suicidal thoughts, low self-esteem, impending divorce, poor impulse control (she was beating her oldest son). She also reported a lack of control over her life, and that she was suffering from extreme guilt and bulimia. After I treated her with several psychotherapeutic approaches that I've learned over the last 15 years, including Transactional Analysis, Bodywork, Gestalt, Reparenting, etc., she managed to clear up some of her depression, raise her self-esteem, get out of an unhappy marriage, stop beating her child, and contain her suicidal impulses. However, the bulimia persisted.
>
> "By highly confrontational group methods and warm, supportive psychodynamic individual treatment, she inched along, "making progress." However, she began regressing steadily. She began carrying around

a stuffed animal she called "Blinky." "Blinky's" debut came after an intense session during which Helga began to understand her extreme dependence upon, and ambivalent feelings toward, her mother. Helga was 32 years old at this time. She had four children of her own. Helga herself is the youngest of three children. She grew up in a born-again fundamentalist religious environment and felt both psychologically and religiously conscripted to her family.

"Bulimia had been called "the emotional disorder of the 1980's", since it received quite a bit of notoriety . . . Many hypotheses exist for its causes. Bulimia is a secret addiction that dominates the thoughts of the person (recent studies show that 95 percent of all bulimics are women). Bulimia undermines the patient's self-esteem and can endanger the person's life.

"The excessive vomiting can cause death from cardiac arrest, kidney failure, and impaired metabolism due to electrolyte imbalance or severe dehydration, according to Lindsay Hall in Understanding and Overcoming Bulimia. Hall states further, "Other serious physical side effects include rotten teeth, digestive disorders, amenorrhea, malnourishment, anemia, infected glands, throat blisters, internal bleeding, hypoglycemia, and ruptured stomach or esophagus." These are only the physical possibilities.

"Current psychotherapies for bulimia seem to focus on a behavior approach along with insight-oriented treatment. One of the key issues with bulimics is an avoidance of growing up. This may be reinforced by parents who unconsciously do not wish to let their children emancipate. In addition, the bulimic who has relied upon the approval of others to validate her self-worth may experience tremendous fear at having to trust inner resources in dealing with the world. These phenomena belong to a syndrome hypnoanalysts call the Ponce de Leon Syndrome: [78] Helga was a classic example.

"Since Helga began treatment with me, she has been receiving therapy based on several frames of reference. As a result of my induction to and subsequent residency in hypnoanalysis, Helga agreed to hypnoanalytic treatment."

From Helga's History

Q. What's the problem?
A. My problem, um, I guess you could say mood swings—a feeling of lifelessness, comatized. I don't know—feeling little in a big world—I'm scared about being normal.
Q. How long has this been a problem?
A. Three years—Actually it began way before—specifically when I was a kid and intensified when I was a teenager.
Q. What makes it better?
A. Sex—it snaps me out of it, snaps me into a different mind set.
Q. Traumatic incidents?
A. Being born (laughs).
Q. Describe your eating habits for me.
A. I try not to eat. Either I don't eat or I binge.
Q. Nervous habits?
A. I suck my pacifier.
Q. Describe your childhood to me.
A. It sucks! It was mediocre, middle, well, it was pretty ordinary: Father's an asshole, mother's a bitch—you don't break any rules, you just do what you're told.

She also seemed to have a sexual addiction and to the question, "When you were born or your mother was carrying you was there any kind of problem?" she responded: "She didn't want me when she was carrying me." So, for an ISE, I would expect prebirth or birth. Her word-association test showed the following:

Fear . . . life
Life . . . death
Death . . . black
Hate . . . death
There must be . . . life after death
Live . . . die
Birth . . . death
All my life . . . nothing
The real problem . . . dying
Hypnosis . . . dying
Being normal is . . . dying
Most of all I want . . . to die
I resent . . . being born
Black . . . sex
It snaps me out of it . . . my kids

These responses seemed to indicate a WZS (Walking-Zombie Syndrome diagnosis).[79] After her birth regression and a regression to three years of age, she did not release the extreme nature of her symptoms. However, she appeared to feel somewhat better and was interested in the origin of her feelings.

The real change took place after I explained to her (while she was in hypnosis) the dynamics of the Ponce de Leon Syndrome and asking what happens after death. The dialogue follows:

Q. What happens after death?
A. I don't want to die.
Q. What happens after death?
A. You go to hell!
Q. Why?
A. For not being good, sinning.
Q. What's your first sin?
A. Being born.
Q. So, there's no way you can avoid it, is there?
A. No.
Q. Then what would a child do caught in this dilemma?
A. I don't know—probably feel dead.

Q. Yes, but there's one other thing a child might do and that's to not grow up, because if you don't grow up you don't have to die. Isn't that so?

A. YEAH!!! But how can I get out of it? I'm afraid.

Q. Suppose that you knew exactly what happens right after death. Would that help?

A. Yes.

Following that session, I age-regressed Helga back to the life immediately preceding her current lifetime. She told me she was an American Indian who was being burned for going against the tribal rules concerning sexual conduct. Helga described the excruciating pain of the fire. Tears flowed and she yelled out; finally calm came over her face; the tears stopped. I asked her what happened. With disbelief in her voice, Helga said the pain was gone now and that she was above the body momentarily, drifting toward a light above.

I asked her about hell, Saint Peter, God in judge's robes and heaven. She replied negatively and reported meeting people (spirits) she had known who had died before her. "What are they doing?" I asked. She told me they were welcoming her. These people were happy to see her. "Do you feel peaceful now?" She said "yes."

Her trance demeanor never changed. The astonishment remained in her voice, and her face displayed the look of wonder.

Since Helga's attention span lasted only a few minutes, I decided to go on immediately. I told her to let go of everything she had experienced and blank her mind. "Now, on the count of three, you'll be at the time right before you entered your current body: one . . . two . . . three . . . where are you?"

Claiming that she had just entered the three-month-old fetus, she told how she already felt the conflict in her mother and already felt rejected and dead. At this point, I tied the elements together and instructed her to put an end to her fear of death, which she did willingly.

As a result of this past-life regression, Helga, who had displayed spiritual zombie tendencies throughout her history and who was raised in a strict Christian fundamentalist home, was able to let go of her fear of dying, her fear of hell, and her fear of growing up. This was the turning point: She began focusing on having an adult life instead of acting out her Ponce de Leon fantasies, and even stopped carrying "Blinky." She wrote a story entitled, "Vanessa Grows Up." With Helga's permission, I'm recounting the first sentence. This sentence is indicative of the changes she made after this regression.

> *"One day it happened. Vanessa looked at herself in a full-length mirror and said, 'I love you; you're beautiful.'"*

Helga's was a fairly difficult case for me; one of the first I treated with hypnoanalysis. Traditionally, she would have been classified as a borderline personality disorder, since she displayed many of the features associated with that diagnosis. Too often, when a therapist treats someone with these issues, the traditional bag of tricks is quickly exhausted due to the associated drama and the therapist experiences burn-out, feelings of helplessness and worthlessness.

With Helga, I had begun to feel as if I were at the end of my rope when, fortunately, as a trained a hypnoanalyst I was able to use these powerful techniques to turn her case around as much as I could.

Helga wanted to be married and have another child. She already had four children from two marriages. By the time she was getting ready to separate from her therapeutic relationship, she was experimenting with relationships. Not long after that, she met a man, married him and moved out of state. As far as I know, she is still married and living a fairly normal life.

Emily was a forty-something-year-old married woman who came in with more pounds than she wanted to carry around. Here is her own story about how we solved her weight issue and how she began running marathons instead:

> *"When I first decided to try hypnosis, I felt like I was at the end of my weight-loss-methods rope. I retained an extra 5-7 pounds with each pregnancy. That doesn't sound like much but after four babies it added up. I had cabbage soup-ed, counted points, new year resolution-ed, made and lost the connection, and even attempted a cleansing fast by drinking only cayenne pepper, lemon juice, and syrup—yuk! (And by the way, didn't make it to day 2 on that one.) I was still in the quick—fix mindset when I*

found Ryan Elliott's hypnotherapy program. I had hoped he could just hypnotize me one or maybe two times and I would be able to get the proverbial monkey off my back and finally be rid of the extra pounds and negative body perception. When getting together with mom-friends, who have also struggled with "baby weight" (which by the way, we still called "baby weight" even after the baby turned 3) we talked about the subject of food, exercise and weight loss ad nausea. Its almost as if we focused on our hurdles such as always being rushed, no time to ourselves, no time to plan and prepare healthy adult food, the baby hates the nursery at the health club, the baby gets sick every time he goes in the nursery at the health club, can't go to the health club when he is sick etc. The list went on and on. We comforted each other with every speed bump we hit. The crying jag in the closet is one we all have experienced when getting ready for an event requiring an outfit with buttons and zippers, or that really terrible feeling seeing ourselves in photos, not wanting to even be in the photos and not wanting to go to class reunions, parties, etc. We spent many playgroups playing therapist to each other, talking about our feelings (Disappointed in ourselves. Exhausted. Undesirable. Embarrassed. Angry. Self-Conscious. Not in control. Jealousy.) I was constantly thinking of what I "should be doing differently".

"When women quit working, they leave a part of their identity with their careers. Body changes from pregnancy add on to that feeling of not even knowing who you are anymore . . . it did for me anyway. I was done obsessing about it, and I was done yapping about it. For me, the awareness part was already there. But just because I already had a sense of awareness of what was not working for me, doesn't necessarily make it go away. Ryan Elliott's book 'Wide Awake, Clear Headed and Refreshed' helped me to understand how it worked, but the Hypnotherapy sessions were what helped me to immediately feel like my old self again. I felt as though I was being set free. I felt

filled with joy and optimism. I felt like I was finally getting to the root of it all. I was starting to question some of my ideas and thoughts that I felt were universal truths. I soon started to feel like my identity was about ME, and not what I produced, accomplished, looked like, and it was not about how great my children were either. (Although they are pretty darn great)

"For the first time in a really long time I felt that I was enough, and that the other stuff (all of the 'should's') could and would have to wait. From the time I started the program, some of the old belief systems went away and the changes I started making became part of that new me. I started making major life choice changes such as getting up to exercise at 5 am, and dropping out from the social groups that pulled from my energy reserve. In one of the assignments after a hypnotherapy session I was asked to tell myself before I went to sleep to "show me what needs to be healed in a dream tonight" I knew at that moment, that this was a scientific experience (as well as a spiritual healing) when I had a crystal clear dream about the exchange of power between people, and the effects of my personal power. It took a while to tie it all together, but my subconscious was teaching me a lesson in personal power, which when it's depleted creates an empty spot. Throughout each of the sessions insights would bubble up while engaged in hypnosis as well as EMDR. These were discussed and, in a non-judgmental way, worked-through and, when necessary, replaced with new beliefs during hypnosis.

"The awareness for me was about being emotionally unfulfilled, and not being the person I really wanted to be. I would not trade staying home with my children for anything. I can't imagine missing all of those special moments. But sandwiched between that precious comment, or the sunny day at the zoo, was the not so sexy days. And prior to hypnotherapy, I felt like I could not say that out

loud. I was constantly reminding myself how blessed I was, that it was all such a gift and that instead of complaining, I should fill gratitude journals describing my joy. What I learned through the program is that it can be both. It doesn't have to be just one way. I could still manifest what I want in a family, and still acknowledge, and feel what is not working. I looked at the real deal, and the reality is that being home all day, every day, with babies and toddlers, was really physically challenging and most days mentally not filled with passion and deep interest. And yes, some days, mealtime and food were the highlight of the day. It's the only time when tangible fulfillment takes place amidst a sea of more or less seemingly mundane tasks. For me, cooking was creative, stimulating, and nurturing. There was a beginning, middle and end to it. At the end of the day, when I was exhausted, and not sure why because all I could see was what still needed to be done, cooking and eating dinner, was that one sure fire, immediate thing that felt some measure of emotional fulfillment.

"Hypnotherapy allowed me to identify and become aware of that, address the missing emotional pieces and peer through the door into a future reality of being in my body, mind and emotions in the manner in which I wished it to be. I wanted to be lean, strong and healthy; someone who liked to get up early and exercise, someone who didn't use caffeine for energy; someone who didn't feel guilt or fear or shame about anything. That became my fuel to continually re-enforce those beliefs, images and feelings. The size of my body was not as important as why I substituted food for love. Emotional pain is what made me 20 lbs over weight, and releasing repressed feelings is what made me look and feel lighter. I concluded that the reason to eat food is to nourish your body and the primary reason to feel your feelings is to nourish your soul. It was time to start to not just acknowledge my feelings but to really feel my feelings. I no longer medicated with food, because that was just the quick fix. And I no longer was Pollyannaish about

my station in life. If putting away laundry and dishes felt mundane, I expressed that instead of pushing down that feeling and instead focused on how grateful I was to be able to have this brand new front-loading washer and this opportunity to be home with my children. Through the program, I learned that love is the permanent solution! It can only come from God, others and me. Nourishing my soul with unconditional love is what's needed . . . not more food! Food is just that . . . food. It's not love, approval, celebration, or reward.

"So today, I'm in the driver's seat. I feel energized and satisfied, content, filled up and not empty. It feels great to finally be in charge of my life. Most days I feel balanced and healthy, I exercise regularly, and while I know it is a journey, I also feel confidence because I know who I really am and trust my authentic self, I like her, and it affects my entire family because hypnotherapy made me a real person. A person who is bound to run into more roadblocks, and hurdles, but it will all be ok, because this is the real deal. And, as a bonus, I'm back in my old jeans, so no tears in the closet while trying to find something that fits."

Self-Hypnosis and Visualization Help in Eating Disorders

The routine I follow with weight-control patients includes taking a client's history, completing a related word-association test, interpreting the patient's weight-related dream and regressing under hypnosis to locate the initial sensitizing event. After the patient recognizes the cause of inappropriate eating patterns and deals with that event, the remainder of the treatment is supportive in nature and emphasizes the de-conditioning aspects of habitual behavior.

I suggest the following behavior for recovery:

- Set realistic short-term, intermediate, and long-term goals for body weight.
- Eat your first meal within one hour of waking.

- Eat several, small, well-balanced meals daily and healthy, raw food snacks.
- Drink no alcoholic beverages when working on weight control.
- Learn about healthy dietary supplements from a qualified practitioner.
- Discover food allergies, such as wheat or dairy products, and eliminate those from your diet.
- Practice self-hypnosis daily.
- Imagine yourself at the weight you want to be.
- Affirm your visualization with positive statements such as, "I am ___________ (sexy, thin, etc.)."
- Remember that the positive image you see of yourself is the one your subconscious will aim for.
- Get regular exercise.
- Continue to grow in self-love, developing an attitude of continuing maturity.

Code Concepts

- Overweight, obesity, and eating disorders are complex matters involving psychological, physiological, social, and physical components.
- Diets alone fail because they do not address the real problem.
- Exercise alone is neither efficient nor effective in reducing weight.
- An emotional attachment to food motivates people with obesity and eating disorders.
- Weight control needs to be attacked on three fronts:

  —Psychological/emotional issues;
  —Eating habits; and,
  —Activity levels.

- Perceived threats to one of our survival prerequisites may be dealt with by overeating, resulting in obesity; by refusal to eat, resulting in anorexia; or by such behavior as bingeing and purging (bulimia) which is a primary defense, or other self-destructive actions.
- Unless the underlying negative suggestion or suggestions to the person's survival is removed, any attempts at dieting and food management will be counteracted by the survival mechanism.
- Through hypnoanalysis, clients not only can receive immediate symptomatic relief from life-threatening eating practices, but also can achieve a permanent resolution of the problem.

Code Breaking Exercises

1. Keep a daily journal defining your relationship to food. Keep in mind the following questions:

- How do you know when it's time to eat?
- Do you eat when you're not hungry?
- How do you feel when eating breakfast? lunch? dinner? snacks?
- What do you do with food when mad, sad, scared, ashamed, or upset?

2. Remember: Diets don't work. Die(t) is the message to your subconscious mind.
3. If you believe you have an eating disorder, consider these questions:

- Do you intentionally limit food intake or starve yourself, eating very little, eating nothing, or trying to eat as little as humanly possible regularly?
- Do you binge, over-eat a lot of food in a short period of time?
- Do you purge yourself, by inducing vomiting or taking laxatives attempting to "get rid of" what you've eaten?
- Do you compulsively overeat, eating even when you're not hungry?
- Do you compulsively exercise, exercising too much and too vigorously? Does exercise interfere in your life? Or do you design your life around exercise?
- Do you consume diet pills, laxatives, diuretics or harmful substances to help you stay thin, eat less, suppress appetite or force purging?
- Do you chew up and spit out food before swallowing?
- Do you lie, hide, or act secretive about your eating habits?
- Do you have a close relationship with your scale?

If you answered 'yes' to one or more of these questions, you might want to seek professional help.

4. A good source for information and to take an eating disorder questionnaire is www.something-fishy.org.

Chapter Ten

Phobias: The Unbearable Fearfulness of Being

Worrying isn't necessarily bad, but ruminating over and over about what awful thing can happen is useless.

Ralph Waldo Emerson

Men are not afraid of things, but of how they view them.

Epictetus

The Plague Of Anxiety Disorders

Anxiety disorders, which include phobias, panic attacks, and Post Traumatic Stress Disorder constitute the number one psychiatric problem in the United States.

- About 18% of the population is affected by at least one anxiety disorder.
- 11% takes anxiolytic drugs for up to 90 symptoms associated with anxiety disorders.
- About 6.5 million women and 3.5 million men suffer from tension that they are unable to deal with effectively.
- Arthur B. Hardy, M.D., publisher of the *Terrap Times*, estimates that about 19 million Americans suffer from some kind of phobia. By some estimates, as many as 8 million of these phobias are severe enough to have serious effects on their victims' mental health and their ability to function socially and vocationally.
- The Anxiety Disorders Association of America in Silver Springs, Maryland, estimates that as many as 40 million Americans—almost 1 in every 7—will suffer from some kind of phobia during their lifetimes.
- As of 2008, the Mayo Clinic suggests up to 12% of the population experiences a phobia during their lifetime.
- The number of phobic people in the country rises to 100 million—about 40% of the population—if you classify as a phobia the most widespread fear of all: the fear of public speaking.
- Here's the worst part—the cost for treatment of anxiety is about $42 billion per year and that's in 1999 dollars.

Some quick definitions:

A **phobia** is an irrational fear or anxiety involving certain objects, persons, places, or situations.

Anxiety is a low-grade, generalized fear or feeling of discomfort.

Panic is a sudden, unreasoning, hysterical fear.

More detailed descriptions of these conditions appear later in the chapter. But for now, let's deal with the common denominator of all these conditions: *fear*.

Fear Can Be Friend or Foe

Dr. Hardy gives us this definition of fear:

> "Fear is a reaction which warns us of danger. This reaction is intended to insure our survival. It is beyond our control. The fear reaction signals the body to run away and hide from danger. If you can't hide, or you are cornered, you will use the energy to fight your way out. The bodily feelings produced by this reaction are generally called 'the symptoms of anxiety.'"[80]

Fear pumps up the body's nervous system, creating the impulse to either fight or flee which symptoms include a rapid heartbeat, heavy breathing, tension, and warmth. These reactions are normal and cannot be consciously controlled as they are part of our nature. Throughout our history, human beings have needed to get pumped up to avoid dangerous animals, warriors, or natural disasters. Fortunately, for most of us, this is no longer the case.

Many people, however, still experience this response, even when there is no real danger. These people suffer from irrational fears. Their bodies react as if threats to survival were imminent, even though they may be quite safe. Consequently, stressful conditions result because of a constant readiness to deal with that threat through either fighting or fleeing.

Much unhappiness ensues from these conditions. Those who learn to control their reality (inner experience) largely determine their quality of life, which accounts for a functional definition of peace. Phobia sufferers cannot control their realities. Hence, they are very unhappy.

Anxiety: Small-Scale Fear

Anxiety is different from a phobia in that it is a generalized, small-scale fear reaction alerting the body to a possible danger. The danger frequently eludes the person, but the feelings are usually undeniable and uncomfortable.

Anxiety causes a dual reaction, both physiological and psychological. The symptoms are connected, impossible to separate. However, depending on some unknown vulnerability, some people tend to experience symptoms of a physical nature while others experience symptoms which are more mental/emotional. A combination of symptoms is more likely.

Humans can experience two basic types of anxiety: *exogenous* and *endogenous. Exogenous* anxiety is the type most familiar to us. It is what you experience when you can clearly identify the threat to your security or safety. When you're driving down the interstate and see a big semi closing in on your rear bumper, you experience exogenous anxiety. When your company is threatened by a hostile take-over and you perceive that your job is in jeopardy, you experience exogenous anxiety. The word "exogenous" means, "originating externally." Your anxiety response is triggered by circumstances outside your body.

Endogenous anxiety stems from conditions within the person. Evidence indicates that it is a disorder to which certain individuals are vulnerable. Endogenous anxiety attacks usually come without warning and the victim experiences anxiety without knowing why. Some of the symptoms are a racing heart, shortness of breath, dizziness, choking, or tingling.

It does no good to tell the victim of endogenous anxiety to relax, take a vacation and forget about the problem. That prescription might work for normal anxieties. While the symptoms of endogenous anxiety may resemble those of normal anxiety, the two conditions are quite different.

The anxiety scale in Figure 9.1 shows the range of anxiety, from full-scale panic to fluttering butterflies in the stomach, along with the symptoms and effects at each step on the scale.

10	Panic; disoriented, spacey, detached, frantic, hysterical, numbness or weird sensations and feelings	AREA OF NON-FUNCTION
9	Dizziness, nausea, diarrhea, visual distortions, numbness, some hysterical sensations, concern for losing control	
8	Stiff neck, headache, feeling of doom	
7	Tight chest, hyperventilation	
6	Lump in throat, strong muscle tension	AREA OF DECREASED ABILITY TO FUNCTION
5	Dry mouth, feeling of need for escape	
4	Shaky legs, feel tremor	
3	Rapid or strong heartbeat, tremor, muscle tension	AREA OF CONTINUED ABILITY TO FUNCTION
2	Sweaty or clammy palms, warm all over	
1	Butterflies in stomach	

Figure 9.1

Reprinted with permission from Arthur B. Hardy, M.D., from page 2 of *Everything You Wanted to Know About Phobias But Had No One to Ask.* For more information, call 1-800-2-PHOBIA.

Phobia: Irrational Fear

Phobias are different from anxiety reactions in that phobias usually involve inordinate and irrational fears, or severe anxiety reactions to certain situations, objects, or people that would not normally create fear in most people. Manuel D. Zane, M.D., and Harry Milt define a phobia as "a disorder in which the individual reacts with irrational dread and panic in a harmless situation, flees to rid himself of the unendurable sensations and feelings aroused in the situation, then henceforward, avoids it and similar situations, to avoid the anticipated recurrence of this extremely painful experience."[81]

The phobic reaction does not stem from some real threat. Rather, it is caused by an onslaught from the imagination which unleashes a frightening salvo of thoughts and images. The body starts pumping away as if these thoughts and images represented reality. If the victim were facing a real threat—an attacking dog, or a car approaching in the wrong lane—his or her mind could order a rational response. But since these are imaginary threats, the mind sees no way to deal with them, spurring the body on in an exaggerated response that can lead to panic.

The word phobia originates from the Greek word *phobos*, meaning fear. Individual phobias get their names by taking a Greek or Latin word for the triggering condition and combining it with the word "phobia." Thus, "phobophobia," describes the fear of fear that Franklin Roosevelt referred to in his first inaugural address, when he reassured the American people during the Great Depression that "the only thing we have to fear is fear itself."

The fear of loud noises and the fear of falling are the only two fears people are born with since virtually all babies experience that at birth. All other fears are acquired or learned. Although phobia sufferers consciously recognize that the situation, object, or animal of which they are so frightened poses no threat to their lives or safety, they often go to significant lengths to avoid the fear-producing situation. It is then that phobophobia develops, causing people to alter their life-styles and relationships in dramatic and crippling ways.

Phobophobia is real to many people. It frequently follows the onset of another phobia, so the sufferer fears the fear itself as much as the situation or object that provokes the fearful response. With some phobias, the symptoms progressively intensify and with agoraphobia preventing some patients from leaving their houses or—in extreme cases—their rooms.

Phobias are not new. Hippocrates described a phobic (a person with a phobia) some 2,400 years ago:

> "He would not go near a precipice, or over a bridge or beside even the shallowest ditch, and yet he could walk in the ditch itself.
>
> "When he used to begin drinking, the girl flute-player would frighten him; as soon as he heard the first note of the flute at a banquet, he would be beset by terror. He used to say he could scarcely contain himself when night fell; but during the day (when people were about him) he would hear this instrument without feeling any emotion."

From historical and literary references, we learn that phobias have existed throughout the world and throughout history. The Anxiety Disorders Association of America estimates that 1 American in 10 suffers from phobias at some time during his or her lives. They live in New York City, La Jolla, California and in Pagosa Springs, Colorado. They live in Miami Beach, Chicago, Seattle, and in Bluefield, West Virginia. They include illiterates and Ph.Ds, Protestants and Catholics, Jews, and Muslims, atheists and fundamentalists. They're found among mechanics, college professors, artists, garbage collectors, and corporate CEOs.

Phobic reactions can be frightening experiences. As Zane and Milt note:

> "A situation sensed by the phobic person to constitute a threat—even though no actual danger is perceived or recognized—sets off an automatic reaction of the entire system, which in turn generates a chain of frightening thoughts, images and secondary bodily reactions. Instantaneously, the mind's attention and the body's reactions are captured to the exclusion, for

the time being, of all else. The response is automatic, comprehensive and consuming."[82]

Panic Breeds Phobias

Phobias frequently grow out of panic disorders. Panic, remember, is a sudden, unreasoning, hysterical fear. Panic attacks are episodes of irrational terror mainly accompanied by symptoms of sweating, heart palpitations, chest discomfort, faintness, trembling, hot or cold flashes, feelings of unreality, or fear of losing control, of dying or of going crazy. Many panic sufferers believe they are having heart attacks and seek emergency-room help. Panic attacks usually begin during times of general psychological distress. As a result, a phobia may develop that is related to the place, situation, or person when the panic occurred. For example, if a panic attack occurs while driving the car on the interstate, the victim may develop a fear of either driving or the area where the panic attack occurred.

The person experiencing a panic attack develops a feeling of total disaster. Emotions seem driven to the wall, with no avenue of escape. The situation seems unbearable and unendurable, and the victim often feels that the only recourse is to faint, go berserk, or die.

The Long List of Phobias

In the play *The Merchant of Venice*, Shakespeare wrote of "some, that are mad if they behold a cat." Anticipating Sigmund Freud by centuries, Shakespeare was describing a phobia. It is through the writings of Freud, the father of psychology, that the most common phobias are known—acrophobia (fear of heights), agoraphobia (fear of public places), claustrophobia (fear of closed places), xenophobia (fear of strangers), homophobia (fear of homosexuality), zoophobia (fear of animals), even—get this—triskaidekaphobia (fear of the number 13). Actually, phobias consist of several categories but the five primary ones are:

1. psychological conditions,
2. non-psychological conditions,
3. prejudices,

4. biological descriptions, and
5. fictional phobias.

For example, acrophobia (fear of heights) is a psychological condition while photophobia (fear of light) can be both a psychological condition and a medical condition (where exposure to light can cause pain). Usually homophobia is a prejudice, while ombrophobia resembles a biological condition or fear of rain (imitating plants repelling water) Venustrabobia (a portmanteau word composed of 'venus trap' and 'phobia') comes from a humorous 1998 article published by the BBC News describing a fear of beautiful women. Some men would describe this phobia as a real psychological condition.

If you want to be left to yourself at a party, memorize these phobias and spring them on your friends:

Aurorophobia—fear of the northern lights
Barophobia—fear of gravity
Blennophobia—fear of slime
Cryophobia—fear of cold
Cyclophobia—fear of bicycles
Diabetrophobia—fear of diabetes
Dikephobia—fear of justice
Gallophobia—fear of French things
Geniophobia—fear of chins
Kopophobia—fear of exhaustion
Leukophobia—fear of the color white
Methyphobia—fear of alcoholic beverages
Mnemophobia—fear of memories
Patriophobia—fear of heredity
Peladophobia—fear of bald people
Panophobia—fear of everything
Phasmophobia—fear of ghosts
Photoaugiophobia—fear of glaring lights
Scabiophobia—fear of scabies
Stygiophobia—fear of hell
Tuberculophobia—fear of tuberculosis
Uranophobia—fear of heaven

You can research additional names yourself. There are about 180 defined phobias. With a little imagination, you can add to the list. Just take any place, object, sound, smell, color, or condition that could possibly illicit fear, find its English, Latin, or Greek name, and follow it with the word "phobia."

Regardless of the number of phobias, there's only one phobic feeling reaction: FEAR. It results in decreased functioning, avoidance, and unhappiness.

The Cause is the Key to Curing the Phobia

"The triple allergenic theory indicates that a person is sensitized or set up for a particular reaction to certain stimuli," writes therapist Nicholas Cooper-Lewter about the initial sensitizing event (ISE) or root cause of a phobia.

> "From this point on the person is a potential time bomb of symptoms and problems. Symptom-producing events lurk in the person's life. Symptom intensifiers strengthen the potential strangle hold a person's disease may bring."[83]

Hypnoanalysis is particularly effective in dealing with phobias as a trained hypnoanalyst will be able to uncover the subconscious origin of a problem and use subsequent sessions to undo this subconscious knot and free the patient to live a healthier, more productive life.

The misunderstandings about phobias and the ways professionals of various disciplines try to classify them are rampant. Classifying phobias into either 180 or 18,000 categories does not resolve the phobia. To resolve the phobia we must first determine how the client first came to accept the fearful suggestion and then determine how we are going to deal with it. Although an individual may be totally reshaping his or her life due to the phobia, the fear itself is a magnification of the root problem. To "cure" the patient of the phobia, we need to search for the initial suggestion that generated the fear—the ISE.

Most phobias are not conscious and tend to remain embedded in the subconscious and continue to cripple individuals for months or years if the phobia is not removed through treatment. Phobias and panic attacks do not usually resolve or go away by themselves, though some cases lie dormant for periods of time.

From my extensive training and experience, both as a psychotherapist and as a hypnoanalyst, I have found that the most effective way of uncovering the root cause of phobias is to conduct word-association tests and age regressions. The word-association tests link ostensibly unrelated words through subconscious recognition, leading the analyst to the target age for the ISE—the first encounter which created the phobia. Once removed, the other stages of treatment must follow (the eight R's referred to in the Introduction).

I agree with Lewter that, like other emotional problems, phobias can always be traced back to an initial sensitising event. Dr. Louis K. Boswell described the cause and recommended treatment of phobias this way:

> "An event sufficiently dangerous to the individual may give rise to a state of anxiety in that individual's mind and continue to influence the personality for a long period of time. Threatening events superimposed on this initial sensitizing event will serve to magnify the intensity of the original anxiety. As each threat produces even greater anxiety, the fear for survival takes on an aura of reality . . . We must pay particular attention to those which produced a real threat to the patient's survival . . . We must analyze each problem in the light of this ultimate fear—physical or emotional death.[84] (I would add "spiritual death" as well.)

The Three Phobia Types

Phobias are generally classified into three groups:

- simple,
- social, and
- agoraphobic.

People with *simple* phobias are afraid of singular, identifiable objects or conditions. Fear of heights, water, particular animals and insects characterize simple phobias.

Social phobias involve public situations. People with such phobias may experience anxiety while attending parties, eating in restaurants, speaking before groups, or in other situations in which they are conscious of being observed by other people. The anxiety manifests itself in the form of physical symptoms such as trembling hands, blushing, perspiring, dizziness, weakness in the limbs, palpitations, and hyperventilation. When the victim experiences these effects, the usual response is to flee from the situation and to avoid such situations in the future.

Agoraphobic is the fear of open places, such as markets, roads, etc. It differs from social phobias in that it is debilitating in the worst case, preventing sufferers from driving or leaving one's home or room.

Fear of Public Speaking

Fear of public speaking is a social phobia. Because 40% of Americans feel victimized by this fear, which is also known as performance anxiety, and because it can be a severe handicap for people whose jobs require them to communicate with groups, I will elaborate on this phobia in greater depth.

I have worked with many people who would rather walk on hot coals than speak in public. I can attest to the self-imposed limitations to career, self-confidence and personal satisfaction this fear causes. But does this fear qualify as a phobia?

Burton J. Rubin, author of the *Stage Fright Handbook*, tells us:

> "By all accounts, more people are afraid of public speaking than anything else . . . [Performance anxiety] consistently outpolls the fear of disease, loss of a loved one and even fear of death itself in fear studies. Perhaps this is not so surprising at all when you consider that communication, speaking and conveying our thoughts, is the primary way by which we interact with others. Every time we express ourselves in one manner

> or another, we reveal ourselves and put our egos, our self-images on the line."

> Further, Rubin says:

> "In contrast to fear, a phobia is an irrational fear. A phobia is also a fear of fear. I believe that anxiety, discomfort caused by sympathetic nervous-system reasons in, or in contemplation of, a public-speaking environment qualifies under either definition."[85]

I agree. Many people deal with this phobia by simply avoiding the opportunity to speak publicly. This is in contrast to other phobic reactions which cannot be avoided by scheduling or by refraining from volunteering.

For some people, though, public speaking is a career requirement. A man named Ken came to me for help after hearing one of my lectures on the subconscious mind. He was embarking on a new career that required him to speak on a weekly basis to different groups of professionals. He told me:

> *"Every time I think of getting in front of a group of people, I freak out. I get scared to death. Not only that, but when I actually do have to start talking, I get diarrhea and sweaty palms, and my armpits get so wet I'm afraid that I'll embarrass myself in front of the group."*

Ken was an intelligent, good-looking man in his thirties. I asked him when his problem began.

"I had it in high school so bad that I would skip school on those days when I was supposed to speak," he told me.

"How did you get through college?" I asked.

"Well, I used a lot of courage and would avoid taking classes where I had to get in front of the class."

"What makes it better?"

"Not having to do it?"

"What will you be able to do once this is cured?"

"Enjoy giving speeches."

During the word-association test, Ken told me his problem began at the age of nine. (The number nine appeared in his history several times. The subconscious always sends clues to the astute analyst.)

During his eighth session, I regressed him back to a time in his ninth year. Relying on the assumption that the subconscious always knows what the problem is, I told him: "On the count of three, we're going back in time to a scene, memory, or feeling that's directly related to your problem." I counted to three and snapped my fingers.

"What's happening?" I asked.

Ken answered: "I'm in the gym. They're all looking at me and I can't talk. I'm crying. I feel terrible, embarrassed. I hate myself." He sobbed. "What's wrong with my voice?"

The scene took place at a Cub Scout Jamboree when Ken was nine years old. He was the master of ceremonies and was to introduce the next act. When he got in front of the packed gym, he froze and couldn't speak. A teacher finally rescued him from the situation.

Once he realized the impact of this childhood scene, he was able to let go of the fear that had paralyzed him in his adult life—the fear of repeating the situation that took place when he was a third grader and of looking foolish again in front of an audience. Ken resolved his phobia and now speaks regularly. He even looks forward to it.

Direct Suggestion May Remove the Fear

Hypnoanalysis revealed the key to Ken's problem. Mary Kullman, a colleague of mine, solved another speech-fright problem through direct suggestion. Sally, a 38-year-old sales executive, who was experiencing anxiety as she contemplated a speech she was to give in her Dale Carnegie course, approached Mary, saying:

> *"My chest gets tight when I start to talk; my voice sounds like it is somebody else's voice. I panic, and when I notice that my voice sounds funny and shaky, I need to take a breath but I can't. When you're up there you can't do it. I get all quivery and my hands shake.*

Mary asked how long she had experienced the problem.

"Probably since high school," she said. "I honestly think it started in grade school. In gym, the teacher would pick on little fat kids, and I was a little fat kid."

Sally had the same teacher for three years.

"When I'm standing," she said, "I still feel like a little fat kid."

Mary resolved this case in two sessions by giving Sally direct suggestions to realize that she was not a little fat kid anymore, and to strengthen her self-image, and to build her confidence, thus enabling Sally to give her Dale Carnegie presentation. Mary also gave her a subconscious trigger mechanism to counteract the symptoms whenever she began to experience performance anxiety. Sally called back and reported that everything went fine.

No Magic Formula, But There Are Techniques

Magic formulas don't exist for overcoming the anxiety associated with public speaking, but confident speakers turn their nervousness to an advantage. They take their anxiety as a sign that they are emotionally ready for the speech.

For most people, though, nervousness compounds the problem. They are convinced that the audience is waiting for them to make a mistake and will ridicule them for every little miscue.

In fact, the audience is not waiting for the speaker to make a mistake. Most audiences don't even notice the speaker's nervousness, and if they do detect mistakes, they are prone to overlook them.

You can go a long way toward overcoming your fear of the podium by revising your attitude toward the speech. People who feel the greatest anxiety about public speaking tend to view the speech as a performance. Alternately, those who are most comfortable with public speaking tend to view it as an exercise in communicating.

Observes Michael T. Motley, Ph.D., professor and chair of the Department of Rhetoric and Communication at the University of California, Davis:

> "Excessive anxiety is especially common among people who view speeches as performances, in which they must satisfy an audience of critics who will carefully evaluate gestures, language and everything else they do.

> Though they can't describe precisely what these critics expect, people with a performance orientation assume that formal, artificial behavior is somehow better than the way they usually talk."[86]

Giving a performance requires that you be an actor or an actress. Since few of us are blessed with that talent, it is better to be yourself. Being yourself does not require you to act. And, what many have discovered is that being yourself is more than enough!

Motley has a technique he uses to help his speech students "be themselves." Here's how he describes it:

> "As the speaker [*student*] approaches the podium, I dismiss the audience [*from the room*] temporarily and begin a 'one-way conversation' with the speaker. I tell him or her to forget about giving a speech and simply talk spontaneously to me, using the speech-outline notes as a guide. In this situation, most people feel rather silly orating, so they start to speak conversationally, using natural language, inflections and gestures. I ask the speaker to maintain this conversational style while the audience gradually returns, a few people at a time."[87]

Using this approach, speakers are usually able to maintain the conversational quality before the full audience. When they do not maintain the conversational quality, notes Motley, "the transition from talk to speech is invariably identified later by the audience as the point when effectiveness began to decrease and by the speaker as the point when anxiety began to increase."[88]

Here are some of Motley's tips on overcoming the fear of speaking:

- Decide on your specific objectives first. Before you think about anything else, know one or two major points you want to communicate. Then, plan the best way to get them across.
- Put yourself in your audience's place. Recognize the differences between yourself and the audience in attitudes, interests, and

familiarity with what you are talking about. Then, speak to them on their terms, in their language.

- Forget memorization and do not read your presentation. Except for a few carefully chosen gems and possibly your first sentence—memorable phrases or examples you know will work well—be as spontaneous as possible. Don't rehearse to the point that you find yourself saying things exactly the same way each time. Use brief notes to keep yourself organized.
- Speak to one person at a time. Looking at and talking to individuals in the audience helps keep you natural. It feels foolish orating at one person. Speak to that person as long as it is mutually comfortable, usually up to 15 seconds.
- Avoid thinking about your hands and facial expressions. Instead, concentrate on what you want to get across and let your nonverbal communication take care of itself. Conscious attention to gestures leads to inhibition and awkwardness.
- Take it slow and easy. People in an audience have a tremendous job of information processing to do. They need your help. Slow down, pause, and guide the audience through your talk by delineating major and minor points carefully. Remember that your objective is to help the audience understand what you are saying, not to present your information in record time.
- Speak the way you talk. Speak as you do in casual conversation with someone you respect. Expecting perfection is unrealistic and only leads to tension. The audience is interested in your speech, not your speaking.
- Ask for advice and criticism. For most people, careful organization and a conversational style add up to a good speech. A few speakers, however, have idiosyncrasies that distract an audience. Solicit frank criticism from someone you trust, focusing on what might have prevented you from accomplishing your objectives. Usually, people can correct problems themselves once they are aware of them. If you don't feel you can correct your problem on your own, take a course in public speaking or see a speech consultant.[89]

Rubin contributes these tips:

- When giving your presentation, stay in the present; don't worry about what's ahead with all the "what ifs" and "how do I knows?" You can stay in the present by concentrating on some object in the here and now, such as a table, chair, sofa, or lectern.
- Concentrate on speaking with emphasis. If you concentrate on the words you intend to stress and the way you will interpret your material, you will not have the mental capacity to think ahead and worry about the "what ifs."
- Calm down if you "go blank." Actually, you haven't gone blank at all. The information and the words you want are there in your brain. You just aren't directing your mental energies toward finding them. Instead, you are caught up in the thoughts of "I am going blank," or "I've just gone blank." Clear your mind of these thoughts and concentrate your mental efforts on remembering the information you need. Often, speakers go blank when they try to keep too much information in their heads at once. Take it one thought at a time, and don't worry about the next three thoughts.
- Accept the fact that you have stage fright, and concentrate on doing the things you are supposed to do. The more that you accept the fact that you have stage fright, the less panicky you will get.[90]

Toastmasters International is an excellent organization for those who want to develop their public-speaking and leadership skills. Toastmasters provide opportunities to speak before a friendly audience of peers in a relaxed and pleasant setting. Chapters can be found in communities throughout the United States. Notices of meetings are often published in local newspapers or posted on public library bulletin boards. More information can be found at www.toastmasters.org or by calling 1-949-252-8255.

An Unusual Phobia: Public Urination

Fear of public speaking is the most widespread of public phobias. Less common, but also less avoidable, is the fear of urinating in front of other people. I have not had a patient who complained of this fear, but I am aware of case histories most commonly involving male patients.

Usually, for men the problem surfaces only when other men are present. As the sufferer approaches a urinal with other men standing beside him and as he feels his urine begin to flow, the sufferer begins to feel more anxiety and fear of not going, or of dripping on his pants. Actually, it seems the issue is related to the fear of coming up short in a penis-size duel, something many men only do metaphorically and commonly call a "pissing contest".

Social Phobias Usually Strike While You're Young

We often find that clients with social phobias were shy and timid during childhood. Adolescence finds them lonely and socially isolated. They usually experience their first attacks between the ages of 15 and 30. After that, their phobias may strike again and again for many years.

Social phobias often are rooted in disturbing childhood experiences and cause the social phobic to be extremely self-conscious and sensitive to the ways others perceive them.

Agoraphobia

The third classification of phobias, agoraphobia, takes its name from the Greek word *agora*, meaning marketplace or a place of assembly. A German psychologist, Dr. G. Westphal, gave it the name after he had dealt with three patients who experienced terror associated with various places where they happened to be. The associated "place" could be a workplace, a certain street, a certain building, or a certain square.

Westphal described the phobia as "the impossibility of walking through certain streets or places or the possibility of doing so only with resultant dread or anxiety."

Some have since characterized agoraphobia as a fear of open spaces, but that is misleading. The anxiety can strike indoors as well as outdoors. A victim may experience anxiety while standing in a grocery checkout line or while waiting at an airport baggage claim. When a person experiences such an attack, the typical reaction is to avoid a similar setting in the future. The anxiety spreads to other locales, and soon the victim may feel safe and comfortable only in his or her own home or immediate neighborhood. Often, a person suffering from agoraphobia finds it impossible to function away from home or outside the presence of a trusted friend or relative.

Alan Goldstein, Ph.D., a psychologist and director of the Agoraphobia and Anxiety Treatment Center in Philadelphia, tells us that agoraphobia often stems from childhood conditions. Agoraphobics frequently come from homes in which the parents were either overprotective or too distant. Often, one or both parents were alcoholic or agoraphobic, or suffered from an illness or condition that required the child to shoulder too much responsibility. Many agoraphobics, as children, were either separated from their parents or felt threatened by separation. Some experienced sexual abuse. Observed Goldstein:

> "Because agoraphobics don't have the power, as children, to change their distressing circumstances, they learn to adapt by habitually denying their family problems and the feelings they have about them. Then, as adult, instead of dealing head-on with conflicts in their relationships, they become chronic avoiders, never complaining for fear of rocking the boat."[91]

Depression is a frequent companion of social phobias and of agoraphobia. Everyone experiences mild depression once in a while—the feeling of dejection when things aren't going right. You've had a run-in with your boss, lost a big sale you'd been counting on, your marriage or romance has hit a few bumps, or a friend has let you down. In most lives, there are enough positive experiences to offset these letdowns, and the blues will pack up and leave after a short stay.

But sometimes, the downers in life are so severe and the reaction is so deep and intense that depression moves in for a long visit. Such long-lived depression often accompanies the loss of a child, a spouse, a sibling, or another person close to the victim. Divorce or the break-up of a long-standing romantic relationship can also trigger depression. So can phobias that cripple one's ability to function normally in situations involving other people.

Fortunately, most people have the resources to recover from the pitfalls of life. For those who cannot recover on their own, hypnotherapy offers a means of uncovering the hidden basis of the depression. In the case of phobias, hypnotherapy can help the patient to expunge from the subconscious the factors that bring on the phobia. When the phobia is dealt with and removed, the patient can then deal with removing the depression.

A phobia is very real and not something that is just "in your head." Phobias often strike intelligent, hard-working people and haunt their lives like waking nightmares. Some phobias will appear without warning and disappear as quickly, but those that last for more than a couple of months hold tenaciously to their victims unless treatment is sought.

Peanuts cartoonist Charles Schulz was a well-known sufferer of agoraphobia. Rheta Grimsley Johnson, author of a recent Schulz biography, credits the artist's chronic condition with his creativity:

> "Most things are sad to him sooner or later. Everything becomes a source of depression . . . His loneliness is not the kind most of us feel when a loved one goes (or passes) away. It is baseless and unrelenting and must be dealt with as a basic bodily function—daily, unremarkably, constantly. And the sad, conspicuous irony is that without this wellspring of grief, there most certainly would not be the humor, the piercingly clear look at human foibles, and insecurities, the Charlie Brownness of life that have made the cartoonist rich, famous, and funny."[92]

Schulz, according to Johnson, is among the agoraphobia victims who suffer panic attacks when faced with strange settings, long-distance travel and some public places—hotel lobbies, for instance. She quotes him: "Just the mention of a hotel makes me turn cold. When I'm in a hotel room alone, I worry about getting so depressed I might jump out of a window."[93]

A young woman's letter that appeared in the Ann Landers advice column described the typical onset of anxiety attacks and received an empathetic reply from the columnist.

Dear Ann Landers:

I am a 24-year-old female who needs your help. Lately I have had what I believe are anxiety attacks. The first one occurred while I was driving home about a month ago. I managed to make it, but was really frightened because I had no idea what was happening to me. My sister told me to sit down and take several deep breaths. She put a cool cloth on my face and I did feel better, but let me describe the feeling. Your body shakes and your heart beats like a trip-hammer. There is shortness of breath, you feel light headed as if you are going to faint, and you think for sure you are having a heart attack. It really is scary. I went to a doctor, who prescribed a drug. I had heard that some of these drugs are addictive and can change your personality.

I don't want to take drugs, Ann. I want to fight this thing on my own. Please tell me what to do.

Sincerely,
Hopeful in Detroit

Ann's reply:

Dear Detroit:

You are courageous to want to fight this on your own, but it may not be possible. I hope you will seek out a mental health professional who specializes in phobias and related anxiety disorders. For additional information, contact the Phobia Society of America (Now the Anxiety Disorders Association of America in Silver Springs, MD). You are not alone. Millions of others have experienced anxiety attacks, and with the proper help they have gotten them under control. You can too. Good luck.[94]

The columnist offered good advice. The fear of panic attacks often moves untreated victims to the next step of severity: *phobic avoidance*—avoiding the situations, people, and places where panic attacks have occurred. Finally, full agoraphobia may result, and suffering individuals will fear being away from what they consider "safe" persons, places, or situations. They will alter relationships and behavior patterns in dramatic and crippling ways. They will redesign their activities and life-styles to avoid fear-producing situations. Depression often accompanies agoraphobia, as does seeking relief through alcohol or drugs.

Joy Considered Suicide

Joy, an agoraphobic, sought my help, complaining:

> *"Well, I have panic attacks. I've had them for a long time. I feel like everything's unreal. I get tense and shake. That started happening in eighth grade. I started smoking pot; I thought I was going crazy through high school. They went away during college. After I graduated, they got real bad. It's gotten worse now that I'm home."*

I wondered what she would like to do that these problems stopped her from doing. Her answer:

> *"Lead a normal life, to feel like I don't have to worry. I hate being alone. I have a strange feeling that I'm two people. I feel worthless and half the time I don't feel like living. I don't know the meaning of life and I feel useless."*

During her analysis, I regressed her several times, taking her back to the womb, to the time of birth, and to traumatic events and accidents that might have been her ISE. Though Joy was improving in all areas of her life, the panic attacks returned. She met a man whom she married, left her parents' home, and began law school. Joy reported greater self-esteem and more zest for life. But those panic attacks were stubborn, and I knew I was missing something.

Joy grew up with an alcoholic father and possessed the qualities of an adult child of an alcoholic. That fact, though, didn't explain the troublesome attacks. The answer surfaced in relation to Joy's mother and how Joy could get her needs met.

During panic attacks, said Joy, "My mother comforts me." During her upbringing, Joy learned that to get her needs met within her family she had to get very needy. Once she understood how her panic met her need for love and attention, Joy learned healthier ways to take care of herself.

This was an interesting and challenging case because I couldn't solve it just by finding and bringing to consciousness the initial sensitizing event and the symptom-producing event. I had to uncover and analyze the secondary gain—the conditioning factors in her relationship that supported her intense fear.[95]

Joy credited hypnoanalysis with saving her life. She wrote:

> *"I probably would have committed suicide if I hadn't sought help. This experience has made me alive again . . . I no longer feel dead and worthless. Although I still have problems, I don't face them with the intense fear and dread that I once did. [Hypnoanalysis has been] the most beneficial experience in all my life."*

Phobias and panic disorders are curable with professional treatment involving client and family education, the restructuring of negative thinking, and support for confronting the feared situation while resolving conflicts that are uncovered. Sometimes, medication is necessary. The important thing is to identify the problem and get professional help to face the fear.

Most of Us Avoid *Something*

Fear is a natural and normal feeling, as are the other feelings humans experience, such as anger, sadness, shame, and happiness, in varying degrees. Phobics, however, are more easily stimulated by their fear and feel it more intensely than other people do. Their fear dominates their other feelings

The following poem puts the condition in perspective. Written by Don Mesuda, Jr., "My Phobic Friend" appeared in a newsletter of The Phobia Society of America:

My phobic friend is a special person,
One who cares without rehearsin'
Some can't drive or be alone,
But would rather prefer to stay at home.
Others feel funny in public places,
And get very nervous when meeting new faces.
My phobic friend needs special attention
Because new situations cause much apprehension.
Sometimes it's hard to understand,
But imagine living in a foreign land.
Or having a constant panic attack
With thoughts of lions at your back.
My phobic friends need people to confide in
So they won't need their shells to hide in.
They've missed some parties and summer vacations,
But are thankful for their family's patience.
For without support, the phobic is alone,
Their dearest resource is the telephone.
They have learned to face their fears,
And look forward to ending years of tears.
After weeks of practice they finally see
How wonderful life is when you're Phobia-free!

The Fear of Flying

I think this poem is clever, pointedly sincere, and timely. I would add just two lines, after "apprehension" in line 8:

"When it comes to boarding a plane to fly,
My dear phobic friend would rather die."

A great many of my clients seek help with aviaphobia (fear of flying). A survey *by USA Today* and Gallop Poll in 2006 found that more than 27% of Americans feel some fear related to flying, down from an all time high in November 2001 of 43%. Since more than a quarter of the American population is afraid to fly, aviaphobia is more common than even I had thought.

Media hype about near misses only increases the panic felt by fearful flyers. The September 11, 2001, tragedy increased people's fear of flying, yet, the reality is that flying is statistically safer than driving a car.

People with aviaphobia have vivid imaginations amplified by horrific fantasies in which they see themselves on a crashing plane, suffering all the lethal consequences in dramatic color. Media coverage tends only to reinforce the fear of flying and the attitude that "I'll never fly again. It's too dangerous."

The real fear is that of crashing, not of flying. Most clients who present with this issue begin getting anxious as they enter a plane, not later. Their fear is mostly related to other subconscious negative suggestions. It has been my experience that most of these cases resolve very simply once the cause of the irrational fear is identified. The following two cases illustrate.

Removing the Aviaphobic Fear

For one middle-aged lawyer, fear of flying had its roots in a difficult birth experience. He came to me complaining of anxiety each time he had to fly or use an elevator. Interestingly, it wasn't the flight or the elevator ride that frightened him; he was quite comfortable during flight. It was the *contemplation* of flight that caused him to break into a sweat. That suggested to me that the problem originated in the womb.

I regressed him back to the womb and he told me:

> *"I feel pushing, squeezing; it's tight . . . a floating sensation . . . pulling . . . stuck, trapped . . . I don't know what to expect. I am being pulled through. It's wet, scary. They put me down."*

When I asked him to identify his fear in the present he pinpointed the moment he was getting onto an elevator or into an airplane. I asked him to leave that fear in the past, and he did. With that suggestion, I was able to de-condition his subconscious mind, relieving it of the fear of moving into closed, tight objects. Some time later, he told me he was still flying and enjoying it very much. His case was a complete success!

This Complex Case Revealed a Few More Interesting Secrets

"Anxiety is the issue and panic attacks recently" complained Donna, a thirty-something woman who sought help after landing her dream job with an airline that required her to fly to unknown locations, places she'd never been before, to meet with new business associates. Her concern was, *"An urge to know where the bathrooms are and urinate but I don't have to."* She said she had had the problem for five or six years [my emphasis]. *"In a group situation, you can't slip away . . . anxiety about talking to people . . .* (Where else do you feel it, I had asked.*) . . . anywhere stuck in traffic"* were complaints she mentioned in her history.

Utilizing hypnoanalysis, Donna's irrational fear was totally resolved. But before I share the process, understand what she said she wanted from her treatment. In her words, *"I want to completely be free of anxiety, at ease with people, live in the moment, be natural, lose weight, go on tours with my family, not have to go (to the bathroom) every time we go someplace new* [again, my emphasis]*."*

The first interesting secret to resolving this case stemmed from the very first time she went "someplace new." Can you guess when that ISE was? Ok, you most likely get it by now.

Here's how she described her birth, *"bright . . . scared, took a long time. Like I want to go back in, not nice—lots of hands getting in my space."* She went on to describe the feeling of asphyxiation or birth anoxia she felt and then identified how these feelings come up at meetings, in airplanes, in cars, etc. Once Donna recognized that the cause of her anxiety and panic resulted from a birth trauma, she was able to let go of those feelings in the here and now. She realized she didn't die from that experience and that there is no reasonable expectation of dying from enclosed places in her present life. Yeah, success! But wait, there's more . . .

In a subsequent session, we followed the feeling of needing to urinate back to its beginning. Here's how she described it: *"I was on roller skates, at 5 or 6 years old* (notice the numbers 5 and 6. These are the same numbers Donna had mentioned as the duration of the problem. This is no accident. The subconscious often reveals ISE information this way). She described how two male relatives were acting "too friendly" when she had to urinate and she picked up a fearful, negative suggestion concerning people she didn't know very well.

Consequently, those two negative suggestions, both of which took place before 7 years of age, produced anxiety symptoms that went away completely once she understood the historical roots and how current situations triggered those feelings.

Tips for Aviaphobics

Since flying is so common in our present life-style, and the fear of flying creeps up in most of us at one time or another, I am including some specific suggestions that may be helpful in dealing with aviaphobia:

- Avoid watching television programs, news coverage, or survivor interviews after a plane crash. There are few benefits from these publicized accounts.
- Confront any grandiose tendency to take air accidents personally, as if luck had it in for you with thoughts of "Just my luck, I've got a flight coming up and wouldn't you know it, there's a crash."
- Recognize your superstitious or magical thinking. Air accidents are not omens, portents, or harbingers of the future. Nobody has the psychic wherewithal to cause an air crash. Air crashes do not happen in numerical sequences such as three in a row; nor do they take place more frequently on Friday the 13th, during a full moon or when Mercury is in retrograde. However, beware of small planes that have less than stellar track records. Think JFK, Jr., Sen. Paul Wellstone, Sen. John Tower, and singers John Denver, Buddy Holly, The Big Bopper, Ritchie Valens, and Wiley Post, Omar Torrijos, Hale Boggs, and Will Rogers—all of whom were killed in small plane accidents.
- Keep in mind that all air accidents are thoroughly investigated by the government and airlines and, after reviewing the findings; changes are policed by regulatory agencies for improving safety and performance.

- Remember that near misses are not narrowly prevented catastrophes. Planes that are miles apart are considered "near miss".
- Keep in mind that not everyone stops flying after a highly publicized crash. Only those predisposed to phobias do. Others just get nervous for a time.
- Self talk like "I only have a number of safe flights in me" is useless and induces more fear.
- Eliminate seeing air-related disaster films such as *Air Force One* or the like. They just feed negative fantasies.
- If you're phobic, then get help. Aviaphobia is one of the easiest to cure.

What Phobias Have in Common

In my practice, I treat many people who are suffering from phobias. It doesn't matter what the phobia is. It could be anything from fear of water to fear of crowds. Basically, the phobias are all the same in that they emanate from the same source—a belief buried in the subconscious mind that is causing this irrational fear.

Through hypnoanalysis, I communicate with the client's subconscious mind. With the client's help, we identify the source of the fear, analyze it, resolve it, decondition it, and remove it.

Remember, you have nothing to fear but fear itself. Conquering fear is simply a matter of going within yourself and bringing to the surface the original cause of your phobia. After that is done, you'll truly understand the last line in "My Phobic Friend," "How wonderful life is when you're Phobia-free."

Code Concepts

Phobias are irrational fears or severe anxiety reactions to certain situations, objects, or animals that do not normally create fear in people.

- The fear of loud noises and the fear of falling are the two fears people feel from the birth experience.
- Most phobias are seated deeply in the subconscious minds and permanent relief may require help from a hypnoanalyst or comparably trained professional who are competent to conduct age regression and concurrent removal techniques by discovering the initial sensitizing event causing the phobia.
- Similar to other emotional problems, phobias can always be traced back to an initial sensitizing event. A time exists in the phobic's subconscious mind before the fear existed.
- Phobia sufferers will redesign their activities and life-styles and will alter relationships and behavior patterns to avoid the fear-producing situations.
- Depression and relief seeking, along with self-destructive behaviors such as controlled-substance abuse, often accompany phobias.

Code Breakers

Refer to the Chart 9.1 on page 145. What areas of your life correspond to the various levels of anxiety?

____

____

Think back to the first time you can remember feeling this fear or phobia, then consider where your initial sensitizing event took place. Ask your subconscious mind to produce hints and memories for you. Keep a journal of your results. Do this for 30 days and if you don't feel better, get help.

If no phobias, be happy!

Chapter Eleven

Defining Depression: Dead Humans Walking

"To my knowledge, this particular syndrome has never been reported anywhere in the annals of medical literature. I am confident that the reason it has not been so reported is not because it is rare, but simply because it has not been looked for, indeed not even suspected, by the medical profession."
William J. Bryan, Jr., M.D.

"The madness of depression is the antithesis of violence. It is a storm indeed, but a storm of murk. Soon evident are the slowed-down responses, near paralysis, psychic energy throttled back close to zero. Ultimately, the body is affected and feels sapped, drained.

In depression . . . faith in deliverance, in ultimate restoration, is absent. The pain is unrelenting, and what makes the condition intolerable is the foreknowledge that no remedy will come—not in a day, an hour, a month, or a minute . . . It is hopelessness even more than pain that crushes the soul."
William Styron

When we remember we are all mad, the mysteries disappear and life stands explained.
Notebook, 1898, Mark Twain

The Walking Zombie Syndrome

When I asked this female client, Terry, what her problem was, she said,

"I'm just going through the motions [of being alive]. I was told it might help to come here to remember . . . I was sexually assaulted, been over-whelmed. I'm a workaholic. Being a math analyst, we're a little unstable . . . having nightmares, very vivid dreams. All I want to do is sleep or I can't sleep at all."

She further stated, "*I feel like there's a void in my life. I never feel anything, never feel a sense of happiness.*"

What this client described is a syndrome related to depression and grief, first identified by Dr. William J. Bryan, Jr. in the Journal of the American Institute of Hypnosis in July of 1961. A serious subconscious syndrome from which many people may suffer unknowingly, a simple and apt description of this condition is: "the patient *has already accepted* the fact that he or she *is* dead,"[96] thus coining this condition: subconscious diagnosis of the "Walking Zombie Syndrome" (WZS). Some of the earlier cases I shared in this book exhibited this syndrome.

From patients Dr. Bryan believed suffered from this syndrome, he discovered a wide and somewhat bizarre list of symptoms. The patients he treated gave him medical histories that included statements such as—

1. I feel dull and listless all the time.
2. I'm completely emotionless.
3. Nothing means anything to me anymore.
4. I really have no vitality.
5. I just don't take any interest in things anymore.
6. I feel like I have lost my personality.
7. I am just existing; I don't get a thrill out of anything.
8. Life has been a problem; I'm very depressed.[97]

These patients did not exhibit a fear of death, as they unconsciously believed that death had already arrived. Of course, this does not mean that every patient who states feelings of dullness and listlessness has accepted the fact that s/he is dead, but many of them could be suffering from undiagnosed Walking Zombie Syndrome.

The syndrome can be particularly hard to diagnose as the patient—feeling dead on a subconscious level—has no waking knowledge that s/he is suffering from WZS. If asked, the patient would deny having the subconscious belief that s/he is emotionally dead. However an analytical interpretation—especially in the word association tests—of that denial would contain phrases that convince the hypnoanalyst that Walking Zombie Syndrome is the correct diagnosis.[98]

The reasons these patients give for visiting a hypnoanalyst are varied: in some cases, it may be for depression, listlessness, loss, or a general lack of vitality. In others, it may be alcoholism or other addictions. Frequently, people seek help to become more successful and authentic. Then again, the patient may be having a sexual symptom. One patient Dr. Bryan treated presented himself as an asthmatic. To diagnose these patients as WZS, however, a very thorough medical, social, and psychological history was used before beginning hypnoanalysis.

The treatment of WZS requires the hypnoanalyst to help the patient acknowledge the difficult emotional event or period of time that led to the problem, then to help him/her to experience a "mental and/or spiritual rebirth." Since the patient's "death" may have occurred at any time during the person's life, a careful history must be taken.

From Terry's word association test (WAT):

Ryan: My problem began at age . . .
TERRY: *ten*
Ryan: It all started when . . .
TERRY: *I was young, 12, my parents divorced.*
Ryan: Death . . .
TERRY: *yes*

Just from those three responses, I put the pieces together that this woman's problem did not begin with her date rape but was exacerbated by it, making the assault trigger her current crisis. Her subconscious "death" took place many years before, between ages ten and twelve when her mother drank, began seeing other men, with a stepfather entering the scene not long thereafter. That situation begs for an answer to the question: was there any sexual inappropriateness with the stepfather?

Again from her word association test:

Ryan: when he did it . . .
TERRY: *I was mad*
Ryan: It got worse when . . .
TERRY: *nobody listened.*

The sad part about this case showed itself and proved to be prophetic.

Ryan: I'll sabotage my progress by . . .
TERRY: *smoking pot*
Ryan: Instead of dealing with my problem . . .
TERRY: *run away and hide.*

And that's exactly what Terry did, she left therapy before dealing with the basis of her problem. In Terry's last session, I regressed her back to the womb to remove some of the negativity she inadvertently accepted from her mother's attitude about the pregnancy. This is what Terry said about her pre-birth experience:

> *"(It's) Long . . . she's carrying another kid . . . a daughter on the way, sad, over-whelmed . . . it has to do with my father, she can't turn back, she's stuck with him . . ."*

Then I asked her when those stuck feelings show up in her life. Saying, "*in my career and with my boyfriend,*" we went back further in time to when I knew she felt like a winner, into the sperm race at conception. During the regression, Terry claimed to feel good and at peace with herself as well as everyone else.

It was important to regress her back to a good feeling in order to demonstrate to Terry beyond any doubt that, she—as was each of us—was conceived with a feeling of peace and self love. Allowing someone to experience that long-forgotten feeling relieves much of the power of negative suggestions.

Generally, going back in time to the first negative suggestion(s), before dealing with the current crisis or reason for seeking therapy (in this case, the date rape) allows the client to feel well enough to continue therapy. Imagine a stack of quarters ten high; if the bottom one is bent, what happens to all the rest? By straightening the bottom one, the other nine quarters come more into balance. That said, when a client is using drugs or alcohol, the bets are off and healing becomes a coin toss instead of a neat stack.

Human beings are very suggestible during the earliest years of life, especially to negative feelings and ideas because the brain has a negative bias without which humans would repeat the same mistakes over and over again. Hypnoanalysts must pay special attention to these areas in a client's past:

1. All acute infectious diseases, especially those life-threatening ones including a high fever;
2. All accidents or injuries in which the patient might have been unconscious or at a very low level of consciousness;
3. Any operations in which the patient may have received a suggestion during the operation that s/he would probably expire;
4. All war experiences;
5. All deaths in the immediate family or of close friends;[99]
6. Difficult or traumatic birth experiences;
7. Unusually long separations from the mother after birth, in infancy, or before 7 years old;
8. Adoptions; and,
9. Traumatic experiences such as being the victim of a crime, abuse, incest, rape, etc.

To treat Walking Zombie Syndrome, we usually age regress the patient to the "initial-sensitizing event"—the cause of the patient accepting the death suggestion. Using this approach, the patient is able to relive the event—all the way though—to arrive at a realization that s/he did not actually die! With that realization, the patient has no need to continue to suffer the symptoms of WZS and can return from the illusion of the grave. Such treatment also involves uncovering the "symptom-producing event" and the events that intensified the illness.

As demonstrated by the above case, the client didn't die physically but accepted a "spiritual death" suggestion, a negative belief about being wanted and accepted by her mother. This spiritual death represents what we call the "Spiritual Walking Zombie Syndrome" (SWZS) or "Identity Problem." Terry's WAT showed the following connections:

Ryan: Fear . . .
TERRY: *myself*
Ryan: Desire . . .
TERRY: *myself*
Ryan: Hate . . .
TERRY: *myself*
Ryan: Unwanted . . .
TERRY: *self*

Recall that the WAT's significance manifests in the formula: If A = B and B = C, then A = C. You'll get how *fear, desire, hate, unwanted* and *myself* all equal one another.

Ryan: They really wanted . . .
TERRY: *someone else*

This last statement indicated to me there was a prenatal problem. Unless overt abuse and much neglect is apparent in the case history, hypnoanalysts know from experience that the feeling of being unwanted frequently stems from negative beliefs mistakenly accepted during pregnancy.

The feeling of deadness shows here:

Ryan: If I could feel . . .
TERRY: *anything*
Ryan: Why can't I . . .
TERRY: *feel anything*
Ryan: If I knew I'd never be punished . . .
TERRY: *I'd feel alive.*

The sad part about this woman's case is that I could have helped her significantly utilizing hypnoanalysis, EMDR and Neurofeedback. I learned a long time ago that we can't help everyone who walks through our doors but that doesn't stop me from doing whatever I can.

People often want me to hypnotize them into feeling better, not being depressed, or feeling ONLY happy most of the time. But I can't do that—this is planet Earth. Pain is part of life. Losses hurt, fear paralyzes, anger raises cortisol levels, joy and love soothe the body and mind. Laughter, excitement and sexual release help bodies feel well and live longer.

When a person recovers from the Walking Zombie Syndrome, he or she feels alive. Alive is feeling. Dead is not feeling. Depression is another kind of deadness. Living involves experiencing *all* our feelings. Happiness is one of three emotions that define us as sentient creatures, a spiritual being having a physical existence. WZS is a *subconscious* syndrome suffered as a drastic result of traumatic experiences. Depression, however, is a *conscious* condition described by symptomatic disturbances in one's feeling, thinking, and/or behavior.

Defining Depression

Depression is an illness that can cause or be caused by an imbalance of two types of brain chemicals, neurotransmitters and neuropeptides, an imbalance that can be genetically determined or that can stem from a host of other reasons such as food allergies, environmental toxins, allergies, and food sensitivities. Depression is not a personal weakness or a character flaw, rather it is similar to illnesses such as heart disease, diabetes, and cancer. Therefore we should not ignore its importance or neglect its treatment.[100]

An episode of depression usually follows a dramatically stressful event such as the death of a loved one. Depression can occur after a divorce, or a major life transition (job loss, a move). People who have recurrent episodes of major depression are said to have "unipolar depression"—what used to be called "clinical depression."[101] These people experience times of low and depressed moods, a continual sadness.

While depression can run in a family, many people suffering from it do not have it their family history. Genetics, a stressful life situation, or both can contribute to a person developing depression.

The following statistics describe unipolar depression:

- More than 19 million Americans suffer from unipolar depression each year. This fact makes it the most common mental illness is the U.S. [102]
- People suffering from depression lose the pleasure of everyday life. Depression can complicate other medical problems. Depression can lead to suicide.[103]
- Anyone of any age, race or sex can develop depression. It is not a normal part of life no matter how old one is or the state of one's health.[104]
- Seventy percent of persons with depression will experience full remission of the disorder after professional treatment; unfortunately, fewer than half of those suffering from depression will seek treatment. Many people do not see depression as a serious illness, or believe that they can treat themselves. Still others see depression as a personal weakness.[105]
- At some point in their lifetimes, an estimated 33-35 million adults in the U.S. may experience depression. It can affect women and men of any age, race, or income level. Studies show women are twice as likely to suffer from depression than men.[106]

Causes of Depression

"If there was ever an outstanding example of man tearing down his physical being with his thoughts, it would be depression. Henry Maudsley stated, 'the sorrow which has no vent in tears may make other organs weep.'"[107]

Depression can wreak havoc on the patient's body and life; and yet, there seems to be no single cause of depression. For some, there may be several factors involved, for others a single cause. Then there are a large number of people who develop depression for no obvious reason. It may be that the interaction between biochemical, environmental, social and genetic factors is the cause.[108]

Many people suffering from depression try to cover up their suffering, however, the daily pressures of living and hiding can play out harshly on the human body. "Often the submerged depression emerges in a host of somatic symptoms and sensations: symptoms that are the psychophysiological reverberations of the emotional state, without basic organic pathology."[109]

The fact is that depression is not a personal weakness or a condition that can be willed or wished away, but it can be successfully treated. Below is a list of possible causes for unipolar depression:

- *Biology*—Changes in brain chemicals called "neurotransmitters," or a low or overly high level of these can contribute to depression.
- *Cognitive Patterns*—A person with negative thinking patterns and low self-esteem is more likely to develop unipolar depression.
- *Sex or Gender*—Women experience unipolar depression at almost twice the numbers as men. The reasons may include changes in hormone levels in pregnancy, menstruation, childbirth or menopause. It may also be caused by the stress associated with a woman holding multiple responsibilities.
- *Co-occurring illness*—Depression is likely to accompany certain diseases: heart disease, Alzheimer's, cancer, Parkinson's, diabetes and hormonal disorders. [Some autoimmune conditions such as celiac can have depression as one presentation of the illness.]
- *Medication*—The side effects of some prescription medication can include depression.
- *Genetics/Family History*
- *Situational*—Difficult life events, including divorce, financial problems or the death of a loved one can contribute to depression.[110]

Social learning habits may also play a role in developing depression. Individuals learn good and not-so-good ways of dealing with stress. Family, education, social circles and work environments all influence the way we deal with stress. Environmental factors also influence psychological development and the habits one uses to resolve problems.[111]

Symptoms of Depression

A clinical diagnosis of depression can be made when a patient experiences two or more weeks of depressed mood along with an expressed loss of interest accompanied by at least four other symptoms of depression.[112] Here are the most common symptoms of unipolar depression:

- Persistent sad, anxious or "empty" mood;
- Sleeping too much or too little, waking at unusual times;
- Reduced appetite and weight loss (or the opposite);
- Loss of pleasure and interest in activities once enjoyed, including sex;
- Restlessness, irritability;
- Persistent physical symptoms that do not respond to treatment (such as chronic pain or digestive disorders);
- Difficulty concentrating, remembering or making decisions;
- Fatigue or loss of energy;
- Feeling guilty, hopeless or worthless; and
- Entertaining thoughts of suicide or death.[113]

Depression is a serious health problem that affects feelings, thoughts and actions, and can appear as a physical illness. Children are not exempt from depression. According to the Center for Mental Health Services, as many as 1 in 33 children and 1 in 8 teens have depression.[114]

The symptoms of depression in children are very similar to those of adults and may additionally include:

- Withdrawal from family, friends and favorite activities;
- Changes in eating and sleeping habits;
- Frequent physical complaints, such as headaches and stomachaches;
- Lack of enthusiasm or motivation;
- Play that involves an undue aggression towards self or others, or that focuses on only sad themes;
- Feelings of excessive sadness.[115]

Adolescents have a particularly difficult time maintaining mental health. There are so many physical, emotional, psychological and social changes that go along with youth. A teen can feel a strong sense of rejection due to seemingly unrealistic academic, social, or family expectations. The teen can overreact when things go awry at home or at school. We hear teens say frequently that life is "not fair," and that things never seem to go their way. They feel confused and very stressed by the conflicting messages they receive from parents, friends, the media, teachers and society overall.

Depression can be difficult to diagnose in teens because adults may *expect* teens to act moody. Also, adolescents do not always understand or express their feelings very well. They may not be aware of the symptoms of depression and may not seek help.

The above symptoms may indicate depression in a teen as well, particularly when they last for more than two weeks. Adolescent depression may also be accompanied by:

- Poor performance in school;
- Anger, rage;
- Overreaction to criticism;
- Substance abuse; and,
- Problems with authority.[116]

Teens may experiment with drugs and/or alcohol, may become sexually promiscuous to avoid feelings of depression or express their depression expressed through hostile, aggressive, and risk-taking behavior.

Types of Depression

There are many names for depression. Psychology Information Online provides much information on the following depressive disorders:

Major Depression—is the most serious type of depression due to the number of symptoms and the severity. Individuals experience wide differences in symptoms. Not all depressed people feel suicidal, for example, nor do they all have a history of hospitalization. Because of the variation, no diagnosis of "moderate depression" is ever made.

Dysthymia Disorder—a low to moderate level of depression that lasts for at least two years, and sometimes longer. The symptoms are not as severe as a major depression, yet they are more enduring and more resistant to treatment. People with dysthymia may develop a major depression at some time.

Unspecified Depression—includes people with major depression symptoms not quite severe enough to be diagnosed as major depression. It also includes people with dysthymia disorder symptoms that have not lasted for the two-year period.

Adjustment Disorder, with Depression—describes a depression that occurs in response to a major life stressor or crisis.

Bipolar Depression—includes both high and low mood swings, as well as a variety of other important symptoms not found with other types of depressions.[117]

Co-occurring Depression—mentioned above, depression could accompany other serious illnesses. Often, this type of depression is overlooked and untreated, assuming the patient is suffering only from the primary medical problem and the patients themselves do not have the information needed to judge their own mental state. Anyone experiencing serious illness should be evaluated thoroughly in terms of emotional state, personal and family histories, and symptoms to determine if one or more illnesses are present.[118]

Other Treatments for Depression

More than 80% of depression patients who seek treatment show improvement. Unipolar depression is highly treatable. The most common treatments are psychotherapy, hypnosis, lifestyle and dietary changes, or antidepressant medication—or a combination of these. The choice of treatment would depend upon the severity, pattern, or persistence of depressive symptoms and the patient's medical history.[119]

Psychotherapy is known as "talk therapy." Research shows this can be helpful for many people with some types of depression. It can be used alone, or in combination with other types of therapy. Mainly, two styles exist: Cognitive-behavioral, which helps by challenging negative beliefs and attitudes; and, Interpersonal, which works to overcome problems with roles, social skills and other factors.[120]

Psychodynamic therapy operates on the premise that a person's childhood experiences and trauma can follow into adulthood, causing problems in the patient's personal and professional life. This therapy works with the understanding that resolving childhood conflicts frees the patient from repeating unhelpful patterns and helps the person to find successful ways of dealing.[121]

The following are some suggestions for a natural approach to a **healthy lifestyle** that may help provide some relief of depression symptoms:

- Maintain proper sleep and hygiene as advised by a health care professional;
- Eat a well-balanced diet;
- Manage anxiety as professionally advised;
- Participate in a structured and supervised exercise program;
- Set realistic goals;
- Create small, manageable tasks; and,
- Let others you can trust (family and friends, for instance) help you.[122]

The Use of Theology in Hypnoanalysis for Depression

Depressed people are not active; the condition itself prevents a person from taking initiative. Dr. Bryan reminds us that the lack of action can be a stopgap measure in protecting the patient during the lowest depressive periods. Once a patient begins to feel "better"—capable of taking action—the danger of harm to self still remains until full recovery. This fact reminds us that the underlying cause of depression needs to be found before it is cured; otherwise the patient may take drastic action.[123] So much of the treatment rendered today comprises palliative care rather than cure. In some circles, "cure" may even be considered a dirty word.

Protecting the patient is good! However, successful treatment requires that the patient not be overprotective of her or himself. Some patients, even after treatment, continue to suffer the symptoms of depression, still convinced, perhaps, that no action is better than taking the wrong action.[124] These patients may easily mistake an everyday occurrence for a harmful situation and thus miss opportunities to move beyond the depression mode.

For these patients, the application of Christian theological principles can be valuable. In both the Old and New Testaments, direct suggestions on dealing with a condition such as depression can be found. Most Americans are familiar with the Christian scriptures, and feel favorable or tolerance towards them.

The most helpful, Dr. Bryan found, were the verses from Philippians 4:4-8. [125] "*Rejoice in the Lord always: And again I say, rejoice . . .*" Excellent advice, Dr. Bryan assures us. The verse does not state, "do not worry" as negative suggestions tend to focus our minds on negative outcomes. A depressed person can learn that s/he can be content when and where s/he is, that your *reactions* to events are different from the actual *happening*.

Your reactions create your reality, as indicated by verse 5: "*Let your moderation be known unto all men. The Lord is at hand . . .*"The cause of a person's depression is not an *action*, but a *reaction* to stimuli. In other words, it is not *what happens to you* that causes depression, but *how* you *react* to the situation. Thus knowing the Lord is at hand can help one realize that emotions of sadness or grief do not have to become a full-blown depression.[126]

Odd as it may seem, a depressed person can be too careful! See verse 6: "*Be careful for nothing; but in everything by prayer and in supplication with thanksgiving let your requests be made known unto God . . .*"It is safe to say that St. Paul did not mean for anyone to be foolhardy, but that depressed people have a tendency to get in their own way by fearing to take action. It is important for recovery that a patient be brave and demonstrate faith in the process.[127] Patients often overlook the fact that if one does not ask God for what s/he wants, s/he will not get it—if one doesn't *ask*, one doesn't *know*.

A natural follow up to this cautionary about caution is verse 7: "*And the peace of God which passeth all understanding, shall keep your hearts and minds through Christ Jesus . . .*" Dr. Bryan says, "[w]hen an insolvable problem is left in God's hands, the patient can then forget about it . . . the patient [can get] back to work and he will realize that he is accomplishing something and pretty soon God will solve the problem for him."[128] Many readers will have heard the expression: let go and let God.

Verse 8 reads, "*Finally, brethren, whatsoever things are true, whatsoever things are honest, whatsoever things are just, whatsoever things are pure, whatsoever things are lovely, whatsoever things are of good report; If there be any virtue, and if there be any praise, think on these things . . .*" As it says, *think* on *these* things: the patient's thoughts control her/his state of mind."[129]

Treating Depression with Medication

The common palliative practice these days is for doctors to prescribe antidepressant medications for their patients who are suffering from depression. Some 189 million prescriptions are written yearly for depression.[130] Prescription drug treatments are divided into different classes. Each class of medication will affect the level of chemicals in the brain called "neurotransmitters." These chemicals are thought to help regulate mood.[131] There are two most commonly prescribed antidepressant classes:

SSRIs (selective serotonin reuptake inhibitors) are believed to treat depression by affecting the levels of a neurotransmitter called *serotonin*.

SNRIs (serotonin-norepinephrine reuptake inhibitors) are believed to treat depression by affecting the levels of two neurotransmitters called *serotonin* and *norepinephrine*.

Both of these drug classes can require up to 8 weeks for their full therapeutic dose to take effect.[132] Patience is needed in taking these medications, giving them time to work, and tracking any possible side effects.

Generally, clients are referred to me after receiving a diagnosis of depression and medication prescribed by their doctor. I work with the client using hypnoanalysis, EMDR, and neurofeedback to remove the subconscious causes of the depression. Once the client feels better, I work with the referring physician who will supervise the reduction and elimination of the client's medication. When someone seeking treatment from me is so depressed that my treatments will not be of help, I refer the client to a psychiatrist who medicates conservatively and then we work together to heal the client.

Personally, I do not like medications because, in my opinion, medications do not really heal anyone but simply make them a little less ill. However, since no one treatment fits everyone, medication has its place, especially for clients who are suicidal or otherwise incapacitated.

Aging and Depression

Many older Americans suffer from depression. Because some symptoms of depression mimic the natural aging process, depression often goes undiagnosed and untreated in this age group.[133] This problem is compounded when their caretakers think depression is a natural part of the aging process. It is not!

To compound this tragedy even further is another fact—that older people are disproportionately likely to die if they attempt suicide.

Here are some facts about aging and depression from the National Institute for Mental Health:

- In 2004, people over the age of 65 comprised only 12% of the U.S. population; however, they account for 16% of all suicides.
- In 2004, 14.3 out of 100,000 people age 65 or older died by suicide—this is a higher rate than the 11 per 100,000 in the general populace.
- Non-Hispanic white men age 85 and older were most likely to die by suicide in that year. The death rate was 49.8 suicide deaths per 100,000 for persons in that age group.[134]

So often we think of teenagers when we read about depression and suicide, but according to the above statistics, older white men constitute the highest suicide rate in the U.S.

On a second look, the causes of depression for older people are obvious—frustration due to loss of memory and physical ability, losing one's dignity to pain and illness, losing one's home and independence, grieving the death of loved one(s), financial insecurity and uncertainty—any one of us would be challenged.

Then there is the loneliness implicit in aging: hearing loss makes phone calls a problem; difficulty walking leads to not exercising, driving or keeping a pet; vision problems can make reading impossible.

Even tougher to face is an embarrassment the elderly feel that they do not talk about—that they are becoming incompetent and need to be in a nursing home.[135]

The good news is that, once diagnosed, 80 percent of the elderly respond to treatment.[136] Age does not have to be an obstacle when treating depression. As a friend used to say, we just need a "shift in perception."

Addiction and Depression

An estimated 17 million Americans are addicted to drugs or alcohol—that is more than 7 percent of the population. Thirty-seven percent of the people suffering from alcoholism in the U.S. also have a mental illness in addition to the addiction.[137]

Alcoholics or addicts are not the only ones who suffer with their problems—each of these people has an enormous impact on the lives of their parents, siblings, children, spouses or other family members, friends or bosses. The affects on those codependents are discussed elsewhere.

An additional challenge for the depressed recovering addict or alcoholic is that they cannot participate fully in any 12-step addiction recovery program—the most successful treatments for addiction. Additionally, the dual-diagnosed people worry about being judged by their luckier peers—those who don't have both illnesses.

We Suspect the Walking Zombie Syndrome

Along with any or all of the above treatments, an astute hypnoanalyst will suspect an underlying WZS or Spiritual-WZS that, once removed, rarely reappears. If the syndrome does reappear, then it usually does so in a milder form related to a stressor that stimulated the ghost of the condition. Hypnoanalysis, along with any of the above-mentioned interventions, can help a depressed person immensely.

Suicide, according to the depressed person, feels like a way out. Killing the pain is the real goal but this solution throws the baby out with the bath. And what if—just *what if*—suicide does not take away the pain but carries it along in the spirit's subconscious to resurrect in the next life? We don't actually know. However, a solution is always available, options exist even when things seem darkest, situations seem hopeless, but not truly serious. Life is precious and needs to be preserved.

S.A.D.

Though many people have probably heard of *Seasonal Affective Disorder* also known as SAD, not all medical professionals recognize this condition as a distinct psychological disorder. S.A.D. is a seasonal depression characterized by a person's mood varying according to the seasons of the year. With the onset of colder, darker winter months, a person with S.A.D. may experience depressive symptoms: individuals may eat more, crave certain foods, sleep more, experience more fatigue and weight gain. In some cases, there may be a social withdrawal as well—almost a hibernation pattern.[138]

For most people, these symptoms abate in the spring once the weather is warmer and the days longer. Though it's still being debated in psychological circles, for the many people who become depressed during the winter months, S.A.D. provides a rational explanation for a chronic and sometimes debilitating psychological problem.[139]

Light therapy is often recommended for S.A.D. based on the assumption that decreased exposure to full-spectrum light may be responsible for chemical changes that trigger depression in some people.[140]

More recent research, according to Dr. Mercola of Mercola.com, suggests that people who live in the northern hemisphere have especially low Vitamin D levels and that many SAD symptoms may be reversed simply by supplementing Vitamin D.[141]

Grief and Depression

Grief is as a natural and healthy reaction to a major loss, leading to emotional healing. It is important to recognize when someone is grieving. Grieving can, however, be a long, drawn-out and intensely painful time, causing significant distress. A grief reaction can last for a few months, or for years. A grieving person will possibly never stop missing a lost loved one, for instance, or regretting a major loss, but the sharpest pain will lessen eventually.

For example, consider the case of M, a college student on Christmas break, who said, "*I built my life around her and now she's gone. I felt worthless . . . almost like a panic . . . I feel like I lost my purpose in life.*" M had lost his relationship with Esther, his fiancée. A few sentence completions from his word association test will demonstrate his underlying Walking Zombie Syndrome.

Ryan: The one thing I need most is . . .
M: *love*
Ryan: sex . . .
M: *love*
Ryan: desire . . .
M: *sex*
Ryan: without love . . .
M: *I'm really hurting*

Get the point about how love and sex were connected in this young man's mind? Remember when A=B and B=C, then A=C. Here's the subconscious thought stream: **Love=sex.** And without that love/sex connection, he feels dead. Love is not sex and sex is not love. But in his mind, they were one in the same.

Ryan: Being with her reminds me of . . .
M: *peace*
Ryan: touch . . .
M: *deep peace*
Ryan: disconnected feels like . . .
M: *death*
Ryan: death . . .

M: *terror*
Ryan: Love comes from . . .
M: *connecting two people's hearts*
Ryan: most of all I want . . .
M: *to truly connect with someone*
Ryan: at the very bottom of it all . . .
M: *I just want to be loved*
Ryan: I really desire . . .
M: *a true love*

While it is natural to want all these things (and most people do), what we found with M was that from an early age (going as far back as the womb), he felt unwanted and not connected to either his mother or father. He even mentioned the idea of karmic connections between the three of them. But there's more to it.

Ryan: guilt . . .
M: *constant*
Ryan: punishment . . .
M: *deserved*
Ryan: My punishment is . . .
M: *to be in pain*

He had the Spiritual Walking Zombie Syndrome where his own self-love died and was replaced with neurotic guilt and self-punishment. Once he understood all these subconscious connections, and after a couple regressions to early times in his life, M realized self-love was the cure. We were able to neutralize the negative womb suggestion by helping M to understand that his parents had had trouble in their lives and that trouble was not his fault: he had been a fetus, they didn't even know him and so how could they not want him? Besides, once he experienced the sperm race, he knew he was created in love and that the Creator wanted him to be here.

M understood that he no longer needed a lover to fill unmet childhood needs nor did he need to continue to grieve the loss of his relationship. M let go of his grief, felt better, went back to school and, since I never heard from him again, I assume he's doing well.

Descriptions of Different Types of Grief

In treating grief, it is important to have an understanding of the different types and what triggers them.

- *Normal grief* (also called *uncomplicated grief*). Grief that is the normal, healthy response to a major loss: the death of a loved one or a pet, miscarriage or stillbirth, divorce, loss of job or home, or serious physical injury.
- *Anticipatory grief.* Grief that begins before a major loss: the initiation of divorce proceedings or a terminal illness diagnosis of a loved one.[142]
- *Anniversary reactions.* Grief responses that occur when faced with reminders of the loss: anniversaries, holidays or other special days throughout the year. (These are usually short term and are not always a setback in the grieving process.)[143]
- *Complicated grief* (or *traumatic grief*). Grief that becomes chronic, disabling and more intense. This grief can progress into major depression, with features of post-traumatic stress disorder such as nightmares and flashbacks. (While the American Psychiatric Association does not recognize *complicated grief*, the National Institute of Mental Health estimates that 10 to 20 percent of people grieving the loss of a loved one experience *complicated grief.* [144])

Grieving is a personal process. Each person grieves loss in a different way. Grieving varies by age, family, culture and region. Some people may express their sorrow openly while others grieve privately. Children, for instance, may not understand the concept of death and may take more time to grieve, or need it explained over and over to them. Adolescents understand death as adults do, but may grieve differently, seeking refuge with their friends in their own peer groups or may engage in more impulsive or risky behaviors such as drug or alcohol use, or impulsive sexual behavior.[145]

The emotional and psychological symptoms of grief include . . .

- *Sadness and low mood.* Feelings of regret are common in grieving people. The grieving person may cry or yearn for what was lost.

Grieving people may experience the proverbial "lump in the throat."

- *Shock, disbelief and confusion.* An initial response to major loss can be denial—the individual may not be able (or may refuse) to grasp the fact of loss. When the actuality sinks in, the grieving person may be confused and unable to comprehend what has happened.
- *Anger and irritability.* After denial, anger may follow. A grieving person may become angry at her/himself or others for allowing the loss. This person may lash out at the world.
- *Guilt.* Guilt can follow anger in the grieving process. The individual may feel that s/he failed to prevent the loss. This may lead to lower feelings of self-worth. A severe decline in self-esteem may be a warning that a major depression could follow.
- *Anhedonia* (loss of interest or pleasure in usual activities). Many people who are grieving lose interest in daily and once-loved activities.
- *Wishing* (a passive wish to be with the loved one). This feeling should not be confused with actual thoughts of suicide. Actual suicidal behavior is more serious and requires immediate treatment.
- *Anxiety.*
- *Obsession with what was lost.*[146]

Grief can have a negative impact on a person's physical health, as well. Existing medical conditions may worsen, or a new condition may develop. Some physical symptoms of grief include the following:

- *Numbness* or an empty feeling in the chest and abdomen.
- *Fatigue.* Grieving people may feel chronically tired.
- *Appetite and sleep disturbance.* People may eat too much or lose their appetite. They may sleep too little or too much or may have nightmares.
- *Substance abuse.* Grieving people may use alcohol or drugs to deal with their grief to deaden the pain.
- *Aches and pains.* Vague complaints in the stomach and head are common among grieving individuals.

- *Trouble concentrating*. Grieving can impair a person's concentration at home and at work.[147]

The grieving process can be long and intensely painful and can result in an overwhelming feeling of emotional distress. Productivity at work or school may be impaired and social function may be lowered. Most grieving people do continue to go to work and to socialize, but with far less enjoyment than before the event.

The Grief Recovery Handbook is a good resource when one is dealing with a loss. The 20th Anniversary Expanded Edition 2008 by John W. James and Russel Friedman is available from Harper Collins Publishers.

Despite the difficulties in the grieving process, it is not a good idea to avoid grief or to try and deny a major loss. Avoiding the grief process could lead to serious physical and emotional problems later. Take heart in that many grieving people will not require psychological or psychiatric treatment during the process. That said, a helpful counselor can be of enormous value in dealing with loss.

Code Concepts

Intuitively, you may sense if you have an underlying Walking Zombie Syndrome. Even though you may not have experienced what you would define as trauma, you may still suffer from WZS and may be asking yourself, "How could I have picked this up?" Since we live in three dimensions of mind, body and spirit, accepting an unwanted death suggestion in any dimension of existence can happen accidentally, before you are ready to defend against it. Therefore, trust your gut feeling, get help from someone who can analyze your subconscious and get to the beginning of the death suggestion and nullify it.

1. Which dimension do you feel is underdeveloped or simply doesn't compute in your life?

   Mind Body Spirit

2. On a scale of 1 to 10 (10 being the most alive), how alive are the three dimensions for you?
3. Do the lowest scores interfere with your life in significant ways?
4. Once you raise your score(s), what could you do or experience that you can't do now?
5. What have you done already to change the score(s)?
6. Did those changes make any significant difference? If not, then what will you do now?
7. If you are depressed, know it, and are receiving help but not getting better, consider other treatment options. Leave no route untraveled to get help.

If neither grief nor depression applies to you presently but are you are curious, below are a couple links to internet sites that will test your depression level. And if you are depressed, reach out. Realize you did not make it happen to yourself; you do not want to be depressed, nor does it do any good to tough it out. Getting help is a sign of a strong character and not a sign of weakness or defect.

Wakefield Depression Test—http://depression.about.com/cs/diagnosis/a/wakefield.htm

Beck Depression Inventory—http://www.encyclopedia.com/doc/1G2-3405700046.html

Chapter Twelve

Codependency:
The Basic Horror Of Identity

Ever since people first existed,
they have been doing all the things we label
"co-dependent." They have worried themselves
sick about other people. They have tried to help
in ways that didn't help. They have said yes
when they meant no. They have tried to make
other people see things their way.
They have bent over backward to avoid
hurting people's feelings and,
in doing so, have hurt themselves . . .
They have believed lies and then felt betrayed . . .
They have worn sackcloth because they
didn't believe they deserved silk.[148]

Melody Beattie

Creative minds always have been known
to survive any kind of bad training.

Anna Freud

A Nation of Codependents

What is a codependent? The term is usually applied to family members of alcoholics and drug addicts, but it can also apply to anyone who has lived in a dysfunctional family or with an abusive person. In dysfunctional families, one or more members of the family are out of balance, addicted to something, or mentally ill. The other family members then adjust their own behavior to compensate, assuming different roles and using this compensating behavior to deal with the addicted or dysfunctional person. Relationships with friends and love interests can also become codependent, with one party attempting to protect the other party who is an addict or abusive.

Notes Donald Brennan in *The Recovery Press*:

> "Many psychologists and therapists in the Recovery Movement, people such as Claudia Black and John Bradshaw, believe that anyone who has been involved, especially in childhood, with chemically dependent persons in long-term intimate relationships has been pathologically affected by those relationships. The consequent mental disorder is called 'codependence,' and it is a widespread malady in any society where substance abuse is prevalent. Therapist Sharon Wegscheider-Cruse estimates that as many as 96 percent of Americans could be affected."

Ann Wilson Schaef, in her book "When Society Becomes an Addict", maintains that U.S. society itself is an addictive system, and that in the 21st century the American people are collectively codependent, with relatively few in recovery. The vast majority of Americans are caught in the throes of this progressive disease, and expend tremendous energy in their efforts to survive the symptoms. It is a majority out of touch with feelings, entrenched in denial, and caught up in role-playing, disordered thinking, enabling, and all manner of debilitating, dysfunctional and addictive behavior patterns. According to Schaef, codependence permeates not only our families but also our institutions and their bureaucracies, including businesses, schools and government.[149]

Humans compensate for many things in many ways. If you develop a near-sighted condition, you unconsciously begin to squint when peering at distant objects. By narrowing the opening through which your eyes peer, you sharpen the distant image somewhat. Of course, the permanent remedy is eyeglasses or contact lenses. Once you have the proper lenses, you don't need to squint any more but you may still do it out of habit. You are still trying to control your eye focus by squinting, even though you no longer need to do so.

When one member of a family develops a significant dysfunction, it upsets the balance in the family arrangement and everybody's role changes somewhat. Everyone has to adjust and may take on different roles (as we shall see in cases later in this chapter). As they adjust, the co-dependency is created.

When Family Balance is Upset

The family unit has been compared to a hanging mobile. The mobile is in delicate balance. If you change the position or weight of one of the hanging units, you disrupt the balance of the entire mobile.

If Dad is an alcoholic, a workaholic, or a golfaholic, he will not exert his full weight on the family mobile. If Mom is a drug addict, a clubaholic, or a shopaholic, she too will throw the mobile out of balance. If the addict is Dad, perhaps Mom steps in, becoming a self-sacrificing martyr as she assumes the roles of both parents.

Or maybe the oldest son assumes the burdens his father won't assume. In such a case, he becomes a family "hero," sacrificing his childhood for the good of the entire family unit. The oldest daughter may similarly assume the responsibilities of a dysfunctional mother—or of both parents. Consequently, the child has become trapped in a behavior mode dictated by the parent's dependency, and the two thus become codependent. By shielding dependent persons from the consequences of their actions, codependents enable them to continue and, even deepen, their dependencies.

Codependents, therefore, are enablers. An enabler, according to Angelyn Miller, "is one who prevents growth and learning in others by assuming their responsibilities. An enabler promotes weakness in others by protecting them from the consequences of their unproductive behavior."[150]

Observes Jennifer P. Schneider, M.D., author of *Back from Betrayal,* in her foreword to Miller's *The Enabler:*

> "Enablers, as adults, often continue to consider themselves innocent victims who are making the best of a bad situation. Surrounded by crises, they 'pull the family through' time and again. They are often seen as heroes by their friends."

Miller cites the alcoholic as "the classic example of the dependent who needs the support of others to maintain dependent patterns." She explains:

> "Alcoholics who find a mate who will accommodate their behavior can spend a lifetime without changing. They have someone strong and capable they can depend upon to hold things together, cover for them, and protect them from the consequences of alcoholism. Dependents believe themselves to be victims of an uncaring world, when actually they are victims of an overprotective one."[151]

The codependent wife tells the kids Daddy is sick when he's actually drunk and calls the boss to tell him Joe is sick and can't come to work when Joe's ailment is a hangover. When makeup won't hide the shiner he gave her last night, she tells friends she ran into a door instead of into the fist of a drunken spouse. The codependent wife is sick and needs help as much as her alcoholic husband.

Codependents feel powerless to stop the addictive behavior or correct the personality vulnerability that feeds their codependency. They seek, instead, to control the behavior that results from the disorders. They assume responsibility for others' behavior and welfare. This self-sacrificing behavior becomes embedded in the subconscious and distorts the codependent's relationship with the rest of the world.

Children who grow up in a dysfunctional home will find it difficult to function in normal surroundings. Their subconscious minds have adapted their behavior patterns to the abnormal environment, and when they take those patterns into normal settings, the patterns do not mesh.

Codependents grow up believing that their mission in life is to be at the service of others. But fulfilling that desire does not lead to a warm feeling of contentment. It frequently leads to unhappiness as they often feel victimized.

Codependency is a much broader problem than drug or alcohol addiction. Codependents, says Schneider, learned their unhealthy behavior as victims of a painful or difficult childhood. Frequently, as the product of a dysfunctional family, the child's nurturing was inadequate. These codependents-in-training learned how to cope with a difficult family life by becoming rescuers and caretakers, thereby confusing being loved with the feeling of being needed. Schneider characterizes adult enablers as "volunteers rather than victims."[152]

Growing a Codependent

Marty, a fifty-year-old optometrist appeared at my office seeking weight loss. After taking his history, I learned that Marty is a codependent, but his codependence didn't grow out of an alcohol or drug environment. It grew out of a dysfunctional home in which Marty had to assume parental responsibilities at an early age.

"I'm mother and father to the world," he later told me. He didn't identify codependence as a problem; he simply felt helpless and too fat.

Marty's father, Luther, was a man of lower-than-average IQ, though Marty's grandparents had never acknowledged it and had never sought special training for their son. Marty's mother, Margie, was a bright woman who had grown up in a poor family with no educational tradition. A large birthmark disfigured her face. As a teenager, Margie had no suitors except for Luther, who was a ninth-grade dropout. Margie herself quit school to marry him.

Marty was the oldest child, and as younger brothers and sisters came along, he had increasing responsibility for their nurturing. Both his parents worked the graveyard shift at a local factory—from midnight to 8 A.M. From the age of nine onward, Marty was left in charge of his younger siblings while the parents were at work. He also had to babysit them during the afternoons following school so that his parents could sleep.

Throughout high school, Marty was not able to engage in extracurricular activities because he had to be home with the younger kids. He was unable to have a typical teenager's social life because that would have conflicted with his child-care duties.

On top of filling in for both parents as the caretaker for his younger siblings, Marty became a partner in the denial of his father's mental handicap. Marty became adept at shielding his younger siblings from his father's temper and became adept at modeling his own behavior so as to avoid rousing his father's anger. Marty became a codependent at an early age.

When Marty grew up, he joined the military, and then attended college on the GI Bill. Though he became a successful optometrist, he did not outgrow his codependence. He married a woman with emotional problems and became a buffer between her and his children. He also tried to keep her problems hidden from their friends.

Marty grew up absorbed in the needs of others to the neglect of his own. He spent the early part of his life living in reaction to his father's moods and behavior. He spent his adult life responding to the needs of his disturbed spouse. Consequently, he resorted to overeating as a way of dealing with his own needs, which needs he was able to identify only after several months of therapy had elapsed.

So, having an alcoholic or a drug addict in the family is not a prerequisite for codependency. Codependency can develop whenever someone is dealing with a close family member, friend or sexual partner who has emotional or behavioral problems.

In her book, *Codependent No More*, Melody Beattie produced this definition of codependency:

> "A codependent person is one who has let another person's behavior affect him or her, and who is obsessed with controlling that person's behavior."[153]

Miller's definition is similar:

> ". . . [P]eople who need and use others to maintain nonproductive and self-defeating behaviors. It is a parasitic relationship—the **dependent** needing (or wanting) someone to take over his or her responsibility

> to society, and the **enabler** needing (or wanting) to take over another's responsibility in order to bolster his or her own sagging self-image."[154]

Often those who seem to thrive on problems are feeling dead inside and therefore, need the drama and excitement that problems create in order to know (subconsciously) that they are alive. Codependents need dependents and vice versa.

Beattie lists these characteristics of a codependent:[155]

- **The need to take care of others:** Codependents feel responsible for other people. They anticipate other people's needs and wonder why others don't anticipate theirs. If you need something that they can provide, codependents feel obligated to provide it. If codependents need something and you give it to them, they feel guilty for accepting it. But after they've done so much for others, they often feel angry, victimized, unappreciated, and abused. Codependents lead sad lives, never realizing they are volunteers in their codependency.
- **Low self-esteem:** Codependents live in abnormal environments, but they pretend that everything is normal. They blame themselves for everything but get angry, defensive, self-righteous, and indignant when others blame or criticize them. They reject compliments but get depressed when they're not complimented. They feel guilty about having fun just to be having fun. In fact, guilt is their constant companion.
- **Tendency to repress feelings:** Codependents are afraid that if they acknowledge their thoughts and feelings they will be overcome by guilt.
- **Worrying:** Codependents focus all their energy on other people and their problems but never find the solutions.
- **Controlling and being controlled:** Because the behavior of other people has brought them sorrow, codependents are afraid to let other people be themselves. To exercise control, they may feign helplessness, or they may try to use guilt to influence the behavior of others.
- **Denying there's a problem:** Codependents don't like to face problems head-on. They prefer to wish them away—to push

problems out of their consciousness and pretend they don't exist. They have trouble acknowledging how bad things are. They believe lies—even the lies they tell themselves. Thinking magically, very often they exhibit symptoms of the Ponce de Leon Syndrome (arrested development).

- **Depending on others for happiness:** Codependents look for happiness outside of themselves and attach themselves to the people or things they think can bring them happiness. Their quest for love and approval often draws them to people with problems. But often, the people they're drawn to are incapable of loving. Codependents eventually feel trapped in relationships that don't work and stay with them long after healthy persons would have walked away.
- **Difficulty in communicating:** Codependents tend to communicate indirectly. If they do not say what they mean, it is often because they do not consciously know what they mean. Their true feelings are submerged somewhere in their subconscious. They ask for what they want or need indirectly, through sighing or pouting or other nonverbal methods of communicating.
- **Inability to draw the line:** Codependents don't know how to set boundaries. They'll draw lines in the sand, and then keep blurring the lines. Eventually, they will put up with what they said they would never put up with, do things they said they would never do. They let others hurt them—repeatedly—then wonder why they hurt so bad. All the while, they feel victimized.
- **Lack of trust:** Codependents don't trust themselves, their feelings, their decisions, or most people. Yet, they try to trust untrustworthy people. They think God has abandoned them and often lose faith and trust in God.
- **Anger and fear of anger:** Codependents are afraid to express anger because they're afraid they'll make other people angry. They get depressed and cry a lot. They may overeat. Eventually, their repressed anger explodes in a "get-even" act of hostility, or in a violent outburst of temper.
- **Problems in the bedroom:** Codependents take their controlling behavior into their bedrooms. They may be more concerned

with pleasing their partners than with pleasing themselves. Sex becomes another act of self-sacrifice.

Things May Get Worse

If a codependent fails to get help, the condition can have serious repercussions. Depression and lethargy are among the by-products of codependency or they may become withdrawn and isolated. Feeling trapped in their relationships, they may begin planning ways out. Sometimes the way out is suicide. They may become violent and seriously ill, emotionally, mentally, or physically. They may overeat, under-eat, or abuse alcohol and other drugs.

Codependency is largely an Identity Problem[156]. John Bradshaw, in his book *Homecoming, Reclaiming and Championing Your Inner Child*, defines codependence as "a disease characterized by a loss of identity."[157]

John Scott, Sr., a colleague and hypnoanalyst from Memphis, Tennessee, characterizes codependency very well in a hypnosis script, a script which I use for codependent clients while they are in treatment:[158]

Who Am I?

One might say, "Who am I?" Codependents do not know what their lives are all about and seem to be floating aimlessly along without specific goals. They do not have much ambition, which in turn indicates that they do not have very much energy either. So as they float through life without aims, goals and ambitions, they are like matchsticks tossed about on the water.

The inner self, which is called the ego, is weak and brittle. In some cases this is indicated by the person saying that he or she feels shaky inside. This shaky or insecure feeling causes the codependent to be afraid about the future as they are not sure what the future holds for them. A person in this position does not have an inner sense of cohesion or connectedness nor do they have a sense of power. Another way to look at it is that the inner self is scattered or fragmented,—that their lives are in bits and pieces.

Some codependents describe themselves in this way:

"I am unwanted."

"I am unlovable."

Others feel that when they were born they were not planned, so feel that they are some kind of a mistake and therefore they have no purpose. They frequently conclude that there is no reason for their existence into the future and reveal that they are unable to cope with life.

Some turn to vices such as drugs, alcohol, smoking or obesity. They frequently have an intense fear of rejection. Many times they feel that their behavior is more childlike than adult. They lack the security and the strength that an adult has. Some people have recurrent depression and grief. Some also feel that they have lost contact with God and therefore have a very empty feeling about themselves, spiritually and emotionally.

Scott says the problem is often traceable to prebirth experiences. He notes:

> "There is a kind of extra-sensory perception in the communication between the mother and the unborn child. It is as if in the last three months before birth the child in the womb is like a mind reader. And it reads the mind of the mother. Severe events in the daily life of the mother can send messages to the unborn child by means of the hormones that are secreted by the mother and in turn flow into the unborn child."

The strong emotions of the mother, which are manifested by fear, anger, hatred or pain, frequently will influence the unborn child. Before the child is born it is very sensitive to these emotions.

Sometimes the mother's feelings are that the pregnancy is unplanned, unwanted and has no purpose; that it is a mistake. And if the mother has these feelings strongly, week in and week out throughout the pregnancy, there is the likelihood that the unborn child will absorb and believe these feelings are its own before it is ever born. If the mother has feelings of bitterness, resentment and disappointment, these strong emotions also produce feelings in the unborn child that are similar. So a person can have an identity problem due to the events that happened before that person was born.

The attitude of the father affects the unborn child indirectly through the mother. If the father neglects or abuses the mother, her attitude is affected and she passes this on to the child.

Identity problems may also arise from conditions in early childhood. As Scott tells us:

> "Before a child is five years old, it is in a perpetual state of hypnosis, which simply means that the child is highly sensitive and picks up quickly on all that goes on around him or her. The events and the feelings that have a strong impression on the child influence that child's feelings about itself. And so, if it is born into a home where it is unwanted and unloved or (what's worse) where it is abused; where there is rejection on the part of mother or father or both, then that too works away on the new infant, and puts within its mind a feeling of not being wanted; of being rejected; of having no cause to be alive. If the child was born prematurely or if it was born too late or if it had an unusual birth situation, this too can influence the child. It doesn't always, mind you, but sometimes it does." [159]

When the child feels unwanted or like an intruder into the world, notes Scott, it may respond through some form of self-destructive behavior. The child may even become accident-prone or illness-prone, which means that it is subject to many illnesses all of the time. In some cases, even more serious illnesses such as cancer and diabetes are likely to develop.

In most all of these situations," Scott observes, "the person is unable to love." This is the one trait that is common to all people who have identity problems. They do not have the capacity to love, especially to love themselves. Even if they start to enter into a love relationship or they have a relationship that looks like it might be love, it doesn't last. Something happens in those relationships, preventing them from getting deeper.

Such people are also unable to enter into a loving, trusting relationship with God. They may belong to a religion and profess belief in God, but they understand neither God nor religion. They do not feel deeply spiritual in their relationship with God, so they are unable to develop a deep love for God, for themselves, for someone of the same sex, or for someone of the opposite sex. Usually these people have a confused relationship with their parents.

Often, it takes time for codependents in therapy to volunteer the information that identifies them as codependents because they submerge themselves so completely in the task of caring for and controlling others that who they are has long ago slipped out of sight. Because they feel that they exist for others, they overlook self-care.

A codependent may have worked hard throughout life to become successful in a career. Having achieved success, the ordinary person would feel perfectly justified and comfortable in indulging in some kind of reward: a trip around the world, an expensive new car, or a nice sailboat. Ordinary people can do that for themselves and enjoy the fruits of their labors.

But codependents can't be carefree. If they spend that kind of money on themselves, they are haunted by feelings of guilt, and they are unable to enjoy the things their labors have purchased. Therefore, many codependents that are outwardly successful, with every apparent reason for happiness, nevertheless feel hollow and incomplete on the inside. They may isolate themselves resulting in depression and loneliness. Not knowing who they are, they overlook the possibilities in themselves and ignore the opportunities for personal growth and fulfillment.

His Spirit Came Back to Life!

Arthur, a codependent 40-year-old male, showed up for treatment after being involved in various forms of therapy groups and modalities for nearly 20 years. Arthur said:

> *"My problem . . . is that I can't stand to be myself. Secondly, I feel stuck in my career. I want to change, but I don't know what to do with myself."*

> I asked what he wanted from me.

> *"I want the freedom to be myself without having to cling to somebody. Also, I want to make a change in my living and working situation."*

Art grew up with an alcoholic father and a very controlling codependent mother. He expressed anger and frustration over having worked on his problems for 20 years, yet still feeling the way he described.

After doing his word-association tests, Art brought in a dream he had. This is it:

> *"I wonder if I have a spirit in me that doesn't belong there. Sometimes I feel like my head is full, as if there's an extra consciousness along for the ride."*

His word-association test showed the classical signs of the identity problem:

Ryan: Complete a sentence beginning with the word "who."
ART: *Who am I?*
Ryan: Unwanted . . .
ART: *Me.*
Ryan: They really wanted . . .
ART: *Somebody else.*

But what really turned this case around was the regression connected to his dream. Art regressed to a scene in which he was in the crib. His mother had just lost his month-old sister, who died of a problem heart. Art described in vivid detail, with tears, the terror of being beaten by a desperately depressed mother. He was helpless and he writhed with pain as each blow reached him. His spirit died during those beatings. He lost the connection and love of his mother.

Once he understood this, relived the experience, and realized his mother had acted crazy, we were able to bring his spirit back to life. With the help of much reinforcement, Art was able to love himself again. It took a while, but he solved his problem, left a dead-end job, married, and moved out of state.

Children are Vulnerable

Children are particularly vulnerable to codependency as they easily fall into the trap of mistaking codependency for love. This mistaken perception can follow them into adulthood and can lead them into marriages or romantic relationships that are built on codependency. Art's relationship to women replicated the one he had with his mother, always trying to please and overly concerned with her needs.

Children of substance addicted parents may express their codependency in a number of ways. They may do it by overachieving such as pushing to be the best in school or in sports to counteract the shame of the addiction by giving the family something to be proud of.

Another way such children may deal with this problem is to try to be entertaining, seeking to relieve the tension at home by being amusing and never taking anything seriously. It is no accident that the best comedians often come from dysfunctional homes.

Children from these families may cope by withdrawing from the family altogether, spending a lot of time alone or with friends. Or they may choose rebellion—acting outrageously in an effort to distract attention from the family's core problem. This had been Art's strategy, which he had resolved before engaging in hypnoanalysis.

Dealing with his family's codependency addiction, Art's spirit had died. He couldn't keep the greatest commandment in the law, according to Jesus, recorded in Matthew 22: 36-40, "Love God with your whole heart, soul and mind. And the second is the same as the first, love thy neighbor as thyself." As a result of recognizing the cause of his problem and taking corrective measures, Art is on his way to loving himself.

Child abuse and neglect have a profound negative effect on a child. When children are abused at an early age, healing requires recognizing the feelings and memory, rehabilitating thoughts and behavior, reeducation (in Art's case, this meant accepting he was a child of God first and of his earthly parents second), and reinforcement and repetition of the positive suggestions. Lastly, healing requires taking responsibility for feelings, thoughts, and patterns, regardless of where they originated.

John Was Addicted to Religion

John Bradshaw's father was an alcoholic and John became the family "hero" after his father abdicated his responsibility, becoming a super-achiever in Catholic school and deciding to study for the priesthood. Now an author and lecturer on family problems, Bradshaw contends that religion can also become addictive when you completely surrender your thinking and creative powers to a set of unyielding beliefs.[160]

Bradshaw identifies religious addicts as those people who are absorbed in religious activities to the exclusion of family, friends, and all secular interests. When a parent becomes a religious addict, the addiction affects the rest of the family much as any other addiction would.

"It's not uncommon in a family where there's religious addiction, where the parent is super responsible, to have the kids become under responsible or underachievers," Bradshaw told a group at the Center for Recovering Families.[161]

When one member of a family gets out of balance, the rest adapt by assuming different roles. "The second you have to play a role," Bradshaw contends, "you no longer can be yourself. You no longer can be real. You start playing the role, and every one of these roles has prescribed emotions that go with it . . . Your very choices are determined by the role . . . A false self arises . . . Once you get into these roles and they get ingrained, you think that's who you are. You think that's your essence. You think that's your identity. The fact is that you don't have any identity. All you have is a role."[162]

Adopting the role comes as a result of families being out of balance. In hypnoanalysis, we very often find that the balance was not there in the beginning, and—by identifying the codependent's ISE—we can accelerate the recovery process.

Shame Is at the Core

Bradshaw identifies the core problem of codependency as shame,[163] shame that has been passed down from generation to generation, from parent to child, from child to grandchild, and so on. The person who experiences shame feels flawed as a human being. Shame, in fact, is identified with the genesis of human flaws. It was shame that Adam and Eve felt when they were driven from Eden, no longer the flawless human creatures God had placed in the garden.

Do not confuse shame with guilt, however. Tony Schirtzinger, therapist from www.helpyourselftherapy.com writes, "When we feel guilt, it's about something we did.

When we feel shame, it's about who we are. When we feel guilty we need to learn that it's OK to make mistakes. When we feel shame we need to learn that it's OK to be who we are!" [164]

It's a terrible burden to feel shame, to be convinced that you are worthless. Shamed people feel a constant fear of discovery—"When they are doing well, they think it's only a matter of time before they are discovered as useless." [163] This pressure is real and unremitting.

Most people experiencing feelings of worthlessness try constantly to prove that they do have worth, are always worried about what others think and believe that others are always judging them. If others are kind to them, they assume it is because they do not 'really' know them, the Imposter Syndrome at its worst.

The Garden of Eden story takes on added significance when codependents realize that the consequence of original sin is judgment. Judging one's self and others creates shame. God reserved judgment for Himself. It seems that human beings are unable to handle being judged and get stuck in polarized thinking, that is, extreme black and white thinking (thinking that is more consistent with children under 7 years old: right versus wrong and shades of gray do not exist), one of the hallmarks of codependence. (Hypnoanalysts describe this state as the Ponce de Leone Syndrome.)

By stopping and relieving the origin of subconscious judgment, codependents can realize who they are and become the person they want to be instead of the one they were conditioned by circumstances to be.

Who Am I, Really?

Incorporating shame is a gradual and complex operation. Art's began with his physical abuse. Marty's began with the relationship to his parents. Others frequently report a womb experience as the onset of their shame. Resolving this problem is commonly done through recovery groups along with hypnoanalysis.

The person who feels flawed also feels hopeless. What do you do with flawed items? You cast them aside and look for one that is perfect.

"Codependency," says Bradshaw, "is a way of institutionalizing shame." "It's a way I can always feel good about myself because I'm always helping others."[164]

In reality, codependents do not feel good about themselves. They struggle through life dealing with their shame, trying to shield the objects of their codependency from shame, taking responsibility for others, but neglecting their own primary responsibilities: the responsibilities for themselves.

Once recovery has progressed and the codependent realizes and feels that he is a child of God first and a child of his parents second, the battle is half over.

Guilt, Loneliness, and Depression

Guilt, loneliness, and depression are the handmaidens of codependency. Guilt sticks to codependents as they have assumed enormous responsibility—the responsibility for the welfare of the family or for the behavior of their dependent partners—and when they are unable to control things for the better, they blame themselves, bringing on guilt.

Guilt can be a healthy force when it warns you in advance of a wrong course, or when it reminds you—after the fact—that what you did was not in your best interests and should not be done again. Healthy guilt is a gut feeling.

Guilt becomes unhealthy when it takes charge of your mind and actions long after the need for remorse has passed. Unhealthy guilt is obsessive and needlessly repetitive.

The codependent's guilt is based on the need to be perfect and on feeling guilty for existing. Codependents are extremely tolerant of imperfection in others but can't tolerate it in themselves. Therefore, when they fall short of perfection—as all humans do—they are unforgiving of themselves.

Joan Borysenko, Ph.D., author, psychologist, and cell biologist writes: "When you overcome the tyranny of black-and-white thinking and accept the range of grays that makes us human, you'll begin to let go of unhealthy guilt."[165]

Borysenko has some other healthy advice that applies to codependents: "Quit people-pleasing, and be true to your own feelings . . . Instead of repressing anger to appear virtuous and kind, express your feelings in a non-hurtful way. Instead of doing things you don't want to do in an effort to win others' approval, stop being a martyr and learn to say no when it's appropriate."[166]

In addition to guilt, codependency breeds loneliness. The codependent feels trapped in a one-sided relationship that provides no emotional nourishment. This spiritual famine is the essence of loneliness.

Codependents are lonely because they are unable to share themselves with others because they have no identities of their own. Their identities are lost in the identities of the people they are trying to control or please.

As Bradshaw writes:

> "The wounded inner child contaminates intimacy in relationships because he has no sense of his authentic self. The greatest wound a child can receive is the rejection of his authentic self. When a parent cannot affirm his child's feelings, needs and desires, he rejects that child's authentic self. Then a false self must be set up".[167]

As one patient remarked to James F. Masterson, adjunct clinical professor of psychiatry at The New York Hospital Cornell Medical Center: "I'm not doing what I want, because my ideas—about how I work, how I think, how I dress—and even my hobbies and how I relate to men are filtered through the perception of what *others* want.

I'm good at perceiving what pleases other people and giving them what they want, but I feel trapped, like I'm suffocating inside my skin."[168]

Codependents are afraid to allow themselves to become close to others because they are afraid of being engulfed on the one hand and abandoned on the other. To break this cycle of loneliness, the codependent must first recognize the problem, and then develop more constructive ways to relate to people and life. Codependents must, almost literally, become new persons, developing interests and friendships on their own, apart from their partners in codependency. Hypnoanalysis, with its unique capacity to speak directly to the subconscious and go straight to the initial sensitizing event, can reduce considerably the time frame for the individuation process.

Guilt and loneliness, of course, produce depression. Depression has many causes—some genetic, many psychological, most subconscious, and some environmental. Difficult relationships often support depression as a person may be drawn into a difficult relationship by psychological-codependent "needs," thus completing the cycle of depression.

Depressed people are persistently sad and anxious. They feel hopeless and pessimistic. Nothing ever turns out right, and nothing ever will. They feel guilty, worthless, and helpless. They have no interest in pleasures, hobbies, and activities they once enjoyed. They feel tired, listless, and apathetic. They sometimes think of death or suicide, and in extreme cases will attempt suicide. They have trouble concentrating and remembering things. They also have trouble making decisions. They are plagued by headaches, digestive disorders, and chronic pain. Basically, they are dead subconsciously as a result of accepting negative death suggestions.

In its pamphlet, *Plain Talk about Depression*, the National Institute of Mental Health, Office of Scientific Information, suggests these methods of dealing with depression (paraphrased below) [169]:

- Avoid setting very difficult goals or taking on a great deal of responsibility.
- Break large tasks into small ones, set some priorities, and do what you can as you can.

- Give your self a break by expecting reasonable behavior from yourself; expecting perfection will only increase feelings of failure. Remember, good is good enough.
- Get out and be with other people, do things; it is usually better than being alone.
- Participate in activities that may make you feel better.
- Try mild exercise; go dancing, to a movie or ball game, or participate in religious or social activities.
- Overdoing simply leads to acting as if you are a "human doing" rather than a "human being." Be kind to yourself if your mood is not greatly improved right away. Feeling better takes time. Tell yourself over and over, "**I'm sorry this is in your life, I love you**!"
- Avoid making major life decisions, such as changing jobs or getting married or divorced, without consulting others who know you well and who have a more objective view of your situation. In any case, it is advisable to postpone important decisions until your depression has lifted.
- Expecting yourself to snap out of depression leads to frustration. People rarely "snap out". Help yourself as much as you can, and blaming yourself for not being up to par only adds to your misery.

There are a number of short-term pick-me-up techniques for pulling yourself out of blue moods to help get you "up" for that special occasion when you can't afford to be down.

First, figure out what is eating you. Often, when you sit down and think about it, you can pinpoint some event in the recent past that is out of your conscious mind but keeps bugging you from its subconscious retreat. Maybe it was a bit of criticism you didn't think you deserved, or some action on the part of a friend that you interpreted as a snub. It may be the weather, or simply loneliness.

By pinpointing the triggering event, you can decide on an appropriate action. It may be that you need only to be told, "I'm okay, even if the boss did criticize the punctuation in that report I submitted. I liked its substance, and that's what counts."

Exercise can help a bad mood. It can physically release pent-up feelings of anxiety and restore a sense of control over events. It also causes your brain to produce more endorphins, which are natural antidepressants.

You can use mental visualization, "self-hypnosis," to replace negative thoughts with positive ones. Remember a happy period in your life and dwell on it. Or think of things that have made you laugh.

For women, shopping might be a pick-me-up. Shopping makes you feel that you are taking care of yourself. For the codependent, shopping also reinforces the idea that you are an individual with the ability to make decisions on your own.

Reading a book or talking with a close friend will let you take a break from problems. but don't choose a book or a friend that will reinforce your depression.

Taking a drive or a walk, or spending time in a natural setting, may give you the change of scenery you need. If your mood is associated with a particular room or office, get out of it for a while.

You can go anywhere you want in your imagination. Try planning an imaginary vacation—to Tahiti, to Monaco, or to Acapulco. Drop by your friendly travel agency and pick up some brochures. If you really want some vivid images, get a travel video.

If all else fails, throw a punch—at a pillow, a punching bag, or some other object that won't feel pain, won't strike back, won't be destroyed, and won't hurt you. You might try buying an inflatable clown that bounces back up when you hit it.

The point is that you have needs apart from the needs of your codependent partner. Indulge those needs. Recognize and accept that you are imperfect, too, and since you share that trait with more than 5 billion other human creatures, you don't have to feel guilty about being imperfect. Discover yourself, make friends with yourself—especially your inner child—and start treating yourself with the same kind of concern you show to others. Take yourself on a picnic, to the zoo, or on some other activity you enjoyed as a child.

Six Suggestions to Help Recovery

Addictions, of course, can be cured. Recovery from codependency is also possible. Human Services, Inc., of Dallas, Texas, lists these six steps toward recovery from codependency: [170]

1. **Being Honest**. Admit that your partner really is addicted to a substance or a behavior, and that both of your lives are being controlled by this addiction.
2. **Detachment**. Give up trying to rescue the addicted partner, to solve his or her problems, make him or her happy, or save him or her from the consequences of his or her addictive behavior. *This isn't within your control.*
3. **Putting Yourself First**. Take care of your own needs. Plan activities and set goals for yourself that are not contingent on your addicted partner's moods or actions. *Only the addict can solve his or her problems; only you can make yourself happy.*
4. **Getting Help**. Reach out to friends, relatives, or a therapist who can help you sort out your feelings and begin living for yourself. Without help, your codependency will, at best, stay the same or get worse.
5. **Talking**. Recognize your own needs and feelings, especially the anger you may feel about the control the addiction has had over your life. Then tell your partner—without apologies—what you want.
6. **Being Patient**. Understand that you won't solve your problems all at once, so don't try. Instead, take one step at a time and feel proud of your strength and courage.

The Alcoholics Anonymous Twelve-Step Program has been a useful model in helping people recover from addictions and their model is helpful in recovering from codependency. As one codependent put it:

> "When I began using a Twelve-Step Program, I heard a lot of talk about people using behavior to control others. They all seemed to know what this controlling behavior was, and they all seemed to agree there was something wrong with it. At first I didn't understand. When I finally understood, I got mad. I felt accused of doing something awful. It made me angry. I had been taught to seem powerless, had learned ways to appease my craving for love, attention and recognition in indirect ways because it wasn't acceptable to want those things, much less ask openly for them. But I was now

> being told it was my own sick controlling behavior that made others miserable and kept me from feeling close to them. Something inside me screamed, 'Not fair! Not fair!' [171]

The Need to Control

Codependents have trouble recognizing that their unconscious need to be in control is compulsive. They don't know they have such a need, they don't know how to get rid of it, and they are surprised when others point it out.

But controlling others is rarely necessary. Others don't need our control. Rather, it is the codependent who has the need to control, a need that springs from the subconscious, is quite destructive and keeps you from feeling and from facing reality.

How do you know when you are using controlling behavior? There are a number of signposts.

One sign is **tension**. If you are doing the controlling, you feel nervous because you are trying to manipulate someone into either doing something to please you or not doing something that displeases you.

Another signpost is **blaming**. You point to someone else as the cause of your unhappiness and try to make the other person feel guilty. When you do that, you are conceding to someone else the right to determine how you feel.

Urgency is another marker. Desperately trying to prevent something from happening, or having an overpowering need to make something happen is a signal that you are trying to control.

Another indication is the **refusal to feel**. This shows up constantly in the codependents I treat. To be a codependent requires that you discount, deny, or ignore your own feelings and the feelings of others. Codependents do not want to know their own feelings or the feelings of others. This sometimes makes it difficult to determine the initial sensitizing event for a codependent person due to codependents' capacity to ignore their feelings and deny their problems. However, with the support of a group and the eight R's of hypnoanalysis (Relaxation, Realization, Reeducation, Rehabilitation, Reassurance, Repetition,

Reinforcement, and Responsibility), the ISE eventually emerges. (See the Introduction for more about the eight R's.)

The treatment plan for codependence has three guiding principles:

1. **The cause is in the past.** There have been experiences, events, and people, or the lack of these, over which the patient has had no control. These have left a hangover or ghost from the past, which has caused current problems.
2. **No blame.** We are not here to blame or point the finger at anybody. We are attempting to understand the past and its effect on your subconscious mind.
3. **Working together.** We work together so that understanding emerges gradually. We can't do everything at once. The pieces will fit together. We are headed in the right direction.

Steps For How to Let Go

Since codependency is an instinctive response, it springs from the subconscious which is why hypnoanalysis is such an effective means of uncovering the ISE and freeing the subconscious mind of the memories and attitudes that result in codependent behavior.

Codependents present the hypnoanalyst with a challenge, however. If hypnoanalysis is to be successful, the patient must have a trusting relationship with the hypnoanalyst. Yet, codependents have conditioned themselves to expect the worst from everyone and are never sure of what others will do if they let down their guards. It becomes doubly important, then, for the hypnoanalyst to establish a relationship of trust with the patient and show the patient how to release the need to control.

How can this be done? The Hazelden Foundation, in its pamphlet, "Letting Go of the Need to Control," gives several suggestions [172]:

1. **Look for behavior patterns.** Because the need to control is instinctive, it resurfaces time and again. Learn to recognize these instinctive reactions and you will soon recognize your controlling *modus operandi.*

2. **Make up your mind that you will trust your own feelings and perceptions.** When you decide to believe in yourself, your self-esteem will rise.
3. **Identify alternatives.** Look at the way things are going now. If nothing changes, what real choices do you have? What are the probable consequences of each choice? You can try to get others to change by communicating with them indirectly—through hints, pouting, withdrawing, and other actions. You can wait until things are different. Or you can look for other choices that lie outside your habitual way of doing things.
4. **Check out assumptions.** Low self-esteem causes you to imagine the worst. You act as though what you have imagined is true, and your imagination becomes a self-fulfilling prophecy. But often your worst fears are groundless, especially when it comes to the way other people regard you. Ask others what they really think and feel about you. When you take the trouble to check out assumptions, you are in a position to act on the basis of facts, not fears.
5. **Decide what you really need and start looking for it.** Take a needs inventory at work and at home, with friends and family. Be candid. You deserve support in your efforts, and you must learn to trust those near you to provide the support. By learning to trust, you build self-esteem and you gain the strength to take risks, the strength that will enable you to let go of your codependency and to recapture yourself for yourself.

The Twelve-Step Program has been an effective route to recovery for alcoholics and other substance abusers and is also an effective program to help codependents recover. The CoDa World Fellowship is the official organization of Co-Dependents Anonymous.[172] Following a Twelve-Step Program, codependents agree to adhere to the 12 Traditions[173]and the 12 steps:

1. Admit that you are powerless over the factor that brought on your codependency.
2. Come to believe that a power greater than yourself can restore you to sanity.

3. Make a decision to turn your will and your life over to the care of God, as you understand God. (In my groups, and in hypnoanalysis, I work with God as "God equals Love".)
4. Make a searching and fearless moral inventory of yourself.
5. Admit to God, yourself, and to another human being the exact nature of your wrongs.
6. Become entirely ready to have God remove all these defects of character.
7. Humbly ask God to remove your shortcomings.
8. Make a list of all persons you have harmed, and be willing to make amends to them all.
9. Make direct amends to such people wherever possible, except when to do so would injure yourself or others.
10. Continue to take personal inventory, and when you are wrong, promptly admit it.
11. Through prayer and meditation, seek to improve your conscious contact with God, as you understand God, praying only for knowledge of God's will for you and the power to carry that out.
12. Having had a spiritual awakening as a result of those steps, try to carry this message to others, and to practice these principles in all your affairs.

These twelve steps, while developed specifically for Alcoholics Anonymous, are used for codependents and a host of other addictions such as Narcotics Anonymous, Overeater Anonymous, On and On, etc. The codependent reared in a dysfunctional family can benefit from these steps and need not be in a relationship with a substance abuser or dysfunctional person.

As Angelyn Miller observed, the families of codependents "need a chance to get out from under the enabling of their caretaker, and their enabler needs to be relieved of the burdens."[174]

A good prayer for all codependents—one that can be used as a self-hypnosis suggestion—is this:

> *"God, grant me the serenity to accept the things I cannot change, the courage to change the things I can, and the wisdom to know the difference."*

Remember, change takes time. Focusing on living one day, hour, minute, or second at a time allows freedom to be in the process of becoming one's self. The following is from Anne Wilson Schaef from "Living in Process."

"Life is a process.
We are a process.
The universe is a process."

Another exceptional resource is *The Seven Jewels of Codependence*[175] where the authors describe the primary traits of codependence as loving, sensitive self-sacrificing, reliability, energetic, self-controlled, and creative. However, those traits can be used in both beneficial and harmful ways. On the positive side, codependent traits can be transformed into the "Seven Jewels" of having an open heart, awareness of what is, mutual sharing, firm foundation, productive power, focused effort, and discovering options. The authors redefine codependence as a potential for wonderfully positive and powerful way of life by simply noting that loving is never a negative but always a positive quality.

Code Concepts

A codependent is a person who has allowed another person's behavior to affect him or her, who adapts his or her own behavior to protect the other person, and/or who is obsessed with controlling that person's behavior.

- The codependent's partner may be a person who is addicted to alcohol, drugs, religion or other substances or behavior.
- When one member of a family develops an addiction or dysfunctional behavior, the rest of the family members assume roles to compensate for the dysfunctional member.
- Codependents submerge their own identities while trying to control the behavior of others. They try to shield their dependents from the consequences of their actions and try to assume responsibility for the actions and welfare of others.
- Codependents are marked by a need to take care of others, low self-esteem, a tendency to repress feelings, a tendency toward excessive worry, a need to control and be controlled, denial that there is a problem, dependence on others for happiness, difficulty in communicating, inability to set boundaries, lack of trust, anger and fear of anger, and problems in sexual relations.
- Codependence breeds loneliness, guilt, and depression. Depression may breed codependence, and a cyclical pattern results.
- Codependence is an instinctive response; hence, the key to overcoming it lies in uncovering subconscious motivation.
- Hypnoanalysis can help by uncovering the ISE through age regression. This requires the building of trust between patient and analyst.
- The steps toward recovery are honesty; detachment; putting oneself first; getting help from friends, relatives or a therapist; and talking openly with your partner.
- To free oneself of the need to control, one should look for the behavior patterns through which one attempts to control, determine to trust one's own feelings and perceptions,

identify alternative ways of coping with problems, check out assumptions to make certain that choices are based upon facts instead of fears, and decide what one really needs and start looking for it.

Code Breaking Exercises

1. Ask yourself whether you identify with the codependents described in this chapter. Be honest.
2. Analyze what you are doing to help yourself.
3. Read books by John Bradshaw, Melody Beattie, and Anne Wilson Schaef. "The Dance of Wounded Souls" by Robert Burney and "The Seven Jewels of Codependence" by Willard and Gibertini are two I especially recommend.
4. If you are depressed, seek professional help immediately, especially if you are suicidal.
5. List your own unproductive, self-destructive behaviors. Decide which ones you want to change.
6. Intuitively, write down the percentage of time you are living for others—from 0 to 100 percent. Do it now, without thinking. ______________________.
7. Intuitively, what percentage of the time are you assuming responsibilities for others? ______________________
8. Intuitively, what percentage of the time do you seek love from?

   God ______________.
   Others ______________.
   Self ______________.

If the answer to Question 6 is over 15 percent, you need help.

If your answer to Question 7 is anything above 0 percent, except for children, you need help.

On Question 8, the ideal score is God 33 1/3 percent, others 33 1/3 percent, and self 33 1/3 percent.

Nobody is perfect—remember that. However, mature people need to spread their need for love among the three sources.

9. Consider this quote:

   "The need to belong to something larger than ourselves underlies many of these pursuits. We long to feel a vital part of some community of others, to have the security that comes through belonging to something larger than ourselves. It is through identification that ultimately we know rootedness."[176]

What do you think?

Chapter Thirteen

Winning Is Mind Over Muscle: If You Don't Mind, Then Muscle Doesn't Matter

It is not enough
to fight. It is the
spirit which we bring to the
fight that decides the victory.

General George C. Marshall

He . . . got the
better of himself,
and that's the best
kind of victory one
can wish for.

Miguel de Cervantes

Mind and Muscle

"Football is played, above all, with the heart and mind," said Pennsylvania State University Coach Joe Paterno. "It's played with the body only secondarily. A coach's first duty is to coach minds. If he doesn't succeed at that, his team will not reach its potential."[177]

"Golf is 90% mental and 10% physical." A quote attributed at various times to Jack Nicholas and also Ben Hogan. Jack is also quoted as saying, "There is no room in your mind for negative thoughts . . ."

Yogi Berra commented, "Baseball is 90% mental, and the other half physical"

"The fight is won or lost far away from the witnesses, behind the lines, in the gym, and out there on the road; long before I dance under those lights." Mohammed Ali

"Some people say I have attitude—maybe I do . . . but I think you have to. You have to believe in yourself when no one else does—that makes you a winner right there." Venus Williams.

"I want to be remembered as the guy who gave his all whenever he was on the field." Walter Payton. [178]

Tiger Woods, the most recognized athlete of all time is quoted as saying, "I'm the toughest golfer mentally." "Mental toughness, I think you could put it into words," he said. "It's stuff like you never give up. You never give in to anything. You never accept anything but the best from yourself. You can always push to get better."[179]

All of the above professional athletes believe that winning in their sport is a matter of mind over muscle. If sports are played with the mind, is it possible to program the mind for victory? Can hypnosis, with proper suggestions, turn a loser into a winner by the power of the mind?

Les Cunningham, Ph. D., Australian hypnotherapist, has used hypnosis to improve the performance of many athletes. He suspects that the use of hypnosis lies behind much of the success of Soviet-bloc athletes in Olympic competition.

As a pool player and golfer, I have used hypnosis to improve my performance at both. Later in this chapter, I will describe how I have worked with sports players to remove the deep-seated subconscious factors that hindered their minds from developing the mental toughness needed to play their best games.

But let's get something straight at the outset: hypnosis will not turn Joe the Plumber into a Joe DiMaggio or Mohammed Ali. It will not turn a weekend or basement pool shooter into the Black Widow, "The Color of Money's" Fast Eddie Felson, or Mike Sigel, nor can it turn an average 16-handicap golfer into a Tiger Woods, Bobby Jones, or Phil Mickelson. Also, enabling the couch potato to rise from the sofa and run the marathon takes an act of God, not hypnotic suggestion.

Hypnosis should not be used to help someone ignore an injury to perform to maximum capacity. Ignoring an injury for the sake of temporary gain can worsen the injury or make it permanent. But hypnosis can help you to use your full potential, to get the most out of yourself that, as Cervantes wrote, is the best kind of victory one can hope for.

Even without hypnosis, many athletes have acknowledged that muscle alone doesn't win the athletic event. Sports history is populated with names of players whose physical abilities were mediocre but whose mental attitudes spurred them and their teams to victory. Billy Ripken of the Baltimore Orioles might not possess the physical talent of Cal, his brother and teammate but his hustle and determination have earned him a respected niche among major-league infielders.

Billy Martin, whose fiery management personality led the New York Yankees and Oakland Athletics to championships, was a spark plug as a player, too. But it was Martin's competitive attitude, not his physical prowess, that made the difference on the field.

Leo Durocher, who also achieved greatness as a manager, enjoyed a playing career marked by smart play that compensated for lack of physical talent. Durocher took the field with a single-minded determination to win. He once remarked:

"What are we out at the park for except to win? I'd trip my mother. I'll help her up, brush her off, tell her I'm sorry. But mother don't make it to third."[180]

"We become what we think we are," wrote Les Cunningham in his book, "Hypnosport: How You Can Improve Your Sporting Performances". We become what we think. "If we think of success, we become successful. If we think of failure, we become failures."[181]

They *Expected* to Score

That was the attitude Paterno, often referred to as "JoePa", a College Football Hall of Fame who coached the Penn State Nittany Lions football team for nearly 46 years, tried to communicate to his players and he took a dim view of end-zone theatrics after a touchdown. "When a Nittany Lion scores a touchdown," he said, "he doesn't dance and go berserk in the end zone. When a Penn Stater goes on that field, he *expects* to make a touchdown."[182]

Paterno knew that a winning coach must also cultivate a winning attitude, and he saw Bear Bryant of the University of Alabama as the epitome of confidence:

> "When Bear Bryant . . . walked out on that football field, self-confidence hung in the air around him like a fine mist. That was worth at least one touchdown for Alabama."[183]

And Paterno saw himself as a winner. He wasn't content to see himself as a good coach, or the Coach of the Year, or even the best coach in Penn State history. "I didn't see why I should leave room in the number one spot for sharing with Bear Bryant or Vince Lombardi or anybody else," he declared. Though Paterno's career ended abruptly as a result of a sex scandal involving one of his assistants, and at the time of his death he held multiple records and had coached five undefeated teams to major bowl game victories. "JoePa" definitely understood the concept of mind over muscle.

The mother of Olympic runner Brenda Morehead urged the same type of attitude when she advised her daughter, "Don't want to win; want a record!"[184] Whether Morehead set the record or fell short of it, that confident determination propelled her to victory in the Olympics.

If you believe you will succeed, you will succeed. If you believe you will fail, you will fail. Imagination is a powerful tool for accomplishment. If you can produce vivid images of success in your mind, those images penetrate to your subconscious, and from there they can light your way to success.

I know this is easy to say. I do not want to oversimplify or mislead you into thinking that programming your subconscious mind for success in a competitive sport is as easy as sinking a four-inch putt or getting on first by taking four straight balls. Besides determination and ability, many factors contribute. Hypnosis, self-suggestion, and hypnoanalysis can, however, make a tremendous difference with a motivated person, as you shall see.

Willie's Prayer: "Don't Let It Be Me"

In the final game of the 1951 National League playoffs, the New York Giants were fortunate that Bobby Thomson came through at the crucial moment. With one out in the ninth inning, Thomson represented the winning run for the Giants. Thomson confidently strode to the plate and knocked a Ralph Branca pitch out of the park, making the Giants the National League champions.

The man scheduled to hit behind Thomson was a rookie named Willie Mays. Mays, praying in the on-deck circle, was not asking God, "Please God, let Bobby get a hit so we can go to the World Series." Willie's prayer was, "Please don't let it be me. Don't let me come to bat now, God."[185]

Would Willie have come through in the clutch? Not likely. He was 1 for 10 in the playoffs, and at the time was totally lacking in confidence.

Later, it was a different story. Manager Leo Durocher took Willie under his wing and, over time, instilled confidence in the youngster. At one point, when Willie was moping around in the clubhouse, feeling sorry for himself because of his poor batting performance, Durocher told him:

> "You're the greatest ball player I ever saw or ever hope to see . . . You can hit it into the bleachers here, over the fence, anywhere you want . . ." [186]

Willie, of course, went on to live up to Durocher's prescient description. Had he possessed the confidence in 1951 that he acquired in later years, he would have been praying for a chance to come to bat.

Durocher's challenge was to get the negative, pessimistic thinking out of Mays' subconscious mind and replace it with positive, optimistic thinking. The manager succeeded through patient reassurance and reinforcement. A hypnoanalyst might have done it more quickly. Had Willie used hypnosis to purge the image of failure from his subconscious, the Giants might not have needed a dramatic stretch drive and a cliff-hanger playoff series to win the pennant.

"Boundless confidence seems to ride hand-in-hand with the success of an individual or a team," says Cunningham in the preface to his book.

Was it pure luck that Babe Ruth, after calling two strikes on himself, was able to point toward the stands, then drive a home run within a few feet of where he had pointed? Not likely. The Babe had superb confidence in himself and that confidence gave him the poise, timing, and concentration to accomplish what he aimed to accomplish.

The Pyramid of Success

Cunningham compares sporting success to a pyramid. Its triangular base consists of three factors: intelligence, physical conditioning, and psychological conditioning.[136] The athlete achieves peak performance when all three factors harmoniously promote the athlete performing at his or her subconscious best.

A good coach can provide the extra intelligence using his own knowledge, training, and experience to serve as guides in setting up the athlete's schedule for training and competition. The tennis player who schedules too many tournaments and not enough training sessions is unlikely to make it to Wimbledon. The one whose schedule brings the athlete to the tournament in peak form is the athlete most likely to win.

Once those schedules are set, the athlete has to stick with them. This calls for discipline. The athlete has to see the schedule of training and competition as a road to success. With that road clearly fixed in mind, the competitor embarks on it with single-minded determination.

Physical conditioning is the next prerequisite to athletic success. As Cunningham notes, a good strong competitor will always beat an equally good but slightly weaker opponent. When athletes in training see themselves getting stronger and fitter, they receive good, positive reinforcement.[187]

Finally comes the psychological conditioning—the mental programming for success. Self-hypnosis can be an effective tool for this programming. Through it, athletes can learn, in Cunningham's words, "to imagine with crystal clarity" the points on the pathways they have mapped out.[188]

We now know beyond any shadow of a doubt that exercising muscles by imagination strengthens the muscles almost as much as if the muscles were exercised physically.

Cunningham divides his inputs into three overlapping stages: long term, medium term and short term. Long-term strategy begins before the season starts. With the help of self-hypnosis, the athlete can concentrate on the ultimate goal. Cunningham observes:

> "At no time should negative thoughts or doubts be allowed to intrude into your imaginings. The only things to think about are positive steps toward the championship. Visions of the crowd, the arena, the sights, sounds and smells, your role in the winning play, the championship-winning performance, the applause and the euphoria associated with victories should be all that concerns you at this stage in your preparation."[189]

During the training period, Cunningham urges athletes to go into self-hypnosis and imagine themselves growing in strength, coordination and stamina.[190]

As the day of competition approaches, medium-term and short-term preparations begin. That is when athletes practice and perfect the correct style. At this stage they can, under self-hypnosis, see themselves performing the correct way. They can feel the correct grip on the bat, the club, or the racquet. They can imagine themselves swimming with the correct stroke.

On the eve of the contest, athletes may experience stage fright. If they know how to use self-hypnosis, they can overcome this by imagining in vivid detail all their activities on the day before the contest. They should start "imaging" a week in advance. If possible, they should plan a routine to be followed the day before the event and stick to it. They should imagine what they will be eating, feel themselves experiencing the pleasant tiredness upon retiring to bed, and then sinking into a comfortable night's sleep. If insomnia sets in, they can use self-hypnosis to relax themselves and fall asleep.

Several hours before the contest, or even just before the contest, they can again relax themselves through self-hypnosis. After taking last-minute instructions from the coach, they visualize how the contest will go. They see themselves performing at top level, their muscles perfectly tuned, their reflexes sharp, their energy fully mobilized.

Peak performance demands an appropriate level of arousal. The rule of thumb is that the simpler the task, the higher the level of arousal necessary to accomplish it. Cunningham suggests that players associate different levels of arousal with different colors.[191] By concentrating on the appropriate color, they can thus achieve the proper level of arousal at the proper time. Self-hypnosis is one way of achieving the desired state of arousal at will.

When the mind is properly *programmed*, the athlete goes into the contest confident, poised, and devoid of negative thoughts. This confidence does not remove the possibility of mistakes, bad bounces or bad calls by the referee, but it does insulate the player from the demoralizing effects of these breaks. The tennis player who makes a bad serve during a match will not be rattled by the mistake. The player with positive programming knows that one bad serve does not lose a tournament.

The Golfer Who Wanted to Be Someone Else

When a twenty-something professional golfer, Jack, said during a history session with me, this is what he said when asked what the problem was:

> "*I think it's just confidence, my main problem is . . . not to the level I want to play . . . not conscious, something internal. I want to believe in myself to play, to have the ability to trust yourself and let go. It's constant. I never thought I was good enough. I got cut my first year in high school. I was always playing catch up.*"

When I asked him what made his problem worse, he said, "*The golf coach said I had no ability in golf and I should play football.*"

Jack had been playing on the mini tours but wanted to get on the PGA tour. Following hypnoanalysis, he made it through some parts of

Q-School and lowered his stroke average about two shots per round. He was thrilled. But the real reason that allowed him to progress was this discovery under hypnosis: When he was 5 years old, his parents divorced and Jack became over-weight. Grade school kids teased him mercilessly about his size to the point where he decided he did not want *to be* (which we discovered in regression; he did not know this consciously). In high school, his coach telling him to play football only made Jack more determined to play golf, which he did very well. After Jack turned pro, this golfer jumped from coach to coach, from mentor to mentor trying to "be" them. His car became his home and he was romantically involved with a Jekyll and Hyde-like alcohol abuser who made his life more difficult.

After a few months of treatment, Jack decided that it was more than OK to be himself and consequently began playing much better golf, gave up his dysfunctional girlfriend, bought a home and worked a finance job in the off season. Basically, he turned his whole life around and stopped *"Always trying to find out what was wrong."* That statement, taken straight from his history, describes how he felt about his golf game. In reality there was nothing wrong with his game. What Jack was describing was his negative subconscious mindset about himself.

Nor should we expect that the athlete who uses hypnosis will never lose. Jack lost plenty of times, as has Arnold Palmer, Jack Nicklaus and Tiger Woods. And remember that no baseball team has ever won a pennant with a perfect season. You win some, lose some, and some get rained out. But athletes who are programmed for victory will not be deterred by the defeats along the way. They will learn from their defeats and, thus, turn them into positive experiences.

To be a success, you have to concentrate your entire mind on being a success. When excellent pianists play, they concentrate their minds entirely on what they are playing. They do not wonder whether, maybe, they'll hit the wrong note. An excellent pilot, when flying a plane, concentrates entirely on piloting the aircraft. It won't do to concentrate partly on piloting the plane and partly on the fear of not doing it right. Self-consciousness is anathema to the pianist, the pilot, and the athlete.

When the 15-year-old San Franciscan, Lynne Cox, swam the English Channel in 1972 breaking both the men's and women's speed record, she concentrated her mind entirely on the challenge she faced.

Her concentration was so intense that, mentally, she had already swum the channel in advance, before she ever got into the water. In her mind, it was an accomplished fact before she ever began, becoming the youngest person ever to swim the English Channel (until 1988 when an 11 year old bested her age record), and Lynne did it under self-hypnosis. Had part of her mind concentrated on the fear of what might happen if she didn't make it, then she would have been sapping her own strength, causing self-defeating feelings and thoughts.

How We Sap Our Strength

The truth of the matter is that each of us saps our own strength to a certain extent, depending on the amount of fear we allow to creep into our minds. We are even afraid to let go of our fear. We think that maybe fear is a good thing; that maybe it motivates us. We may think, "Maybe if I'm afraid I'm going to be poor, then I'll have to strive to be rich; maybe if I'm afraid I'm going to lose the game, I'll play better." But nothing could be farther from the truth. When can you accomplish what you want to do? When you rid yourself of the fear that you might not accomplish it. Remember: Fear creates that which one is afraid of.

Three negative emotions must be eliminated before you can get started toward becoming a better athlete. Hypnoanalysts call the three negative emotions the "unholy triumvirate:" fear, anxiety, and guilt. These emotions do no good; they hold you back. Before you can remove them though, you have to learn to recognize them so that you can prevent them from moving back in.

The first and biggest negative emotion is fear. It usually creeps back in the form of motivation. You say, "Oh, it's good for me to be afraid; it motivates me." But that's ridiculous. Fear motivates people to panic. Justice Oliver Wendell Holmes ruled that the only limitation to free speech is that no one has a right to yell "fire" in a crowded theater when there is no fire. Why? Because it makes people afraid causing them to panic. They lose their reason and rush for the exit, even though it's blocked. Emotion comes to the door and reason flies out the window. Whatever you are afraid of, the fear must go.

The next negative emotion is anxiety, or worry. Business people worry, and that gives them ulcers. All successful people have ulcers, right? Far from it. The really successful people handle their business without ulcers. The amount of energy used to make your stomach secrete the acid that create the ulcers is working against you, not for you. That means you are sublimating other drives, such as hostility, by injuring yourself. Fear and anxiety are negative emotions that injure you. Channel the hostility into the business itself instead of into your body.

The most insidious of all the negative emotions is guilt. Guilt is an after-the-fact emotion. You feel guilty because you made the wrong decision; therefore, you punish yourself. You feel guilty because of something that happened a long time ago, perhaps in your childhood. You feel you did not do the best for your mother or your father, or for your brother or your sister; or you could have done this, or you could have done that. The guilt makes you certain that you do not deserve to be a success. Therefore, if you do not deserve to be a success, you must find a way to avoid success. This all happens on a subconscious level.

Guilt tells you that you don't deserve to win. It calls for punishment. How do you punish yourself? By never achieving the goals for which you are striving, by never winning. Clearly, you can do without fear, anxiety, and guilt.

Guilt In Action

Walter, a 37-year-old pool player was having difficulty sinking the winning ball in competitions. His only symptom was his arm shaking. Once the shaking broke his concentration, he would then worry and frequently miss pocketing the winning ball.

In hypnoanalysis, Walter recalled a time at age 15 when he was losing a pool game and tried to win it by cheating. His opponent caught him. To save face, Walter beat up his opponent resulting in being barred from the facility for six months. The guilt brought on by the cheating and by the beating of his opponent led Walter to punish himself. He hated himself for the way he had acted and decided—unconsciously—he should not win any more.

Once we brought this scene into his consciousness, Walter realized that it was not within his jurisdiction to punish himself and he was able to let go of his self-hate and tendency toward self-punishment.

When working with clients, after I clear the negative emotions from the subconscious, I replace the negative emotions with the following

14 principles, principles that were developed by hypnoanalysts and that successful winners in every walk of life must exhibit:

1. Everything will work out okay.
2. You will have enough time to fulfill your goal.
3. You will be able to acquire the necessary power to do what you need to do.
4. You can acquire the necessary knowledge to complete your goal.
5. Over the long haul, good thoughts prevail.
6. You believe in being merciful, and that means winning quickly.
7. You believe the whole world in which you compete is within your personal domination.
8. You believe that you deserve to win wherever you play.
9. You believe in yourself and in your ability to overcome your obstacles.
10. Winners love themselves. You love yourself.
11. Winners always feel as if they have won, even when they have lost, because they have learned something from losing.
12. Winners avoid self-indulgent, victim-like feelings. The world loves a winner.
13. When you are playing, you are no longer aware of yourself. You seem to lose yourself completely in your play.
14. Relax and win.[192]

Both Tim Gallwey, author of *The Inner Game of Tennis*[193] and coauthors James M. Rippe, M.D., and William Southmayd, M.D., of *The Sports Performance Factors,*[194] emphasize that the body/mind has wisdom of its own, that it can execute extremely coordinated movements of all kinds on its own without thinking or being told how to do them. This so-called wisdom of the body is actually the subconscious in action, which remains untested due to conscious thoughts of the "should" or "ought-to" nature overriding the subconscious, mind/body know-how. Consequently, in hypnoanalysis, I remove the negativity first, the district of one's own mind/body second, and then implant the subconscious positive suggestions.

Beating the Voodoo Hex

A fellow hypnoanalyst, Dr. Earl Taylor, used hypnotherapy to bring a major-league baseball player out of a batting slump.[195] The player—we'll call him Slugger—had grown up in a big-city ghetto in a strongly religious environment. After three new players from the Caribbean who joined the club told Slugger that they had put a voodoo hex on him, Slugger's batting average began to plummet.

Dr. Taylor found a number of negative experiences in Slugger's background that made him susceptible to the negative suggestion. Here are two of them:

1. When he was in high school, Slugger discovered that the woman he thought was his mother was actually his grandmother. He had been led to believe that his real mother was his sister. When he discovered the truth, he had felt abandoned. This was the symptom-producing event.
2. The initial sensitizing event came earlier. When he was a boy, he got into a fight with another child. Slugger was a big kid, and he hit his opponent so hard he thought he had killed the other child.

Now Slugger was in the big leagues. He had a million-dollar contract, was married, and had a couple of children. But his bat and glove were not the only things he was carrying onto the field. He was also carrying a bag of guilt, guilt that he had not been paying enough attention to his family and the residual guilt from when he thought he had killed a boy. This made Slugger susceptible to the suggestion that he was about to become the victim of a voodoo hex.

Dr. Taylor identified the problem and through regression under hypnosis, he helped Slugger analyze the cause of his problem and to locate and remove the fears.

The day after his first treatment, Slugger went three for four at the plate. He was later traded to another team, but he stayed in touch with Dr. Taylor. On one occasion, Dr. Taylor hypnotized him over the telephone, telling him he would have a wonderful day at bat. Slugger came to bat with the bases loaded and drove the ball into the stands.

Negative Thoughts in the Corner Pocket

My personal interest in both pool and golf has led me to develop a program for helping players improve performance through hypnosis which I offer as a week-long, intensive-subconscious analysis. Using this program, I am able to analyze the player's subconscious mind to determine exactly what is happening in the subconscious that is causing problems with their game. Sometimes, the issue that is interfering with the player's game is the same issue interfering with the player's happiness in other areas of his or her life.

Hank Wanted to Play Up To His Potential

One pool player who sought me out was Hank, a 43-year-old self-employed contractor from Minnesota. "The problem is that I don't make all the balls I am supposed to make," Hank said. "It is extremely difficult for me to run a rack [sink 9 to 15 balls consecutively]. Sometimes I can run four or five balls. It's very frustrating."

About 15 years earlier, Hank had operated a pool hall for about five years after graduating from high school.

"One of the reasons I quit was that I wasn't getting any better," he said.

I asked him how long his playing had been a problem.

"Probably ever since the first few years," he said. As we talked, he told me: "I think I know why. I think I have a problem with embarrassment."

Hank told me the embarrassment is compounded by the fact that he likes to play with his friends watching. "I don't enjoy it unless people are watching; nobody watching is what makes it worse," he said. Yet, he told me, he gets embarrassed and feels stupid when he misses a shot. In other words, Hank plays for people's approval.

"What makes it better," I asked.

"When I am really in my element. People watching, and playing for a lot of money."

"What could you do, if you were cured, that you can't do now?" I asked.

"I am probably, even now, capable of being the best player in my town if I can only make the balls I am supposed to make. I want to run a rack and I want to run out and I can't."

If you're not a pool enthusiast, you may need a little explanation here. There are certain shots that a pool player at a given level should be able to make without too much difficulty. These are shots the player has made hundreds of times before. Hank was missing the shots he should have been making.

Hank plays a game called Nine Ball—the game Tom Cruise played in the movie *The Color of Money*. The object in Nine Ball is to sink the balls in succession, starting with the one ball and going through the nine ball. The player who sinks the nine ball is the winner. When Hank refers to "running out," he means dropping the balls in succession, including the nine ball for the victory.

The number five seemed to be significant for Hank. He told me he had been divorced five years. When I asked him about his friends, he said he had had four or five over the past few years. He said he had enjoyed good sex except for about four or five times. He had five children.

Hank had enjoyed an "extremely happy" childhood.

No Responsibilities As a Child Ruined Hank As an Adult

"I played all the time and had no responsibilities," Hank said. "It ruined me as an adult. I could do anything I wanted." How many of us can do anything we want?

I asked about his father. Hank didn't like him very much. "The last time I saw him, I was five or six." His parents had divorced when he was an infant.

We were looking at some stuck places. The word-association test was revealing. Here's how it went:

Ryan: When I grow up . . .
HANK: *I'll be a star.*
Ryan: I would rather __________ than win.
HANK: *Play.*
Ryan: In order to survive . . .
HANK: *I must play.*

Ryan: I don't want to grow up because . . .
HANK: *Of responsibilities.*
Ryan: Punishment . . .
HANK: *Discipline.*
Ryan: I punish myself because . . .
HANK: *I don't like it.*
Ryan: Seeing things through . . .
HANK: *Accomplishment.*

The word-association test made this clear: Winning at pool wasn't the important thing to Hank. The important thing was playing. Playing all the time is something little kids do. So like a child, Hank had been playing for people's approval and consequently was not really taking the game seriously, though that is what he wanted to do.

Being a carefree child had been delightful. Accepting the responsibilities of adulthood had been painful. I pointed out to Hank that he had a Ponce de Leon Syndrome, a suggestion which Hank accepted.

Additionally, Hank had married the high-school homecoming queen, but life didn't have a storybook ending. He was still a child, emotionally, in no position to handle a marriage. He was never home; he was always playing pool. Then came the divorce.

"For the next three or four years, all I wanted was the money in the pocket. Now that I am going back to pool, the subconscious is saying, 'This is death.' Pool is worse than cancer."

In his mind, Hank associated pool playing with a negative period in his life. He believed that to be good at pool was worse than death, and his identity was tied up in what he did.

During several regressions, we followed Hank's feelings surrounding playing pool back to his childhood and relieved the feelings in those stuck places, allowing Hank to move on.

In about his 10th session, Hank remarked, "I think yesterday was terrific; I still feel like a kid. The problem is this death thing, not the child thing. During the time when I was playing, it was horrible. For about three years, no one knew where I was. If my subconscious believes pool is bad, then I'm not going to do it."

In subsequent session, we relieved those negative suggestions and helped Hank to break his bond of identity between pool and his bad feelings. Hank also had negative attitudes about God, religion, and punishment which we reviewed and identified the areas in which he needed to grow up, as well as other areas in which he needed to take care of himself. I gave him many positive suggestions to replace the negative ones and made a tape of those suggestions for him to play at home.

In his last session, Hank told me he was feeling "super" and was very satisfied with his progress.

Inhibited by Low Self-Esteem

Alicia traveled all the way from Alaska to Illinois to seek my help because she wanted to become a world-champion pool player. Pool filled a space in her life that had been empty since her divorce.

"I'm addicted to it," the 40-year-old woman told me. But her game was suffering because she was unable to concentrate on her playing.

"Sometimes your mind is thinking about so many different things that you are trying too hard," she said. She would become tense, her arm would tighten up, and she would miss the shots she should have been able to make with ease.

"I want to sort things out and get the direction that I need to get rid of my inhibitions," she said. "I'm always concerned about what people are thinking and my low self-esteem."

Through our sessions I learned of a number of terrible experiences that Alicia had been subjected to. She was an adult child of an alcoholic who had been abused by her father. She had been raped twice and her boyfriend left her while she was pregnant.

The word-association test showed that Alicia felt stuck at the age of 16—around the age of her first rape. She said she lived "in a fairy-tale world" and did not want to grow up. We were again dealing with the Ponce de Leon Syndrome.

I regressed her to the womb and discovered the initial sensitizing event. It was birth itself. She had felt comfortable and secure in the womb but as the time for birth approached, things got scary. She was not eager to be separated from her mother. That experience translated into a scare each time she got close to someone or any time there were changes in her life. It also got scary for her when she began to play pool really well.

So Alicia was afraid of change. Growing up meant changing and that was scary for her. She had already experienced several unpleasant changes. Once we removed this negativity from her subconscious mind and raised her self-esteem, she was ready to return to Alaska and polish her pool game. I gave her the name of a doctor in Fairbanks and urged her to continue her treatment.

Alicia was suffering from two of the biggest problems in sports: fear and lack of concentration. Once we identify the initial sensitizing event, the problem usually resolves itself and the fear is removed.

Lack of concentration is another matter. I have worked with several golfers who have this problem. For many people, it's simply a matter of learning how to concentrate and how to focus all their energy on what they are doing.

But for other people, concentration can be disrupted by feelings of guilt, anxiety, anger, and other negative emotions. Frequently, self-hypnosis will free a person from these negative feelings and open the door to concentration.

Blowing It Under Pressure

Cliff, a 28-year-old Californian, was another pool player with a problem. "I play a decent game of pool until I get under pressure," he said. "I talk myself out of it, it seems. More often than not, I lose it. I just start losing my confidence. I doubt myself; I feel a lot of embarrassment if I miss it."

How long had this been a problem?

"Forever, I guess. When I was younger—at 15 or 16—I don't think it bothered me. I've only started going to tournaments for the last two years."

What makes it worse?

"When I want to win."

What makes it better?

"I don't know. I still play a good game around the guys I have known all my life. But the closer I get to the money spot, the more I start dogging it. Then I feel the pressure."

I asked what he would be able to do once the problem was solved that he couldn't do now. His reply, *"It stops me from winning. I blow it."*

This was an easy case to work on. Cliff said he played a decent game until he was under pressure. In his first sentence, his subconscious mind tipped me off to what I was looking for. I wanted to find his very first experience with pressure and how it was associated with pool.

"More often that not," he said, *"I lose it."* From experience, I suspected that he had experienced a birth trauma.

Here's how his word-association test went:

Ryan: Life . . .
CLIFF: *Live.*
Ryan: Death . . .
CLIFF: *Live.*

So life is like death. I say live and he says die. So he had a death suggestion. The test continued:

Ryan: The real problem is . . .
CLIFF: *Nervous.*
Ryan: Insecurity . . .
CLIFF: *Nervousness.*
Ryan: Pressure feels like . . .
CLIFF: *Nervousness.*

So insecurity, nervousness, and pressure are synonymous with each other, and with his problem. The real problem equals nervousness, anxiety, and insecurity. The test continued:

Ryan: Embarrassment feels like . . .
CLIFF: *Shame.*
Ryan: Underneath it all . . .
CLIFF: *I am ashamed.*

When Cliff would get close to winning, he would begin to doubt himself, feel ashamed, feel the pressure, and blow the shot.

Ryan: Doubt begins . . .
CLIFF: *When I'm close to winning.*
Ryan: Complete a sentence that starts with the word "who."
CLIFF: *Who am I?*

Cliff had an identity problem.

Ryan: Sometimes I feel I am stuck at age . . .
CLIFF: *Twelve.*
Ryan: I punish . . .
CLIFF: *Myself.*
Ryan: I have always been ashamed . . .
CLIFF: *For wishing bad things on my friends.*
Ryan: My punishment is . . .
CLIFF: *Losing concentration.*
Ryan: It all started . . .
CLIFF: *When I was a kid.*
Ryan: It got worse when . . .
CLIFF: *I got well.*

So here's where we were: Cliff felt very much that he didn't know who he was. At the very bottom of it all, he was scared. He was punishing himself for something he had done a long time ago. He was also punishing himself for wishing bad things on some of his friends. His punishment was his loss of concentration.

When I explained this to him, Cliff became quite excited and agreed that it sounded reasonable. I suggested that Cliff dream about his problem and here is what he described:

"A white wall was standing by itself with black words written on it. As I walked toward it, trying to read it, I was almost ready to make out the words when the wall fell backwards."

Here's how we interpreted the dream: The wall, with the writing on it, was keeping him from doing well. He was going to get well and solve the problem. The feeling he associated with the dream was connected to a scene when he was about 12 years old in a car with friends. He had two groups of friends. He didn't know how to choose between the two groups. He wasn't sure how people felt about him. He had a lot of mixed emotions. He kept telling himself to "quit giving a shit."

To help him improve his pool game, we had to make him see that he was not playing pool to please anybody. The 12-year-old did not have to choose among friends. When he was playing pool, he was playing an opponent. If that opponent was a friend, he did not have to choose between winning the game or keeping his friend. He could do both.

Subsequently, I searched through his subconscious looking for "the pressure." Lo and behold, we were back at birth.

As he remembered emerging from the womb, he said, "I don't want to go through it. I'm scared; I guess . . . I can feel the pressure. It's closing in all around me."

Under hypnosis, Cliff realized that he felt this same kind of feeling during his pool game. Things were closing in around him and he didn't want to do it. The pressure in a pool game tipped off his subconscious mind: He didn't want to be born; pressure from playing pool was like being born; consequently, he didn't want to play pool. Using hypnosis, we wiped out those negative connections, completely removing them from his subconscious and desensitizing his mind to the feeling of being pushed out of the womb when he was not yet ready.

In a subsequent session, we learned more about the guilt feelings that arose from Cliff wishing bad things on his friends. Cliff had a friend who had mistakenly hurt him. Cliff had wished a lot of bad things on his friend. The friend died when he was about 16.

The guilt from this experience spilled into his pool game. When he was playing pool, he was wishing for the other person to lose. It would trigger his guilt feelings over his dead friend. We talked about his guilt feelings associated with his "wish" coming true which enabled Cliff to separate his pool game from the guilt feelings.

In his 14th and final session, Cliff said, "I am ready to go out and compete." He did.

Losing Can Be Positive

To go out and compete is not the same thing as to go out and win. I cannot hypnotize you into winning every time, and you certainly cannot hypnotize yourself into becoming an unbeatable winner. But you can learn to convert losing into a positive experience.

Will Rogers has been quoted as saying, "Everything is funny as long as it is happening to somebody else." Losing is a lot easier to take if it is the other person who is doing the losing. For most Americans, the word "lose" is a cussword, a four-letter obscenity that ranks up there with obscene descriptions of bodily functions and parts.

We are a success-obsessed culture. Only dieters and masochists enjoy losing. Yet, for every player who wins a tournament, there is at least one who loses. While most of us would rather go to hell than admit it, we lose more than we win.

Winning and losing are both part of the human predicament, but the first is vastly more popular than the last. Losing is so undervalued that most people would rather pretend it doesn't exist. They would like to wish it into oblivion.

Somewhere along the way, the win-at-all-costs attitude became the American religion. Vince Lombardi gave this religion its Golden Rule: "Winning isn't everything; it's the only thing." By making winning the only thing, we make dropouts of people who are capable of contributing to our society.

Since there are only so many places at the top and competition to achieve them is so fierce, many will lose. Then what?

Failure: A "Crime" That Pays

"Failure seems to be regarded as the one unpardonable crime, success as the all-redeeming virtue," lamented nineteenth-century statesman Charles Adams. Conventional wisdom tells us crime doesn't pay. But if losing is a crime, then the payoff is in increased self-knowledge. In the 1979 Sugar Bowl, with the national championship at stake against Alabama, Penn State coach, Joe Paterno, called for a run on a goal-line play when his gut instinct told him to go for the pass. Penn State lost. Four years later, again in the Sugar Bowl and again with the national championship at stake, Paterno's gut told him to pass on a key play for short yardage against Georgia. Remembering 1979, he called for the pass. The play worked, and Paterno had a national championship, thanks to a bit of self-knowledge gained in defeat.

As I write this, two people come to mind who, by most appearances, were very fortunate men, and winners to boot: W.C. Fields and Mark Twain.

I remember W. C. Fields from two hilarious movie scenes involving the game of pool. In one, he rolled a pool ball around by running the cue along the top of the ball. In another he used a crooked cue.

Fields was a masterful comedic actor. Was he successful? You could say so. He certainly won fortune and acclaim. But the consensus was that he was an alcoholic.

Did he enjoy pleasing people with his comedy? He once said, "I am free of prejudices. I hate everyone equally." The "everyone" must have included himself.

Mark Twain? Fantastically talented author and humorist, was also a billiards buff. Was he a success? Twain wrote, "Byron despised the human race because he despised himself. I feel as Byron did, and for the same reason." He also wrote, "We all feel inferior, just about different things." Twain was famous, but was he a winner?

History, literature, and folklore spill out famous losers: Romeo and Juliet, Shakespeare's losers in the game of love; the fabulous Casey, who left Mudville without joy when he struck out with the bases loaded in the ninth; General George Custer, a dandy of a general until he met his Waterloo at the Battle of Little Big Horn; Adolf Hitler, whose book *Mein Kampf* drew a blueprint for his Reich expected to last for 1,000 years but ended in its 12th year amid the rubble of a collapsing empire. And how about Robin Hood the bandit; Davy Crockett and his fellow losers at the Alamo; and Christopher Columbus, who failed to find a new trade route to India but unknowingly stumbled across a new world? From an earthly standpoint, even Jesus Christ was a loser: He had no permanent home, no permanent job, and no extensive religious organization. He died ignominiously as a criminal; accused of sedition against the Roman Empire and blasphemy against the very God in whose name he spoke.

Not everyone can be a famous loser, and how many of the just-named people would you trade places with if you could? I wouldn't trade my life with a single one. So why even examine the subject of losing? Several things about losing are worth considering.

First of all, losing a game is not such a fearful thing once you have faced the fear squarely. Today's loser can be tomorrow's champion. "There's always next year" is one of the most hallowed and comforting expressions in the world of sports.

Far more important than the objective fact of winning and losing is your subjective judgment of your own performance. Regardless of how others rate your performance, if you do not measure up to your own standards, then you will tend to think of yourself as a failure.

As Les Cunningham expressed it, "Remember, the whole world can classify you as a failure, but you never become one until you admit it to yourself."[196]

People often use a double standard in rating their performances against the performances of others. They will be tolerant of the errors and shortcomings of others, yet hold themselves to the most exacting standards. Remember, that was the same issue for most people concerning public speaking.

Many explanations have been advanced for this phenomenon. The point I want to make is simply this: Take a look at your performance and learn as much as you can from your losing as well as from your winning.

Eric Berne, the author of "What Do You Say after You Say Hello?" and "Games People Play," said, "A winner knows what he'll do if he loses, but doesn't talk about it; whereas a loser doesn't know what he'll do if he loses, and only talks about what he'll do if he wins."[197]

Along Berne's lines, here are a few ways to think about losing, as paraphrased from Les Cunningham:

- Life is a gamble. If you don't risk losing, you have no chance of winning. If you can eliminate the fear of losing, you can increase substantially your chance of winning because the mind is focused on the task, not on the feeling.
- If you never lose, you can't appreciate winning. Without losing, the competition would be meaningless. If you won all the time, competing would soon become boring, and you'd take up something more challenging in which you run the risk of

losing. You need to lose occasionally just to feel the exhilaration of winning.

- Competition can be enjoyable in itself. It can motivate you to play a better game and surpass yourself, to transcend your limitations in some way. This can yield much satisfaction and fun.
- Learning to lose will help you overcome failure. If you understand the cause of your loss, you will be motivated to avoid that cause in the future.
- You can improve your performance by playing opponents who play better than you do. Losing to a better player can push you to greater achievements. It's more gratifying to lose to a better player than to beat a player of inferior ability.

Code Concepts

- Sports are played with the mind as well as the muscles. Athletic success is built upon a pyramid, the base of which consists of physical conditioning, psychological conditioning, and intelligence.
- Psychological conditioning is done in three stages: long term, medium term, and short term. Long-term conditioning starts in the preseason or at the beginning of training with positive suggestions to the subconscious and total avoidance of negative thinking. Thoughts of fear, anxiety, and guilt must be banished. In the medium term, athletes should imagine themselves growing stronger as training progresses, executing plays and developing their techniques perfectly. In the short term, they should use positive suggestions to overcome stage fright and to bring themselves to the proper state of arousal. Self-hypnosis is helpful at each of these stages.
- The mind, programmed for victory, will not be defeated by temporary setbacks such as a poor serve, an error in the field, or a fumble. It will learn from the mistake and renew its determination to win.
- Self-hypnosis should not be used to suggest that the athlete ignore injuries.
- Athletes should realize that no one wins all the time. The important thing is to perform to your maximum potential and to learn from your losses.

Code Breaking Exercises

1. List new ideas for your success pyramid

   a. Physical conditioning ____________________
   b. Psychological conditioning ____________________
   c. Intelligence ____________________

2 Are you satisfied with what you have? If not, what are you willing to do about it?

____

3. Plan your long-, medium- and short-term psychological conditioning.

____

____

4. Make a list of what you learn from every loss.

____

____

5. List the criteria you use to judge your own sports performance? How does it compare to the criteria by which you judge others?

____

____

6. Psychologist Fritz Perls once said, "The human species has the unique distinction of being the only species on the planet that is capable of interfering with its own growth." Review the ideas in this chapter and list the ways in which you get in the way of your own sports performance.

____

____

____

Chapter Fourteen

The Problem with God: It's Not The Most Important Thing, It's The Only Thing.

God is creative energy.
That we experience this energy
as love,
that within us it promotes order,
happiness, life-energy,
and all other things
that we feel as "good,"
that we can receive this energy
from those close to us
and pass it on to others,
is simple enough and easy to discuss consciously
with depressed people
or those with behavior problems
resulting from depression.

Thomas A. Ritzman, M.D.

At Some Time, We All Ask: Who or What is God?

Self-image shapes reality! Intimately connected to self-image and self-esteem lies our conception of God, a connection which frequently is unconscious. In my practice I frequently treat patients with symptoms of depression, low self-esteem, chronic guilt, and codependency. In about half the cases I find that the subconscious cause of the problem involves God—who or what God is. Part of the problem these patients are struggling with involves the dual—and conflicting—concepts of God as judge, jury, and executioner juxtaposed against the image of a loving father figure.

People are plagued by such questions as "Who is God?" "What's He like?" "What does He expect of me?" "What is sin, really?" "Am I guilty of sin against God?" "What is my punishment?"

According to our Judeo-Christian heritage, in Old Testament times, we heard directly from God,. He talked to us through a sort of hallucinated voice. The Ten Commandments were received directly from God in that fashion.

Between 1000 and 300 B.C., the concept of consciousness developed, and we stopped listening to the part of our minds that would hallucinate voices. We now think of God as being in heaven or within us, guiding us through prayer—not as a hallucinated voice.

As Dr. Gerald May said in *Care of Mind—Care of Spirit*:

> "From the time of Christ until well after the Reformation, little differentiation was made between psychological and spiritual disorders . . . With the advent of Freudian psychoanalysis, however, drastic changes began to take place . . . Today's secular psychology addresses a great deal about how we come to be the way we are . . . However, it can offer nothing in terms of why we exist or how we should use our lives."[198]

One reason for this lack may be the difference in spiritual alignment between therapists and their clients. Dr. Daniel Zelling reported in the *American Journal of Psychiatry* that 95% of Americans polled believe in God, compared with only 5% of the members of the American Psychiatric Association and 43% of the American Psychological

Association.[199] So well over half of the mental care providers are, in effect, denying God or the role of spirituality to those who seek treatment from them. This could account for the lack of success secular psychotherapists have had in treating spiritually based problems.

C. Alan Anderson, Ph.D., cites an experiment at the University of Redlands in California in which the effectiveness of prayer therapy was compared with that of psychotherapy. The subjects in prayer therapy showed a 72% degree of improvement while those in psychotherapy showed only 67% improvement. Those praying in only a random way experienced no improvement.[200]

One reason prayers may seem to go unanswered is that they are not directed toward the individual's real needs. Until we confront our true needs, we cannot pray effectively. The participants in the prayer therapy study just mentioned were subjected first to psychological testing to determine their weaknesses—the matters needing attention in prayer. Unsurprisingly, most participants were plagued by those familiar villains: fear, guilt, inferiority feelings, and misguided love (hate in disguise). These villains are precisely what hypnoanalysis is so helpful in undoing. And if hypnoanalysis is to help patients come to terms with who and what God is, it goes without saying that the hypnoanalyst must believe in and have a reverence toward God, Spirit, The Universe, etc.

From the outset, let me emphasize that there seems to be only one God, regardless of what religion or spiritual philosophy one believes in and regardless of the name by which He or She is called.

In his book *The Problem Is God*, C. Alan Anderson quotes an unnamed scholar, "Rightly understood, the problem of God is not one problem among several others; it is the only problem there is." Anderson comments, "The problem of God is so all-embracing that everything else must be seen in relation to it."[201]

I support this idea, yet in about 50% of the cases I see, the GOD problem looms very large.

I realize that many volumes have been written about God. I believe there are two broad categories in which God is viewed. These categories are not along any religious lines because my experience indicates that even people from the same religious background may still view God differently.

My work has shown that God is subconsciously thought of in two simple classifications: as either a loving image or as a disciplinarian parent figure. For my purpose, living in a largely Judeo-Christian culture, this simplification works.

God is anthropomorphic, meaning that human characteristics are attributed to God. God is created in the image and likeness of man and not the reverse. If God is love, then the believer feels loved by God, has freedom, takes responsibility for self, and doesn't blame God for circumstances in the world. If however, God is seen as a disapproving parent figure, then God becomes judge, jury, and executioner. The personal believer feels wrong, guilty, enslaved, and insecure.

In my opinion, believing that God is love is preferable to believing that God judges and sentences souls to hell, and since love is a feeling/attitude, then God is the feeling/attitude of love. If A = B, and B = C, then A = C.

With this belief in mind, I help people feel that God is love. In the English language, the word "love" has multiple meanings ranging from romantic love to deep feelings for another to self-love. By finding out where in a person's life that feeling of love died—the feeling that God died—and by bringing the feeling of love back to life (assuming it was there in the first place), a person is able to plant the seed of God-Is-Love in the subconscious mind.

When God is viewed as an external parent figure—Good Old Dad—then G.O.D. becomes an acronym. Many problems arise from this idea, which nourishes such beliefs as:

- God is the cause of misery, punishment and trouble in the world.
- God must be pleased or placated before love is delivered.
- We are subservient and, therefore, not responsible for our circumstances.
- We must adhere to laws and beliefs that may conflict with what is in our best interest.

And according to Dr. Menahem, "dealing with such a God has all the problems of dealing with other people plus other complications."[202] Oh my God, how can anyone win with such a God!?!

The Bible tells us at Genesis 1:26, "You are created in the image and likeness of God." Consequently, what we believe God to be is of utmost importance. Helen Street Paredes states it thusly:

> "It is done unto you as you believe. If you believe in a judgmental God, you are judgmental and judged; if you believe in a loving God, you are loving and loved."[203]

It is from this understanding that I work with my patients. Nearly 100 years after Freudian psychology separated the psychological and spiritual aspects of mental health, the spiritual movement and the Recovery Process have now begun to reconcile these two halves of the human psyche. Medical hypnoanalysts have been doing this since Dr. Bryan began the treatment in 1955. J. Gordon Melton, Ph.D., Director of the Institute for the Study of American Religion and author of the *Encyclopedia of American Religions*, credits the New Thought with the "ability to empower people who feel, for whatever reason, that they are powerless."[204] He writes:

> "New Thought has shown an amazing ability to speak to these people and teach them about their inner resources, to teach them what their own negative approaches and vision of the world is doing to them. By getting a more positive outlook on life, these people are developing a greater sense of their own worth and a greater sense of their own capabilities. They are empowered to make use of their inner talents and to turn sickness into health."[205]

Throughout this chapter, my references to God are synonymous with "love". Many of the emotional problems people suffer stem for a lack of God in their lives, a lack of love from others and, most importantly, a lack of love for self.

For Cassie, Every Man Was "Mister Right"

Cassie, 32, came in complaining that she experienced trouble verbalizing her thoughts, had a short memory, and got attached to people. Her self-image was low and through therapy she had completed elsewhere, she recognized her Ponce de Leon Syndrome with spiritual overtones.

I asked what made it worse and she said, "If someone interrupts me or becomes forceful, or if I don't feel comfortable with someone, in crowds or social gatherings."

When I asked what made it better, she said, "When I have had my grief, been close, or even if I have had a good interaction, it restores my faith."

Both of those responses are what you what would expect from a scared kid, so I asked what she would be able to do once she was cured that she couldn't do now. She said, "Leave home, start to take care of myself, feel confident, have relationships."

Grow up, in other words. Other things in her history pointed to a Ponce de Leon diagnosis. Cassie was emotionally stagnant standing in the fountain of youth, if you will, outside the stream of life. She said that she scared men away because, naively, she treated everybody she had sex with as a potential "Mr. Right."

The attitude that every man was a potential Mr. Right indicated an underlying addictive need for love and comfort that was not getting fulfilled. Of course, clinging, childlike behavior on Cassie's part would drive men away.

Cassie was reared Catholic[206] and had developed feelings of personal guilt and inadequacy because of her behavior. Here are some of her responses to questions during the history-taking period of our first session:

Ryan: What was traumatic for you?

CASSIE: *My mother. She always escalated. I was very much afraid of her.* (She looked up to heaven.) *I think I was sexually abused. Also, I just recently had a relationship and it was scary.*

Ryan: When you were school-age, did you sleepwalk or have nightmares?

CASSIE: *I sleepwalked, but I also would cry on the way to school. I didn't feel connected and wanted to stay home.*

Ryan: Did you have repeated or recurring dreams?

CASSIE: *I often dreamed that there was a gloved hand under the bed trying to grab me.*

Ryan: Tell me about your childhood.
CASSIE: *I was angry and depressed.*
Ryan: Tell me about your parents.
CASSIE: *They were constantly fighting.*
Ryan: What do you feel most guilty about in your life?
CASSIE: *I used to feel guilty about masturbating.*
Ryan: What's the worst thing that happened to you?
CASSIE: *It's my mother. She destroys me verbally.*
Ryan: Is there anything you haven't told me that I should know?
CASSIE: *When I was in the city, I was pretty promiscuous. And I used to do a lot of drugs.*
Ryan: What do you want from me?
CASSIE: *I don't want to feel strange about sex, I want not to be afraid of bitchy, dominating women, and I want to plan my future so I'll have a good job.*

Cassie's responses indicated some spiritual concerns in addition to the Ponce de Leon tendencies. People who behave promiscuously, do drugs, and drink frequently are, among other negative compulsions, trying to make themselves feel more alive.

Under hypnosis, I regressed Cassie to the time when was about nine months old. At that age she experienced sexual abuse from her mother.[207] It took several sessions to work through this experience and to associate the problems she had in relationships in the here and now with that frightful experience when she was small. After relieving the anxiety, fear and anger, we were able to help Cassie free up her subconscious, to grow up and to no longer be afraid of relationships and of other people. Both she and I thought she was finished.

A year later, she came in with another problem. Here is our conversation:

Ryan: What's the problem?
CASSIE: *It's peer-related.* (Then she looked up to heaven.) *Just that. I'll stick to that. Being accepted by a group. I feel like a tag-a-long. I can't compete in conversation. I get scared, clam up, and feel inadequate. I am a pleaser. To make up for other people's lack of interest in me, I get needy. That is part of the problem with the relationship I was in. I was putting all this*

energy into other people, thinking they would come back, and they wouldn't. I would have to stand on my head to get what I wanted—attention and recognition.

Ryan: How long has it been a problem?

CASSIE: *All my life. It was very troublesome when I was in high school. I was a lost puppy. My whole family was against me. I never felt adequate. It comes up again and again.*

Ryan: What conditions cause variations in the problem?

CASSIE: *It's generally the voice in my head, the scary critical voice.*

Ryan: What makes it better?

CASSIE: *Attention from my boyfriend.*

Ryan: What will you be able to do once you are cured that you cannot do now?

CASSIE: (She looked up to heaven.) *Feel confident with myself, have lasting relationships, consistent friendships and a strong sense of self.*

Once again, we worked through her childhood trauma, her use of drugs, her guilt feelings, and ways she was punishing herself. In two prenatal regressions we helped Cassie recognize her mother's negative attitude about the pregnancy. Cassie was able to accept that those feelings belonged to her mother, not to her. Cassie was also able to identify some of her own early feelings of peace and confidence that she experienced in the womb that she could bring back to the present. I suggested that she increase her feeling of being connected to God and the universe, helped her to identify with nature and develop feelings that she belonged in the world. Uncovering the initial sensitizing event—in the womb at three months after conception when she felt unwanted—provided the solution to Cassie's problem. Her story has a very happy ending.

Once we relieved the anxiety causing her underlying identity problem, she was quickly able to mend the hole in her spirit. She began to feel connected with the world around her and was able to finish her education, even earning an advanced degree. She met someone and they fell in love. The last contact I had with her she was happily married and looking forward to the birth of her second child.

Cassie had finally been able to overcome a lifetime of spiritual illness and recover her spiritual health. Spiritual Walking-Zombie problems such as Cassie's, as you'll remember, frequently begin in the womb and often indicate a lack of connection with "God" and to the universe. After all, to a fetus or child, who—if not mother—is God?

Mental Health Requires "Being Right With God"

History shows us that "being right with God" has always been a precondition for physical and mental health. Before the advent of medical research, the absence of health was considered purely a spiritual matter, to be rectified through spiritual practices, faith healing, laying of hands, praying, casting out demons, oils, rituals and sacrifices. The source of many guilt feelings and emotional disorders uncovered in my patients can be traced back to misinformation and distortions that were received by the patient before the patient was able to discern negative suggestions.

Thanks to Dr. Bryan's contributions, therapists and clients alike can benefit from a mind-body-spirit union concept. Being a very spiritual man, Dr. Bryan melded his knowledge of law, psychology, and medicine with religion to produce a consistent and practical approach to psycho-spiritual health.

The Bible tells us that much of our anxiety amounts to a denial of God, which equates to a denial of peace and love coupled with the acceptance of guilt. We deny ourselves peace and love when we indulge in judging others or ourselves, and judging results in guilt and self-punishment.

Bryan went back to the original Biblical passages to define a person's relationship to God—to find what was required to be right with one's Maker. Likewise, people experiencing the psychological effects of guilt need to re-examine the source of those feelings. In my experience, the best way to get back to the source of guilt-producing events in your life is through subconscious analysis to pinpoint the time and place at which the negative thought was accepted.

Bryan reminded us that humans, once created, were given responsibility for their own lives:

> "So God created man in his own image, in the image of God he created him; male and female he created them. God blessed them and said to them, 'Be fruitful and

> increase in number; fill the earth and subdue it. Rule over the fish of the sea and the birds of the air and over every living creature that moves on the ground.'"[208]

In seeking to combat people's attitudes about guilt, Bryan also examined the Apostle Paul's interpretation of Christians' frequent guilt response to breaking the Ten Commandments in light of the purpose of Christ's act of atonement. Paul, who was also a lawyer, explains in his letter to the Galatians that adherence to the Jewish law cannot save any person's s existence soul, but that faith in Jesus Christ is what saves them.

> "We . . . know that a man is not justified by observing the law, but by faith in Jesus Christ. So we, too, have put our faith in Christ Jesus that we may be justified by faith in Christ and not by observing the law, because by observing the law, no one will be justified.[209]

> "I do not set aside the grace of God, for if righteousness could be gained through the law, Christ died for nothing!"[210]

> Paul then explains that God made a promise to Abraham:

> ". . . He believed God, and it was credited to him as righteousness."[211]

In the same chapter, Bryan notes that Paul, in writing to the Galatian congregations, invalidates the claim that the Ten Commandments have anything to do with salvation and, therefore, with guilt:

> "The promises were spoken to Abraham and to his seed. The Scripture does not say 'and to seeds,' meaning many people, but 'and to your seed,' meaning one person, who is Christ. What I mean is this: The law, introduced 430 years later, does not set aside the covenant previously established by God and thus do away with the promise. For if the inheritance depends

> on the law, then it no longer depends on a promise; but God in his grace gave it to Abraham through a promise."[212]

In the paragraph preceding this selection, Paul wrote that Christ had brought us out from the doom of that impossible system, meaning living in strict compliance with the Jewish laws of that era. Consequently, people today who feel depressed about their lack of righteousness under the rules and regulations of the Ten Commandments are judging themselves by a standard that does not apply. Since Christ's death, the commandments are null and void. They do not count. Well, then, you may be thinking, why are they there? Paul explains:

> "What, then, was the purpose of the law? It was added because of transgressions until the Seed to whom the promise referred had come . . .
>
> "Is the law, therefore, opposed to the promises of God? Absolutely not! For if a law had been given that could impart life, then righteousness would have come by the law. But the Scripture declares that the whole world is a prisoner of sin, so that what was promised, being given through *faith in Jesus Christ*, might be *given to those who believe*[213] [italics mine]."

Paul then asks in chapter 3, verse 21 if God is confused, first making promises and then contradicting himself with laws. "Of course not," he says. And, at the end of this chapter, he sums up the whole matter by claiming that we were in **protective custody** by the law until Christ arrived, who thereupon freed us from the bondage to law, freed us to be heirs to God's promise as descendents of Abraham—through faith and belief in Jesus Christ.

> "Before this faith came, we were held prisoners by the law, locked in until faith should be revealed. So the law was put in charge to lead us to Christ that we might be justified by faith. Now that faith has come, we are no longer under the supervision of the law . . . If you

> belong to Christ, then you are Abraham's seed, and heirs according to the promise."[214]

And, that is that. An act of faith, not strict compliance with the law, merits salvation. Guilt is neither virtuous nor desirable in the eyes of God. The commandments are not our means of salvation. And since we are imperfect and make mistake after mistake, it is implicit that God loves us despite our imperfections. Consequently we benefit not one iota from neurotic guilt arising from our actions, mistakes, emotional blunderings or accidents.

Instead of internalizing guilt, depressing our spirits and compounding our emotional problems as a result of our behavior, it is more appropriate to ask who gave us the right to punish ourselves? Or even to judge ourselves? Isn't that God's job? Didn't God send Jesus to atone for all the sins committed by all the people who ever lived or ever will live? And isn't that forgiveness available for the asking? Yes!

So it follows that judging ourselves is usurping God's jurisdiction. It is like telling God that he didn't do enough by sending Jesus. He should have done more! Maybe a sequel is necessary—Jesus II, or "Jesus died for everyone's sins except yours!"

Guilt Carried From Lifetime to Lifetime

Often, guilt and depression stem from incidents that took place in a personal history, long forgotten and subconsciously activated. When a person suffering from depression seeks my help, I use hypnosis to analyze the subconscious mind, to identify the negative suggestion, and determine when the suggestion was taken in. In other words, I search out the initial sensitizing event. This locating process involves age regressions and sometimes past-life regressions, either spontaneously or directed by request. In the process, we have frequently discovered that guilt carries from one lifetime to another.

Frequently, depressed people who seek past-life therapy are consciously convinced they have been taken advantage of or mistreated. When we do such regressions, I have found that usually people first go to lifetimes where they were victimized, where they were murdered or raped, for example. The natural tendency is to return to traumatic experiences that left them with fear. In those cases where we continued regressions, eventually patients recalled past lives during which *they* were the perpetrators of evil or wrongdoing, where they inflicted hurt on others. But that is where the guilt lies—in those lifetimes where they inflicted wrongs on others.

The value of past-life therapy is that, through viewing several lifetimes, those who believe in past lives expand their own awareness of the permanency of the soul, which helps in spiritual development.[215] In my past incarnations, I have been both male and female, a Spaniard, an Atlantean, a farmer, a pirate, an Eastern Indian, and a Native American. Many of my earlier lives were negative. It was very difficult and humbling, for instance, to review myself slaying my decrepit mother. In this life, therefore, I feel the need to serve mankind and make a positive impact.

Kitty's Guilt Spanned Across the Ages

Kitty came to me bearing a burden of guilt. Having been brought up in a strict Catholic environment, she had plenty of guilt, but she didn't know why. Kitty called it Catholic guilt.

Our search for an answer led us back to an incident that happened when, at 17, she had gotten drunk and had sex with two men at the same time. Now she was middle-aged and the guilt still clung.

We explored her present life through age regression and found nothing to explain her present feelings. Then we began exploring past lives, and the ISE finally surfaced.

Kitty's subconscious mind held memories of a life several centuries in the past. As a young girl, she had romanced two young men simultaneously. She had married one while carrying the other's child. She never told her husband that the child she bore was fathered by another lover, and the guilt from that deception followed her into her present life.

Once we had identified the source of her guilt, Kitty was able to let it go. She began living the life she wanted to lead, unshackled by the guilt her subconscious harbored over an indiscretion subconsciously remembered from another life centuries before.

The Baby and the Bath Water

Past life regression is usually not necessary. Many spiritual problems stem experiences that occurred in our present life, experiences that are long-forgotten—long forgotten, that is, to our conscious minds.

Martin was a friend of mine, and in the course of our friendship he told me he was unable to get close to the opposite sex. When he tried to get close to women, he felt smothered.

Martin began treatment with a fellow analyst who regressed him to the first year of his life. Martin's subconscious memory took him to a scene in which his mother was apparently stimulating his penis while he was in the bathtub. His father walked in on the scene and threw a fit. During the argument, his mother started taking it out on the infant by holding his head under water.

During the regression, Martin described the sheer terror he felt at being helplessly submerged by his mother. And that is how he felt in relationships with women as an adult. His subconscious mind was returning him to that feeling of having his head under water and being smothered by a woman—his mother.

Martin had been experiencing a death suggestion on many levels. On the spiritual level, he felt that he had been rejected. On the physical level, he felt as if he were dead. That incident in the bathtub was the beginning of his problem with self-esteem, and it set him up for problems with women as well as for problems in several other areas.

Hypnoanalysis helped Martin eject that feeling from his subconscious mind. With repetition and reinforcement of positive suggestions, Martin was freed to enjoy his associations with women and began dating.

Are You Already Dead?

"Most people die around 55 and are buried very much later," George Bernard Shaw said. That thought is worth considering as we examine faith and spirituality and their impact on mental health.

People with mature faith are curious. They are alert, looking ahead, and excited about life. When people become static, when they don't ask questions, when they are willing to settle for existing conditions rather than seeking an abundant life, or when they become depressed and negative, those people turn into spiritual walking zombies.

When that happens, it is time to search for causes, ask questions, and probe into events earlier in their existence. Medical hypnoanalysis is the best vehicle through which to conduct the search. The hypnoanalytic approach that has grown out of Bryan's work can best be described as psycho-spiritual. The psychopathology of spiritual walking zombies is that they have already accepted the suggestion that they are dead spiritually.

Max Was a Zombie

Max had a spiritual problem presenting as a sexual dysfunction. When I asked Max, "What's the problem?" he responded:

> *"Okay, well, I enjoyed listening to you speak the other day. It struck a chord as you being a person who could help me with my problems relating to circumcision. I was circumcised when I was born. It's a barbaric practice. I had something done to me. For one thing, I am gay. I'm in tune with the male's body. I like the uncircumcised penis. It's very difficult to find sexual partners who are uncircumcised."*

When I asked how long this had been a problem, he said, "Well, I have been aware of it almost all my life. It's been more of a problem the last 10 to 15 years."

I asked what makes the problem worse and he said, "Nothing that I can think of. If I start reading some of the books I have."

To the question, "What makes it better?" He responded, "Finding a man who has a nice foreskin."

Then—and this is the important part—I asked, "What will you be able to do once you're cured that you can't do now?"

He said, "Well," and he looked up to heaven and continued, "I guess something I've noticed, if one focuses on lack, then one has a lack in their life. It stops me from really enjoying who I am right now. That anger and resentment comes up, stops me from enjoying other men completely who are cut."

Max, 35, had been focusing on his lack and that was the bottom line on where his problem lay. Focusing on his penis was only a symptom of the problem.

I asked about siblings. He had two brothers and a sister and commented that for a time Max believed that his parents wanted a girl instead of him. About his childhood, he commented that, off and on, he had had some unhappy times and often did not get along with his father. Concerned about Max's attitude, his parents had sent him to a psychologist when he was between 8 and 10 years of age.

In talking about problems surrounding his birth, he said he was born a month early and spent five or six days in an incubator.

"The doctor held me and said, 'If he'll eat, he'll be okay.'"

I asked Max what he wanted from me, and he said he wanted to feel more relaxed about being circumcised. Then, he looked up to heaven again and said, "Just to get over the feeling of lack."

I felt I was on the right trail supported by the word-association test.

Ryan: Death . . .
MAX: *Life.*
Ryan: Live . . .
MAX: *Life.*
Ryan: Birth . . .
MAX: *Death.*

So I could conclude that life was somehow connected in his subconscious mind with death, and the connection was coming from birth. That this fellow was gay also had to be considered in his responses.

Ryan: Exciting . . .
MAX: *Men.*
Ryan: Depressed . . .
MAX: *Excited.*

Remember the rule of logic that applies in our word-association tests: If A=B and B=C, then A=C. So excited, depressed, and men all equal each other in Max's mind. That has a connection, subconsciously, to his feelings about himself and other men.

Ryan: This is where the problem came out . . .
MAX: *A girl.*
Ryan: Complete a sentence with the word "why."
MAX: *Why am I here?*

That was an indication that he had an identity problem, the fact that he thought his parents really wanted a girl.

Ryan: When did it start?
MAX: *When I was born.*
Ryan: Punishment.
MAX: *I punish myself when I don't succeed. My punishment is denying myself.*

He also brought up that he was not really doing the kind of work he wanted to do. We reviewed his history and word-association test, from which Max understood that he had an identity problem, that he felt unwanted and was a spiritual walking zombie because he was punishing himself.

Max's Dream

As with all my patients, I requested that Max bring in a dream. His dream was short and reflected his dissatisfaction with both his job and his homosexuality. He said, "The boss kept wanting this one cowboy type in tight blue jeans, with a cute butt, to talk about the weather on the news. I kept avoiding him. Finally, I acquiesced and got the interview."

Max said that after he wrote the dream down he forgot what it meant to him. "I sort of felt, at the time, like I feel in my life—like I am an observer and lonely." While he was under hypnosis, I asked him to go back to a time when he first felt that way, and he described a childhood scene in the family kitchen:

> *"My dad's up on a ladder. I'm on the floor. It's after my teacher told my mother I was lying. He yelled at me. He wouldn't believe me. I felt angry. I cried. I begged and I pleaded. I shut off and said, 'I am not going to tell anything to anybody, ever.' It mattered because I was right. I wanted him to believe me and to be loved by him."*

We discussed that his decision, based on that one particular situation with his father, was in essence to go dead in his feelings. This was typical of what was happening in his life. He would cut his feelings off and go completely dead. Using hypnotic suggestion, I asked Max to bring himself back to life, which he agreed to do. In a subsequent session, I regressed him to the womb and got this response:

> *"I feel tense, I felt tense all the way to today's experience. I'm scared, at five months. Maybe she's afraid that there isn't enough money, I don't know. It's just too cold. I don't have enough to pay the bills."*

Max described that when he lacks money to pay his bills, he experiences feelings of coldness. It was significant that he identified these feelings both in his present life and as belonging to his mother, since in the womb he did not have the ability to think separately and independently.

The next step was to bring him through the birth experience, from five months to nine months intrauterine. During the experience, he said:

> *"Sometimes, I get this feeling the world is on top of me and I'm just squooshed."*

He went through a good deal of physical discomfort and was wiggling around on the chair and crying slightly, so through suggestion we wiped out what is called the "birth trauma." I also wiped out, removing from his subconscious, the "weight of the world" so he would no longer have to carry that weight around. We also removed the negative suggestion that was focused on his foreskin as a symbol of something he lacked. I gave him positive suggestions about being peaceful and calm and eliminating thoughts that his mother had had about him, feelings that he was supposed to have been born a girl, and feelings about not belonging in the world. As a result, Max realized he was a child of God first and a child of his parents secondly.

Max came for a total of 14 sessions, three more after the womb regression, and each of those last three times said he was feeling better, more peaceful, and that his work was good. Once we removed the negative suggestions and he was able to feel loving towards himself, or God's love, he was cured. He changed jobs and the circumcised foreskin was a forgotten issue.

Let's Take a Holistic View

Each individual is a combination of body, mind, and spirit. If any aspect is neglected, the person is in trouble. We each have the power to shape and control our destinies. Faith is the tool with which we try to understand our being and our place in an ever-changing world. Faith is a human activity, not a thing we possess. It is part of our being.

"Confession is good for the soul" is more than a cliché. Holding negative feelings inside does, indeed, kill one's spirit, but it also affects the body. In his research on body image among women with eating disorders, Dr. James Pennebaker, a Southern Methodist University professor, concluded that confession of a burdensome secret resulted in dramatic physical effects.[216]

One of those burdensome secrets involves sexual trauma. Pennebaker found that women who have undergone sexual trauma before age 17 are more prone than others to develop medical problems later in life. He concluded that this phenomenon arises from the shame and guilt these women usually associate with the events. The negative feelings prevent them from discussing their ordeals with anyone. Abuse survivors are unable to let go of something that needs to be cleansed because frequently they believe they caused the abuse to happen.

Pennebaker followed that finding with laboratory studies to measure the immediate effect that confiding heavy secrets had on the body and learned that when volunteers disclosed a secret, their blood pressure and heart rate dropped and their sweat reflexes diminished.

One young woman whom I'll call 007 had suffered numerous hospitalizations for her eating disorder, anxiety, and depression. She purged routinely and her word association test went like this:

Ryan: purging feels like
007: *good!*

This woman had a history of oral sexual molestation (very often bulimics have experienced oral abuse in their history) at 6 or 7 years old and raped at 16 by a neighbor in her own basement. She never told anybody, her therapists, her parents, or her friends about these events, instead preferring to keep the secrets to herself, hiding this information even when she was hospitalized in eating disorder programs. After sharing appropriate parts of my background with her and through the use of hypnoanalysis, 007 felt compelled to finally tell her parents about her abuse. The confession alone helped her deal with her shame and moved her towards feeling relief. Her parents finally had a clue to understanding why she had behaved the way she did all those years.

Faith's Power is Amazing

Studies have shown that patients who believe in their doctors do better after surgery than those without faith in their doctors. Such patients need less pain medication and have shorter hospital stays. Even ignoring the recorded incidents of people "thinking" themselves well, our profession is beginning to reluctantly admit that faith is intricately related to healing and that our bodies have a built-in healing system.

Faith is not religion, although religion is often the result of faith. People can be religious without having faith, even getting caught up in the rituals of religion. Faith gives meaning to our lives and means acting on something we do not know and do not fully understand.

The classic faith story involves a tightrope walker who strung his rope across the American side of Niagara Falls during the 1930s and crossed it pushing a wheelbarrow. When a crowd gathered to watch the spectacle, the artist asked, "How many believe I can do it again?" They all nodded in support, but when he called for a volunteer with enough faith to ride the wheelbarrow across the chasm, only a child whose parents were not present stepped forward.

The opposite of faith is worry. A lack of faith can lead to narcissism (worry about oneself), anxiety (worry about all sorts of things), or embittered pessimism (the belief that everything will turn out wrong). Happiness is a by-product of faith.

Dr. Thomas A. Ritzman wrote, and I concur:

> "Religion is only one person's path to understanding God, and it may be very different from another's. The trouble comes when we try to force one religion upon somebody who thinks he has a better one, and it doesn't really make any difference what religion he has as long as it leads to the same place.
>
> "God is creative energy. That we experience this energy as love; that within us it promotes order, happiness, life-energy, and all other things that we feel as 'good'; that we can receive this energy from those close to us and pass it on to others, is simple enough and easy to discuss consciously with depressed people or those with behavior problems resulting from depression.
>
> "It helps to prepare the way for getting the concept of God as a judgment-day monster out of the minds of those with jurisdictional problems."[217]

Silver Needed to Mend His Connection with God

Silver's case was unusual. A 30-year-old male medical student with acute myelogenous leukemia, he had heard me speak on subconsciously accepting and acting out death suggestions. Since his illness was not responding to traditional medical treatment and his medical doctors threw up their hands and gave him up for dead, he had decided to follow up on the possibility that he was subconsciously trying to cause his own death.

When I asked my usual, "What's the problem?" Silver responded:

> *"Acute myelogenous leukemia. Or that may be the symptom of the problem. Fatigue. Bleeding from the nose, gums. Susceptibility to many infections."*

I asked how long he had had the problem. He said, *"Two years."*

Silver had a life-threatening illness and I already sensed he was subconsciously giving up his existence to maintain something which was of greater importance to himself. My goal was to find what that important something was.

Without my prompting, he picked back up on his response to my "What's the problem?" saying:

> *"I am out of remission and they tell me that time is running out. Right now, I am having supportive treatment."*

Silver had had two years of treatment in another state. Having recently attended a mind-programming seminar, Silver was interested in exploring what the power of the mind could do in his case.

When I asked him what he would be able to do once he was cured that he couldn't do now, he said:

> *"Well, my goals are to start a family. I have been married a year and a half. And I am not sure of my choice in the medical profession."* (He was a resident.)

The number "two" and personal guilt kept coming up in the history-taking portion of the visit:

- He had had **two** years of treatment.
- **Two** days after his supportive treatment he was back at home.
- On a scale of zero to ten, his life now was a one or **two**.
- He said he had completed close to **two** years of residency.
- He drank a beer or **two** every **couple** of days.
- He had been married almost **two** years.
- I asked him about suicide and he looked up to heaven and said, "When I thought about it, it was pretty fleeting—a minute or **two**."

- He talked about a **two**-year age difference between him and his brother.
- I asked if his parents had ever been really concerned about him. He said, "**Twice**. I had an eye injury in fourth grade, and now."
- There was some heavy petting with a cousin about **two** years ago. (This information combined the number two and guilt feelings, since he was reared in a very strict orthodox religion.)

The last history question also provided useful information. I asked what he wanted from me, and he said:

> *"See if there is something in my past that is causing me to want to kill myself if, indeed, that is what I am doing. Also, another thing, my brother brought up low self-esteem. I've been an overachiever all my life."*

Silver had thrown out several points that caught my attention, and I pursued them under hypnosis in a word-association test:

Ryan: I would rather die than . . .
SILVER: *Be unhappy.*
Ryan: The unhappiness began when . . .
SILVER: *I started medical school.*
Ryan: All my life . . .
SILVER: *Work.*

So all his life, Silver had been overworking to achieve. Through further word associations, it became clear that fear, worry, security, anxiety, self-esteem, death, and life were associated in his subconscious mind; that guilt equaled bad; that punishment equaled discipline; and that discipline equaled death. His life, therefore, was primarily focused on fear, anxiety, and death.

Silver had no self-love and was punishing himself. He was a spiritual walking zombie. Why? With Silver still under hypnosis, I continued the word-association test:

Ryan: I hate myself because . . .
SILVER: *I am causing pain to others.*
Ryan: Pain . . .
SILVER: *Disease.*
Ryan: Leukemia feels like . . .
SILVER: *Pain.*

He evidently felt guilty because, through his illness, he was causing other people to suffer.

Ryan: It all started when . . .
SILVER: *I went to school.*
Ryan: It got worse when . . .
SILVER: *I wanted to get married.*

Remember, this was done under hypnosis. These responses were coming from his subconscious mind.

Ryan: They really wanted . . .
SILVER: *A puppet.*
Ryan: The person I would most like to make happy is . . .
SILVER: *Dad.*
Ryan: Dad really wants . . .
SILVER: *A success.*

Through the word-association test, we obtained a sketchy outline of what was happening in Silver's subconscious mind: He was punishing himself for some kind of problem. He felt his parents wanted a puppet. For a long time, he had been overachieving, trying to please them. He was unhappy with himself for doing that. The unhappiness began when he started medical school. And he would rather die than be unhappy. The picture that came from his subconscious, then, was of a person who was indirectly killing himself.

Silver's Dream Supported the Word-Association Test Results

Silver's dream was set in the medical center:

> *"There were three offices in a row in a hospital. These offices were between two parallel hallways; hence, each had two doors: the main entrance off the main hallway, and the secondary entrance off a smaller hallway on the other side.*
>
> *"I had the office on one end. The middle office was empty. Dr. Miguel (supervising physician in the residency program) had the office on the other end.*
>
> *"I opened the secondary exit door, not knowing where it led to, and found myself in a large, luxury-type hangout with kitchen and entertainment facilities. Dr. Miguel greeted me and took me on tour. He made it known that I was privy to this set up, but was to keep it secret from the other residents as it was a special place for a select few.*
>
> *"At this time, two girls sneaked into the secondary hallway and into the hangout. I slammed the door shut, but they kicked a hole through it. I replaced the door quickly and kept them out, then I forced them back down the hall and into my office.*
>
> *"Through the back hall, I found more people, friends, in my office wanting to come into the hangout. I left them there, went back to the hangout to check it out. Found a bathroom. Had to urinate and did so."*

When asked to interpret his dream, Silver said, "I was finally led into the inner group. It was good, but I was also worried about keeping everyone else out."

He related the dream to his college years and said the two girls represented his mother and his aunt. They would not accept his girlfriend and he was angry about it. Consequently, he had a lot of resentment bottled up inside, especially since this girlfriend eventually became his wife.

Silver was intelligent and very good at analysis. He realized that the resentment was part of what was eating away at him, and, under hypnosis, agreed to stop sacrificing his feelings and his physical self for the approval of his mother and aunt. He had described how both of them had controlling personalities and how they dominated and overwhelmed him.

This case was a challenge to me because, though this part of the treatment went fairly well, I was frustrated by difficulty in regressing this client. I felt sure some early experience or situation had contributed to that problem, but I was reserving my judgment. Silver was extremely motivated to get better, and since he had a life-threatening disease, I very much wanted to help him create a mind-set for healing his leukemia.

After discussing the dream, I talked to him about leukemia being a cancer of immature cells and, in a transcendental kind of association, connected it to the Ponce de Leon Syndrome. He picked up on that and said that the parental pressure relented after he got sick. The situation began to make more sense: His subconscious had developed an extremely rare, life-threatening sickness. A secondary gain from his illness was that by staying sick he was keeping his parents off his back.

That satisfied the primary subconscious analysis in the word-association test: He would rather be dead than cause others pain. It also satisfied the secondary proposition: keeping his parents from pressuring him to get well and to be a doctor, things he was not sure he wanted to do.

He experienced subconscious resistance during regression attempts, however. Regressed to seven months in the womb, he spoke of a problem, pain, and probably fear. Then, he stopped reporting and resisted any communication.

So I tried regressing him back to the first time he felt he was killing himself off. He said:

> *"It's all jumbled up. There are flowers. Nowhere. Black. Nothing, really. All of these jumbled words in my head, but I can't make them out."*

I interrupted suddenly and asked him to go back to the womb:

> *"A lot of pain. Anger. Maybe Dad is hitting Mom. She is crying. Me. 'Cause I am there! Cause Mom is sick. Mom is too sick to cook!"*

I interrupted again and asked him to move up to the birth. He did not; he said only that he was not feeling anything and resisted further. He did say that he understood Dad was hitting Mom because he, Silver, was there and that he was responsible for his mother's pain.

By tying that reaction to the word-association response that he would rather be dead than cause pain, I concluded that this was probably the initial sensitizing event for his decision to kill himself off. I removed that negative suggestion and the responsibility for believing that he caused his mother to get hit. He accepted my interpretations and felt relieved and very curious about these memories.

In a subsequent session, we talked about his recurring fears that he was not getting any better. At the first sign of his blood count changing negatively, he would become frightened and depressed. I explained that he was interfering with his self-healing abilities by negatively programming his subconscious mind with fear.

Childhood Regressions Were Productive

Through regressions to Silver's childhood, we discovered several death suggestions that he had experienced. One was a time when he almost lost an eye. Another time his grandmother had shouted, "If you children don't behave, I'll poke my eyes out." The child in Silver took that to heart, thinking he was hurting her by rebelling. Talking about times when he felt victimized and sorry for himself allowed us to visit a time when he was beaten up as a child and we noted how he had internalized his anger. In therapy, Silver agreed to take responsibility for and to express his feelings, especially anger.

Working with Silver was emotionally intense. His blood count would change almost weekly and he was in and out of the hospital on a regular basis. It was nip and tuck. I had grown attached to him. His battle became my battle but I realized his improvement was his responsibility and not mine, a tightrope walk in this case.

We worked on his extreme desire, even willingness to sacrifice himself, to get his parents' approval. That factor weighed heavily on his mind.

One time I wanted to find out at what age his subconscious mind was operating and had him do an imagery in which he was in a movie theater. Instead of a movie, the theater lit up with the number 12, the age of the child within him. I regressed him to that age. He was in sixth grade, fat, not very popular in school, and experiencing fear of losing his mother. We identified that fear as a feeling still influencing him in the present. His mother and aunt's dislike of his wife was forcing him to choose between them, again raising feelings that he was losing his mother. Consequently, he had subconsciously decided that he could satisfy his need to please everybody, keep the family together, get the attention he desired, and fulfill his need to be himself by dying.

Using hypnoanalysis, I did as much as possible to remove his negative thought and behavior patterns. And we removed the initial sensitizing event along with several symptom-producing and symptom-intensifying events from his subconscious. Through this process, Silver developed a good understanding of himself and his relationship with God, and an understanding of his relationships with various family members. This allowed Silver to take charge of his feelings and thinking.

When I last talked with him, he was still fighting the leukemia, but with a different attitude. He had decided that it was up to him and God at that point, and he terminated medical treatment. He still had ups and downs that were beyond the comprehension of the medical profession but Silver had developed a stronger faith and was working on healing himself through mental imagery and positive suggestions. Silver, his wife, and his brother all expressed the belief that his hypnoanalysis and his strong new-found connection to God had played the crucial role in his self-healing.

One day, after the first draft of this book had been written, Silver's brother called to tell me that Silver had died. The brother told me that I should know that both he and Silver felt that the treatment had extended the patient's life by two years, two years of life that he wouldn't have had otherwise. There was that number two again . . .

I felt extremely sad to learn of his death, but it brought to mind once again something that Dr. Bryan said—a comment I think about when I have done everything possible for a patient: "Leave something to God."

We are the Experiment

Science is now recognizing a basis for what mystics, some religions, and metaphysical people have been preaching for a long time: We are what we think. We affect our lives and the lives of others in ways we don't fully understand. We are the experiment. We are evolution in process, and we can affect our internal and external environments through the focus of our minds, our thoughts. When we change our minds, we change what will occur around us.

The story line of a television series airing in the late 1980s, "Quantum Leap," explored time travel and took its story line from this idea. In the show, a physics professor was caught in an earlier time warp and could not come up with the formula to get back to his present time and place. Weekly he found himself in the body of a different person who was facing a life crisis. Knowing the future, the physicist was able, through relationships and behavior, to influence history. A fanciful story? Not entirely. By our thoughts and actions, we do, indeed, control our piece of history.

God created each of us with a mind. It is unfortunate when we misuse our mind because of our failure to recognize its power. Yet, the subconscious mind is perhaps the most underutilized and most ignored part of the mind.

Fear, depression, hate, failure, anxiety, deceit, self-doubt, and guilt are all negatives. Much of what we hear around us is negative. We can't change everything; however, we do have control over what we allow to get to our subconscious.

Because we are not perfect, we do things of which we are not proud but we can be proud of what we are. We are children of God—God's ultimate creation, created in His image. If we cannot love ourselves first, we cannot love anybody else. So our experiment begins with programming love into our subconscious minds.

In response to a question from a learned man about the greatest commandment in the law, Jesus replied:

> "Love the Lord your God with all your heart and with all your soul and with your entire mind. This is the first and greatest commandment. And the second is like it: 'Love your neighbor as yourself.' All the Law and the Prophets hang on these two commandments."[218]

Many people, however, learn to love others better than themselves, which contradicts Jesus' message.

We develop personal power by balancing and directing our creative energies. Writer Eli Wiesel, a survivor of the Holocaust, responds to the question "Why are we here?" in this way:

> "Our obligation is to give meaning to life and in doing so to overcome the passive, indifferent life. A person who is indifferent is dead without knowing it. I believe that life has meaning in spite of the meaningless death I have seen. Death has no meaning, life has. We must make every minute rich and enriching, not for oneself, but for someone else, and thereby create a bridge between beings that limits the domain of nothingness. Life is a gift and meaning is its reward. The meaning of life is to be found in every encounter. Every moment is a moment of grace."[219]

We can make our lives different if we want to. We have the power to bring about change in ourselves and in our environments though self love, and by devoting our mental energies to positive pursuits. There is an old Chinese proverb that says, "If you don't change your direction, you'll get exactly where you're heading."

God Is Not to Blame

Dana needed a change in direction when she came to me suffering from depression and chronic substance abuse. She complained that her life had little meaning, that everything seemed void and empty, and that she "did not fit in."

> *"My depression and substance abuse were masking underlying problems which I refused to acknowledge. I had worked unsuccessfully with other counselors, but continued to block many emotional injuries and aspects of my upbringing in a dysfunctional family.*
>
> *"I was spiritually empty and blamed God for allowing things I could not control to happen. Before I could change my attitude, I needed to acknowledge what it was, face those painful experiences and reprogram old belief systems."*

Effective hypnoanalysis starts with identifying the thoughts and related reactions accepted at the time of the initial sensitizing event, and reinforced later, thought which block acceptance and use of divine energy, i.e., love. After removal of these beliefs and thoughts, a new concept of self can be presented and reinforced.

Dana went on:

> *"I now realize that I have control over my own life and have accepted total responsibility. I have made and continue to make necessary changes in order to free myself from the curses of my childhood.*
>
> *"The hypnoanalytic process has been extremely worthwhile for me. Now, I feel alive."*

Dana was brought up in an abusive family with a mother who required her children to adopt the same fundamental Christian beliefs that she had. As recourse to the fire-and-brimstone upbringing, backed by the fury of an ever-present "switch", Dana began using drugs as a teenager. She continued her drug use through two marriages, even marrying a fellow who was a user like herself. When she came to me for treatment, her problem was "sustained alcohol and drug abuse."

Dana's treatment was intense, and more protracted than my usual cases. For all practical purposes, Dana's emotional and spiritual growth had ceased when she grew into puberty. Being well-motivated, she stopped the marijuana use and cut down on her alcohol consumption as a result of her therapy. Then, we worked on her identity and immaturity problems. The following is her description of her problems once she stopped her substance abuse:

> *"When I have to talk about myself, I get real anxious and uncomfortable. I get worse when I have to discuss feelings."*

When I asked her what she wanted, she said:

> *"To be true to myself; to be assertive; to honestly and openly state how I feel."*

After five months of working on Dana's goals, I received this letter from her:

> *"Dear Ryan:*
>
> *"A year and a half ago, I came to see you, a shell of a person burned out on life, probably not caring whether I ever saw another sunset or sunrise. The void I lived with was [there] because I had lost all faith and thus all hope in this seemingly cruel, lifeless existence, and felt helpless to do anything to ease the pain in a constructive way.*
>
> *"But since then, there have been many changes. The most important has been the spiritual awakening that I have most recently begun exploring. This spiritual journey has become the most exciting venture I have ever experienced. Working on my past religious upbringing has freed me so that I may now learn and explore without feeling guilt and without displaced anger. Most recently, I do not live, act and feel like a spiritual zombie, but instead like a spiritual embryo—alive and growing."*

This is why I do what I do. It fills a need I have to be involved in helping others as well as myself to learn to "love your neighbor AS YOURSELF." I added the capitals to emphasize what we all know instinctively: that love begins at home, with oneself.

"For I am convinced," wrote Dostoevsky in *The Brothers Karamazov*, "that the only hell that exists is the inability to love." I would add "the inability to love one's self, especially."

Dana "got it," so to speak. She was healed and helped due to the power of love, which is another word for God.

She learned God does not micromanage her life and is not the source of her problems.

We Can Do It

Remember, problems are mind over matter, to borrow from Mark Twain. If you don't mind, then they don't matter. Change has a cumulative effect. There is a divine principle operating inside each of us. We are all connected in some fundamental way, and when one person changes, it brings change in others.

You may know the story told in *The Hundredth Monkey*. According to Ken Keyes, who reported the phenomenon, one young monkey of a tribe in a remote setting started taking his food to the water's edge to wash the grit off before eating it. Other monkeys saw the action and gradually followed the young one's example. Monkeys at other locations were observed continuing to eat unwashed food, however. At the exact moment that the hundredth monkey (a metaphor for some number) in the original colony began washing his food, the practice was begun by primates at other sites all over the world. Without being taught or observing the washing activity, the knowledge and practice had spread through the monkeys' collective intelligence.[220]

If enough of us devote our mental energies to removing our personal negativity and focusing on positive pursuits, we will, through our collective consciousness, bring about a better world, one without war, poverty, and the ills that torture humans. William Bramley says it best in his book, *Gods of Eden*, where he writes that spiritual salvation will not be found in war. "War is the institutionalization of criminality (primarily arson, battery, and murder). War can never bring about spiritual improvement because criminality is one of the main causes of mental and spiritual deterioration." Belief is the key. If we believe we can make a better world, we can.

W. Clement Stone, Chicago philanthropist and CEO of the Combined Insurance Companies, is famous for having said,

"Whatever the mind can conceive and believe, it can achieve."

One person's mind is a microcosm of the whole world. And who knows? You may be the one hundredth human who turns the tide in the world.

Code Concepts

What we feel in relation to our self-image and self-esteem results from how much God we have in our lives.

- In some 50 percent of the cases of depression, low self-esteem, or chronic guilt, and nearly all cases of addiction and abuse, the subconscious root of the problem refers to people's concept of God. Man has created God in man's image.
- History indicates that "being right with God" has always been a precondition for physical and mental health.
- Humans, once created, are given responsibility for their own lives. Life is for the creating.
- People today who feel depressed about their lack of righteousness under the Ten Commandments are judging themselves by a standard that no longer applies.
- Guilt is neither virtuous nor desirable in the eyes of God.
- The value of past-life therapy is that, through viewing several lifetimes, our awareness is greatly expanded and we can more clearly evaluate our lives and the primacy of the soul.
- Each individual is a combination of body, mind, and spirit. If any aspect is neglected, the person is in an unbalanced state. All areas need to be fed.
- We are evolution in process. When we change our minds, we change what will go on around us.
- We develop personal power by balancing and directing our creative energies.

We are all connected in some fundamental way, and when one person changes, it brings change in others and to his or her environment.

Exorcise Your Secret God Code

1. State in a sentence or two what you think God is. What is God like?

   ____

   ____

2. Are you sure you want to hold on to that view of God?

   ____

3. How much does that view resemble someone important to you in an earlier life? Good Old Dad or Good Old Mom?

   ____

4. What transgressions do you feel guilt over? List them.

   ____

   ____

   ____

5. Point out the transgressions on this list that Jesus didn't die for.

   ____

   ____

6. Are you punishing yourself? How?

   ____

7. Do you intend to continue to punish yourself?

   ____

8. List 7 things you can do to put more love (God) in your life.

   1.
   2.
   3.
   4.
   5.
   6.
   7.

Chapter Fifteen

Wide Awake, Clear-Headed and Refreshed

Good judgment comes from experience.
And where does experience come from?
Experience comes from bad judgment.

Mark Twain

A Few Last Words

This chapter title is the title of my first book. Usually, this statement is the last thing I say to a client as he or she comes out of the hypnotic state. Being consistent then, I believe these words should be the last words I share with you, the reader, because we are all in our own trances. If you have read this far, you have learned about "trance" reformation as well as read about people who changed their trance, underwent transformation and began to live the life they were meant to live—their destiny, as it were. True freedom is the ability to change one's trance. The inability to change one's trance is neurosis.

The Roman Emperor Marcus Aurelius said it centuries ago, "If you are pained by external things, it is not they that disturb you, but your own judgment of them. And it is in your power to wipe out that judgment now." John Stuart Mill said it thusly, "No great improvements in the lot of mankind are possible until a great change takes place in the fundamental constitution of their modes of thought."

So, *Wide Awake, Clear Headed, and Refreshed* . . . to me means that happiness is our own choice once we **Wake Up** to the power of our minds, **Clear Our Heads** of the baggage, negative suggestions and misinformation, and finally **Refresh Our Spirits** with our God-given ability to create ourselves and our lives the way we desire.

The question then is: how does one know what to create? The following passage sheds some light.

> "The greatest margin of success is achieved by anyone doing what they want to do more than all other things . . . do what brings the greatest happiness, whatever it is. For when you are joyful, that creates the aura of abundance from the Divine Source. When you're happy, God the Father gives you everything you want . . ."

Ramtha the Enlightened One, by J.Z. Knight

A Few Last Words

Appendix A: How You Can Tell If You Were Hypnotized

When you awake from sleep, you usually know you've been asleep; you are aware of the return of consciousness. But hypnosis is not sleep. While under hypnosis, you are aware of the things happening around you. You are relaxed, but your mind is concentrated. There is no "waking" in the sense of a return to consciousness but there is a sense of coming back from deep relaxation. How, then, can you know when you've been hypnotized? The following sensations demonstrate:

1. Physical relaxation (Body muscles feel relaxed).
2. Fluttering of eyelids when entering and coming out of hypnosis.
3. Mental relaxation.
4. General feeling of drowsiness as if ready to doze.
5. Eyelids heavy (extreme effort to raise them).
6. Eyes smarting and/or tearing. Remove contacts; they create dryness.
7. Eyelids locked together, unable to open.
8. Jaw muscles relaxed.
9. Teeth unclenched.
10. Tongue loose and natural. When tense, the tongue goes higher.
11. Dryness in mouth.
12. Desire to swallow.
13. Moisture at corners of mouth.
14. Desire to scratch an itch, but not sure of doing it.
15. Twitching or jerking in any part of the body.
16. Euphoria (state of well-being).
17. Tingling or numbness in any portion of body.
18. Heavy feeling in any portion or entire body.
19. Desire to laugh, smile, giggle, or cry.
20. Lack of desire to open eyes (relaxation feels too good).

21. Body warmth or chill.
22. Feel personal freedom, carefree or uninhibited.
23. Sexual/sensual stimulation or awareness.
24. Time distortion (minutes seems like hours and vice versa).
25. Voice sounds fading in and out.
26. Letting go as if falling asleep.
27. Occasional involuntary sigh.
28. Feeling of lightness.
29. Feeling of floating.
30. Partial body detachment as if part of the body is not there. Some folks even feel as if they are floating above and out of the body

Under hypnosis, you may feel numb or tingling, light or heavy. Your eyes may water and your eyelids may flutter. Your saliva glands may overproduce, causing you to swallow frequently.

You may have a feeling of daydreaming, of floating, of detachment.

As the hypnotist gave his suggestions, you may have thought to yourself: "I didn't have to follow the suggestions; I just felt like it. I could have resisted, but it was so easy to go along with it." Under hypnosis, you do not carry out the suggestions because you are required to obey. You may act on the suggestions out of a compelling desire to do so. You may even carry out the suggestion without knowing it.

As you are entering hypnosis, there will be an extreme concentration on the hypnotist's voice. If you hear other sounds, they will not bother you. They may be faint or beyond your awareness. To you, the only pertinent sound is that of the hypnotist's voice.

Under hypnosis, you will be hyperaware. You may hear clearly sounds or voices that you were unaware of in the normal state.

You may experience a strong belief that you can carry out the suggestions, from the hypnotist or from yourself, or that you can reach your goal. That feeling will remain after you have returned to the normal state.

You may lose track of conscious time. Twenty minutes may seem like five minutes. You may or may not remember everything or anything that happened while you were under hypnosis.

You may achieve a state of such relaxation that you didn't feel like opening your eyes on command and may even have resented the suggestion. You may have tried to open your eyes before the command but found that you couldn't.

Sometimes, people under hypnosis may be in an uncomfortable position, may have an itch or an urge to swallow cough or sneeze and do nothing about it because it requires too much effort.

You may experience things that don't normally occur. For example, you may be unaware of your body.

All these phenomena are indications that you experienced hypnosis, but they are not always present during hypnosis. The true test is whether you are making progress toward the goal you have set for yourself. By picking a certain time, giving yourself the same or similar suggestions and doing so for 30 days, you should find the change in yourself that you desire.

Let me know what happens by writing to:
Ryan Elliott, 165 S. Church St., Winfield, IL 60190
or email seelight@juno.com

Appendix B: Methods of Self-Hypnosis

The Self-Hypnosis Blackboard. This method was suggested by George Honiotes, M.D:

You want to enter a suggestion into your subconscious mind. The suggestion may be, "I'm going to wake up at 6 o'clock tomorrow," or "I'm going to slim down so I can wear the bathing suit I saw in the store window today," or "I'm going to cut a second off my best time in the 1000-meter race."

Once you have decided on the suggestion, find a good bed or sofa, and make yourself comfortable. Pick a spot on a wall or ceiling and stare at it. If you stare at anything long enough, you'll get tired of staring. When you reach that point, tell yourself that you are going to count from one to five, and at the count of five you will let your eyes close and will let yourself relax.

Remember: You do not close your eyes and you do not relax yourself. You *let* your eyes close and you *let* yourself relax. After you let your eyes close, you let yourself begin to relax, and as you relax you imagine a blackboard with the numbers 50 to 0 written on it in iridescent chalk.

In your imagination, visualize the numbers, and also visualize two or three key words from your desired suggestion, written in iridescent chalk at the top of the blackboard and above the numbers.

In your imagination, begin to erase these numbers, one at a time, from 50 down to O. As you do so, imagine that those key words glow brighter and brighter, like neon signs.

Each time you breathe, erase a number. You will take 50 breaths as you erase from 50 down to 0. While you are erasing the numbers, the words from your suggestion glow brighter and brighter.

You now have complete control of yourself. You are permitting yourself to do this for yourself, so that after you have all the numbers erased and have breathed 50 times, say to yourself, "I will now count myself up to 3 and be wide awake and alert, refreshed, full of life and relaxed."

And you will. This exercise should be practiced regularly, at least twice a day, every day.

The Hypnotist In The Mirror. This method suggested by Thomas J. Hopwood:

Imagine that you are a famous hypnotist. It could be someone you actually know of, but don't know personally. Or it could be someone from your imagination.

Now put on a pair of slippers and get comfortable. Imagine how this hypnotist would hypnotize a person using the direct gaze technique. Stand before your mirror, looking at the reflection of light in one of your eyes.

Now imagine that you are another person—someone about to undergo hypnosis by your imaginary hypnotist. You may name the person to be hypnotized if you wish. Call her Pat. Or call him Pat. Remember, you are not going to hypnotize yourself. Your imaginary hypnotist is going to hypnotize your imaginary friend, Pat. You are simply a detached observer.

Now let your hypnotist talk to Pat, using any well-known hypnotic pattern. Don't just think the words; *speak* them, and form them clearly with your lips. This imparts more feeling to the words than thought alone. As you speak, try to imagine yourself in the roles of both Pat and the hypnotist, now one, now the other or, even better, both at once.

If the eyes grow cloudy for a second, it means Pat is going under. If you find the eyes beginning to wander, it's the hypnotist checking the progress of the subject. Now focus the eyes back on the light reflection in the iris as the hypnotist proceeds.

When you feel your body swaying slightly, it means, again, that Pat is going under. The hypnotist will hear any noise or distraction, but Pat pays very little attention to these, hearing only the rhythmic sounds. Imagine that the hypnotist is now ready to bring Pat completely under. This has no effect on you, of course; you are a detached bystander.

"I'm going to count from 10 to 1 very slowly," the hypnotist tells Pat, "and during this count your right arm will begin to rise so that by the count of one, it will be straight out from your side. Ten, your arm is slowly rising, just an inch or two from your side; nine, your arm is still rising, slowly, steadily, it forms a slender "A" with the rest of your body; eight . . ." With each count the rising suggestion will be given, with variations.

As the hypnotist counts, Pat will be imagining how it would feel if the right arm did begin to rise. While Pat is imagining, the arm may make some movement other than that of rising. It may, for instance, make a small circular movement. The hypnotist is unperturbed.

"Seven, as it slowly rises, your arm is moving in small circles . . ." When the count of one is reached, Pat's arm will be at right angles to the body. As a detached observer, you know that this was not entirely brought about by the hypnotist's suggestions. The hand could have remained at the side as easily as it rose, but Pat was merely going along with the hypnotist to get the sensation of being hypnotized.

The hypnotist now tells Pat that the arm is becoming rigid. "It's becoming as stiff as a board. It will not bend. When I count from three to one, it will be so rigid that you will be unable to bend it."

When the count of one is reached, the hypnotist challenges Pat to bend the arm. Pat finds the arm is not as easy to bend, and tries harder. The arm will not bend. The hypnotist now tells Pat to stop trying. "Your arm will become relaxed . . ."

The hypnotist may now deepen the trance, by a count, or by suggestions, or in some other way. Pat will be reminded that background noises will be audible, but attention should be focused on the hypnotist's voice. The hypnotist may now tell Pat to resume some relaxed position, and may give any suggestion deemed desirable. He will suggest that the next time Pat is hypnotized, a deeper and quicker hypnotic state will be attained.

In this exercise, you are not trying to hypnotize yourself. You're merely trying to imagine the feelings of hypnotist and subject. And you weren't hypnotized. Were you?

About the Author

Ryan Elliott, MSW, Co-Director and Founder of the Lightheart Center.

As a Board Certified Medical Hypnoanalyst, Ryan specializes in healing people by redirecting their subconscious mind towards greater *Prosperity, Performance, Peace of Mind, & Success.* He accomplishes this by changing consciousness from victim to victorious as well as removing negative suggestions interfering with one's life that manifest in anxiety, depression, phobias, guilt, shame, low self esteem, fear, behavioral problems, addictions utilizing three modalities: Hypnoanalysis, EMDR (Eye Movement Desensitization and Reprocessing) and Neurofeedback.

Recognizing that humans are spiritual beings having a physical experience, Ryan specializes in helping people remember who they really are! Ryan specializes in alternative health, is a member of the International Medical and Dental Hypnotherapy Association, holds a Masters Degree in Social Work from George Williams College, and has more than 35 years experience helping people unlock the secrets in their subconscious minds.

Having helped hundreds of clients over the years, Ryan has discovered several secret areas of the mind that interfere with living one's best life from which he has developed a unique process for helping people of all ages and backgrounds transform the problems resulting from negative subconscious programming into positive programming which resolves the problem.

Ryan is the founder and co-director of the Lightheart Center, an alternative health center located near Central DuPage Hospital in Winfield, Illinois. He also serves as Marketing Consultant, Carpenter, and Production Manager at the center as well as being an avid golfer who is dedicated to playing his age.

This book, *The Secrets from Your Subconscious Mind* can be purchased, in paperback form at www.thelightheartcenter.org.

More and more professionals realize the mind and body interact to cause illness. The practitioner of medical hypnoanalysis requires a background and training in the basics of psychology, developmental psychology, psychopathology, and psychotherapy as well as hypnosis, subconscious understanding, and listening skills. In 1974, The American Academy of Medical Hypnoanalysts was formed to foster and stimulate interest in medical hypnosis as a specialty, and to provide physicians, psychologists, social workers and allied health professionals with new knowledge in the treatment of psychological, emotional, and behavioral problems with hypnoanalysis.

Training Available

Ryan offers, besides hypnoanalysis intensives, training, consultation, and classes on the Secrets Method of Hypnoanalysis. Contact him if you are interested.

An Opportunity for Personalized Intensive Rapid Hypnoanalysis

If you live a distance from our location and are unable to maintain a regular schedule of sessions, it is possible to get a rapid hypnoanalytic intensive in about 10 days, over two weekends and the five days in between.

Many people, including sports players, musicians, and others with issues compatible with the method have stayed in a nearby hotel and received their hypnoanalysis over the ten-day period. Usually arriving on Thursday night, we get started on Friday morning and continue on Saturday. Sunday is off and the work begins again on Monday. After having worked with many clients, we have discovered that this schedule helps the process work its magic on the subconscious mind.

If you are interested in the process and want to change your life, simply email me at seelight@juno.com or call **1-800-421-2717** and we can discuss the options available.

Author's Special Offers

Free Consultation on a subject of your choice. Simply email me at seelight@juno.com to set up a time to talk about how you might benefit from a Secrets Hypnoanalysis, training in the method, or whatever you desire to discuss

Birthday and Special Offers Notification: Just email me with your birthday and I will add you to the Lightheart Center Newsletter, Birthday, and Special Offer Program where we will remember your birthday with a card and special discounts available only to our members.

50% Discount on my latest 30-minute Re-Program Your Mind Hypnosis CD with free shipping in the U.S. Regular price $20.00, now only $10.00. Air Mail Shipping outside the U.S, add $8.00. Place your order at www.lightheartcenter.org or by email.

[back cover copy]

The Secrets from Your Subconscious Mind: Interpret the Code and Change Your Life!

Hypnoanalysis: A tested and proven system to unlock the secrets stored in your subconscious and reveal them to your conscious self. By unlocking those secrets, you will be able to overcome:

- Limiting or destructive behavior,
- Unwanted feelings, and
- Intrusive, repetitive, useless, or guilty thoughts

Once you have unlocked those secrets, you will be able to:

- Strengthen desired skills,
- Boost performance,
- Learn to love, especially yourself,
- Reconnect with your spirituality, God or your higher self,
- Develop new life enhancing feelings.

By revealing, examining, and ending the power your subconscious secrets have over you, ***all*** dimensions of your life can improve.

About Ryan Elliott, MSW: Recognizing that humans are spiritual beings having a physical experience, Ryan specializes in alternative health, helping people remember who they really are! Ryan holds a Masters Degree in Social Work from George Williams College and has more than 35 years experience helping people unlock the secrets in their subconscious minds. He is Board Certified by the American Academy of Medical Hypnoanalysis and was recognized for his gifts on the Oprah Winfrey show.

Having helped hundreds of clients over the years, Ryan has discovered secret areas of the mind that interfere with living one's best life. Using this knowledge, Ryan has developed a unique process for helping people of all ages and backgrounds transform and dissolve negative subconscious programming causing their problems, thus allowing one's creative intelligence to reprogram their mind towards greater creativity and increased life enhancing options.

What others say:

"Ryan Elliott's sessions took me from a confident kid to a confident adult! It might not seem earthshaking, but it's a big thing to me. Thanks Ryan!"

Steve Beck, author of "How to Have a Great Day Everyday!"

"Ryan is a highly skilled practitioner and pioneer in the field of hypnoanalysis. His book on medical hypnoanalysis was groundbreaking. I highly recommend him."

Dan Lippmann, Owner, Counseling & Wellness Innovation

"Ryan is incredible. He has walked me through a number of challenging times in my life. What I like best is that he is present with me, has incredible integrity and helps me go to the level I need to be at to find solutions. He also has a great sense of humor, which helps in difficult times. If you really want to create a different life—he's the therapist!"

Lynne Murray

Footnotes

1 *The Road Less Traveled: A New Psychology of Love, Traditional Values and Spiritual Growth* (Simon & Schuster, 2003).

2 www.emdr.com

3 www.rossinst.com

4 While visiting the Casa de Dom Inacio on one of my many trips to Brazil, Joao (the Portuguese name for John) asked me to sit in a rocking chair named The Chair of Solomon. I did so and he came over to me and put his hand on my head, transporting me immediately to a mental vision of the spirit world, the ineffable world I had always wondered about. I gripped the rails of the rocking chair to make sure I was still alive and in the real world but my mind was in the spirit world where I was talking to and communicating with spirit beings telepathically. They were chatting with me and reassuring me of the reality of the spirit world and even offered to get me something to drink. This amazing experience confirmed to me what I desired to learn, that we do not ever die but change form after leaving our earthly body.

5 Sabrina Young, Psy.D at the Sinha Clinic in St. Charles, IL is the psychologist who performed neurofeedback for me. www.sinhaclinic.com 1-630-762-9602.

6 *Letters from Lexington: Reflections on Propaganda* (Paradigm Publishers, Boulder, Co. 2004).

Chapter 1

7 http://dankennedy.com/index.php/aboutus/dan **Dan S. Kennedy is the provocative, truth-telling author** of seven popular "No B.S." books, thirteen business books total; a serial, successful, multi-millionaire entrepreneur; trusted marketing advisor, consultant and coach to hundreds of private entrepreneurial clients running businesses from $1-million to $1-billion in size; and he **influences well over 1-million independent business owners annually** through his newsletters, tele-coaching programs, local Chapters and Kennedy Study Groups meeting in over 100 cities, and a network of top niched consultants in nearly 150 different business and industry categories and professions. His books are

available at amazon.com, BN.com, bookstores, and free information is available at www.NoBSBooks.com.

8 According to Dwight Damon in the 2007 Presidents Message to the National Guild of Hypnotists Membership, he quotes the 1958 endorsement by the AMA and the subsequent retraction in 1987, "*The use of hypnosis has a recognized place in the medical armamentarium that is a useful technique in the treatment of certain illnesses when employed by qualified medical and dental personnel…the report is no longer included in current AMA policy. In June 1987, the AMA's policy-making body rescinded all AMA policies from 1881-1958 (other than two not relating to hypnosis).*"

9 Gregg Braden, *Awakening To Zero Point.* Sacred Spaces Ancient Wisdom; 2 edition (1997).

10 Barbara Marciniak, *Pleiadian Times,* June, (2008).

11 Glen Clark, *The Man Who Tapped the Secrets Of The Universe,* The University of Science and Philosophy, Swannanoa, Virginia, p. 7 (1946).

12 www.brucelipton.com/article/the-wisdom-of-your-cells--part-3

13 Two phenomena exist, closely related to the Pygmalion Effect, suggesting that the expectation of the client influences the outcome of treatment as much or in some cases more than the treatment itself: the Placebo and Nocebo Effects. Placebo describes the client's positive expectations affecting outcome, while the Nocebo describes the client's negative expectations affecting outcome.

Chapter 2

14 Swami Kriyananda, *Awaken to Superconsciousness: How to Use Meditation for Inner Peace, Intuitive Guidance, and Greater Awareness* (California: Crystal Clarity Publishers, 2008).

15 When Mozart was five years old, he could both read and write music and had precocious skills as a keyboard and violin player. Dying at 35, he composed some 600 pieces of music widely accepted as the zenith of classical music. Nicola Tesla, the inventor of AC electricity, held many patents, was a Serbian scientist who died in America in 1943. (Lomas, Robert (1999). *The Man who Invented the Twentieth Century.* London: Headline. Albert Einstein, a German born theoretical physicist who published over 300 scientific works and in 1999 *Time Magazine* named him, "The Person of the Century."

16 Case studies drawn from my files will be included throughout this work. In each instance, fictitious names or initials have been used to protect client identity.

17 "Abraham Maslow: the hierarchy of needs": An article from: *Thinkers* [HTML] (Digital 2005).

18 Matthew 22:36-40, *The Thompson Chain-Reference Bible,* New International Version, (Grand Rapids, Michigan: B.B. Kirkbride Bible Co., Inc., 2007).

Chapter 3

19 Dracula movies portray hypnosis as Count Dracula's tool for controlling people. If you know a producer working on such a movie, please put the producer in touch with me to get the facts straight about hypnosis. Please contact me if you want to make a movie portraying the truth about hypnosis and healing.

20 http://www.rossinst.com

21 Joseph Murphy, D.R.S., Ph.D., D.D., L.L.D., *The Power of Your Subconscious Mind* (Englewood Cliffs, N.J.: Prentice-Hall, Inc., 2008).

22 *Encyclopedia Britannica* (2007), vol. 9, pp. 133-140.

23 William J. Bryan, Jr., M.D., in letter to Dr. Chong Tong Mun of Singapore, Malaya, *The Journal of the American Institute of Hypnosis* (Jan. 1963): p. 4.

24 Dr. Bruce Goldberg, *Past Lives Future Lives,* North Hollywood, California: Newcastle Publishing Co., Inc., (1997).

25 Goldberg, p. 22

26 Arthur S. Freeze, "The Power of Hypnosis," *Arthritis Today* (Jan.-Feb., 1988): p. 10.

27 Herbert Benson, M.D., *The Relaxation Response* (New York: Avon Books, by arrangement with William Morrow and Company Inc., New York, 2000).

28 It seems the AMA only endorsed hypnosis administered by physicians and dentists at that time. Hypnosis and hypnotherapy have attained a solid reputation outside of standard medicine with thousands upon thousands of cases documented and illustrated by various authors, several organizations exist nationally and internationally attesting to the efficacy of hypnosis and hypnotherapy with members numbering in the thousands.

29 Benson, p. 24

30 Benson, p. 25

31 Benson, p. 25

Chapter 4

32 David Boxerman and Aron Spilken, *Alpha Brain Waves*, (Milbrae, California: Celestial Arts, 1975), p. 12.

[33] *ibid*

[34] The word-association test works on the mathematical principle that if A = B and B=C, then A =C.

[35] In my practice, I deal with different religious denominations and help the spiritually depressed reunite with their conceptions of the higher power.

[36] Reported by Ellen J. Langer, Ph.D., in "Mindfulness" (Reading, Massachusetts: Addison-Wesley Publishing Co., 1989), and excerpted in *Psychology Today* (April 1989): p. 51.

[37] Barbara Reynolds, "Treat Whole Person, Not Just the Disease," *USA Today*, Jan. 4, 1990, sec. A, p. 11.

[38] *ibid*

[39] Reynolds, p. 12

[40] Robert Ornstein, Ph.D., and David Sobel, M.D., *The Healing Brain* (New York: Simon & Schuster Inc., 1999).

Chapter 5

[41] *Webster's New Collegiate Dictionary* (Springfield, Massachusetts: G.& C. Merriam Company, 2008), p. 509.

[42] An antigen, in medicine, is a toxin or enzyme capable of stimulating an immune response

[43] From a taped course given in 1973 by Dr. Bryan, *The Bryan Method of Hypnoanalysis* (Clinton, Missouri: Christopher M. D'Aunoy, 1979).

[44] *The Bryan Method of Hypnoanalysis*

[45] *The Bryan Method of Hypnoanalysis*

[46] *The Bryan Method of Hypnoanalysis*

[47] *The Bryan Method of Hypnoanalysis*

Chapter 6

[48] Hans Selye, M.D., *The Stress of Life*, rev. ed. (New York: McGraw-Hill Book Co., 1978), p. 1.

[49] Peter Brill, M.D., and John P. Hayes, *Taming Your Turmoil* (Englewood Cliffs, N. J.: Prentice Hall, Inc., 1981), p. 128-29.

[50] Greg Risberg presented a seminar on touching at the Single Professional's Society at the Glen Ellyn Holiday Inn, December 1987.

[51] Louis K. Boswell, M.D., "Baby Stress," *Subconsciously Speaking* (Spring/Summer 1988): p. 1.

52 Dr. Ross states on his web site, *"At present, the trauma model is marginalized and has no impact on the majority of research, clinical practice and theory in psychiatry...*" This unfortunate situation keeps mental health in the hands of the drug companies and Biopsychiatry and, psychologically stuck in a previous century. A paradigm shift is needed.

53 Louis K. Boswell, M.D., p. 2

54 Margaret Paul, Ph.D. is the best-selling author and co-author of eight books, including *Do I Have To Give Up Me To Be Loved By You*" (2002) www.innerbonding.com.

Chapter 7

55 Serge King, *Imagineering for Health* (Wheaton, Illinois: The Theosophical Publishing House, 2006).

56 Charles M. Citrenbaum, Mark E. King, and William I. Cohen, *Modern Clinical Hypnosis for Habit Control* (New York: W. W. Norton & Company, 1985), p. 35.

57 Erich Fromm, *Escape from Freedom*, (New York: Avon Books, 1994).

58 According to Wikipedia, "**Sleep-learning** (also known as **sleep-teaching** or **hypnopædia**) attempts to convey information to a sleeping person, typically by playing a sound recording to them while they sleep. This now-discredited technique was supposed to be moderately effective at making people remember direct passages or facts, word for word. Since the Electroencephalography studies by Charles W. Simon and William H. Emmons in 1956, learning by sleep has not been taken seriously. The researchers concluded that learning during sleep was 'impractical and probably impossible.' They reported that stimulus material presented during sleep was not recalled later when the subject awoke unless alpha activity occurred at the same time the stimulus material was given. Since alpha activity during sleep indicates the subject is about to awake, the researchers felt that any learning occurred in a wake state." Since the alpha state is consistent with hypnosis, the waking state and the sleep state, it can be said that hypnopaedia works and it doesn't work depending on how you define sleep.

59 Thomas Budzynski, "Tuning in on the Twilight Zone, " *Psychology Today* 11, no. 3 (Aug. 1977): pp. 40-41.

60 *ibid*

61 *ibid*

62 *ibid*

63 Dr. Leo Louis Martello, "Sleep Learning: Education of the Future," *The New Journal of Hypnotism* (June 1988): pp. 16-18.

64 *ibid*

65 Jackie Tschetter, a workshop leader and lay hypnotist who lives in Lake Geneva, Wisconsin, provided this exercise.

66 Charles Thomas Cayce, the grandson of Edgar Cayce, suggested this in a seminar he presented at the Unity Church of Oak Park, IL

67 "Relaxation Revolution: the Science and Genetics of Mind Body Healing" by Herbert Benson M.D. and William Proctor, J.D. Scribner 2010

Chapter 8

68 Steven Reinberg, "U.S. Cancer Rate-Death Rate Combo Drops for 1st Time," *Health Day News,* Tuesday November 25, 2008 and American Cancer Society.

69 Philip M. Bonelli, M.A., "Smoking Therapy: A Composite Approach," *Journal of Medical Hypnoanalysis* (Nov. 1980): p. 165.

70 From Ellen J. Langer, Ph.D., Mindfulness. (Reading, Massachusetts: Addison-Wesley Publishing Co., 1989), as quoted in *Psychology Today* (April1989): p. 51.

71 Small Business Report, July 1985, p. 91.

72 *You Can Quit Smoking and Live a Longer, Healthier Life* (Business & Legal Reports, Inc., Madison, CT 06443), Consultant: Harlan M. Krumholz, Assistant Professor, Dept. of Internal Medicine, Yale University School of Medicine.

73 "Annual Report to the Nation on the Status of Cancer, 1975-2005, Featuring Trends in Lung Cancer, Tobacco Use, and Tobacco Control", *Journal of the National Cancer Institute, Vol. 100, #23.*

Chapter 9

74 For an adult, a BMI between 25 to 29.9 is considered overweight and a BMI over 30 is considered obesity. Your doctor can help you determine where you stand.

75 The first three letters of the word diet spell "die," and who wants to die; consequently, the idea of dieting triggers a subconscious survival response.

76 Louis K. Boswell, "Eating Poor, Feeling Poor," *Subconsciously Speaking* (Winter 1987): p. 4.

77 Ryan Elliott, MSW, "Past Life Regression in Treating a Ponce de Leon Syndrome," *Medical Hypnoanalysis Journal 2,* no. 4, (Dec. 1987): pp. 148-50.

78 William J. Bryan, Jr., M.D., "Ponce de Leon Syndrome," *Journal of the American Institute of Hypnosis 5*, no. 1 (Jan. 1965): pp. 34-43.

79 William J. Bryan, Jr., M.D., "The Walking Zombie Syndrome." *Journal of the American Institute of Hypnosis 2*, no. 3 (Mar. 1961): pp. 10-18.

Chapter 10

80 Arthur B. Hardy, M.D., *Everything You've Ever Wanted to Know about Phobias . . . But Had No One to Ask* (Menlo Park, California: Terraps Programs, 1989), p. 46.

81 Manuel D. Zane and Harry Milt, *Your Phobia: Understanding Your Fears through Contextual Therapy* (Washington, D.C.: American Psychiatric Press, 1984), p. 16.

82 Manuel D. Zane and Harry Milt, p. 48.

83 Nicholas Cooper-Lewter, M.S.W., ACSW, "Initial Environmental Experience: A Powerful Tool for Psychotherapy and Hypnotherapy," *Medical Hypnoanalysis* (Nov. 1981): p. 158.

84 Louis K. Boswell, "The Initial Sensitizing Event of Emotional Disorders," *British Journal of Medical Hypnotism* (Spring 1961): p. 12. As quoted in *Medical Hypnoanalysis* (Nov. 1981): p.158.

85 Burton J. Rubin, *Stage Fright Handbook* (Saratoga Springs, New York: Decision-Making Systems, Ltd., 1986), p. 2.

86 Michael T. Motley, "Taking the Terror out of Talk," *Psychology Today* (Jan. 1988): p. 47.

87 Michael T. Motley, p.48

88 Michael T. Motley, p.49

89 Michael T. Motley, p.49

90 Burton J. Rubin, *Stage Fright Handbook*, pp. 28-47.

91 Denise Fortino, "Conquering Phobias," *New Woman*, May 1990, p.125.

92 Rheta Grimsley Johnson, *Good Grief, The Story of Charles M. Schulz* (New York: Pharos Books, 1995), p. 38.

93 Rheta Grimsley Johnson, p.39

94 Ann Landers, "Anxiety Attacks Need Right Professional Care," *Greensboro News and Record*, Jan. 25, 1990, sec. B, p. 3.

95 In many cases, by finding, understanding, and undermining the negative suggestions, a singular phobia or panic attack case can be cleared up and resolved. Sometimes, secondary gains (meaning that the person experiences an unavowed, secondary benefit as a result of the behavior) make the case more complex.

Chapter 11

96 Bryan, Dr. William J., M.D., Journal of the American Institute of Hypnosis, July, 1961, p. 10.

97 *ibid.*

98 *ibid.*

99 *ibid.*

100 http://www.dbsalliance.org/site/about depression overview (page updated February 5, 2009). (DBS)

101 *ibid.*

102 http://www.mentalhealthamerica.net/index.cfm (copyright 2010 Mental Health America). (MHA)

103 *ibid.*

104 *ibid.*

105 *ibid.*

106 http://www.pristiq.com/depression_symptoms.aspx (copyright 2010). (PCD)

107 Bryan, Dr. William J., M.D., Journal of the American Institute of Hypnosis, January, 1966.

108 http://www.mentalhealthamerica.net/index.cfm.

109 Bryan, JAIH, 1/66.

110 MHA

111 http://www.psychologyinfo.com/depression/sad.htm#features#features (copyright 2003). (PI)

112 PCD

113 MHA

114 *ibid.*

115 *ibid.*

116 *ibid.*

117 PI

118 Jacobs, Dr. Douglas G., M.D., "Lecture on Depression" prepared for National Depression Screening Day, 1994, p. 5. (Jacobs)

119 MHA

120 PCD

121 Jacobs, p. 7.

122 PCD

123 Bryan, JAIH, 1/66, p. 29.

124 *ibid.*

125 *ibid.*

126 Bryan, JAIH, 1/66, p. 30.

127 *ibid.*

128 *ibid*

129 Bryan, JAIH, 1/66, p. 31.

130 Gordon, Dr. James. *Unstuck: Your Guide to the Seven-Stage Journey Out of Depression.* The Penguin Press, New York. June 16, 2008. (Gordon)

131 PCD

132 *ibid.*

133 http://yourtotalhealth.ivillage.com/grief.html (updated 11/12/07). (YTHV)

134 http://www.nimh.nih.gov/health/publications/older-adults-depression-and-suicide-facts-fact-sheet/index.shtml (reviewed May 18, 2009). (NIMH)

135 YTHV

136 *ibid.*

137 http://www.ehow.com/about_4812419_dual-diagnosis-treatment-criteria.html (copyright 2010).

138 PI

139 *ibid.*

140 *ibid.*

141 http://www.mercola.com, "How You Can Overcome SAD (Winter Depression)," Dec. 10, 2006.

142 http://cannontherapy.com/grief/types.html. (copyright 2009).

14348 *ibid.*

144 *ibid.*

145 Lister, Elena, M.D. http://teenadvice.about.com/library/weekly/aa040501a.html. (copyright 2010).

146 http://cannontherapy.com/grief/symptoms.html. (copyright 2009).

147 http://www.wrongdiagnosis.com/g/grief_or_loss/symptoms.html. (Oct. 6, 2010).

Chapter 12

148 Melody Beattie, *Codependent No More* (New York: Harper & Row, by arrangement with the Hazelden Foundation, 2001), p.33.

149 Donald Brennan, *The War for Codependents*, (The Recovery Press, April 1991), p. 16.

150 Angelyn Miller, *The Enabler: When Helping Harms the Ones You Love* (Austin, Texas: Hunter House, 2001), p. 7.

151 Angelyn Miller, p.29

152 *ibid*

153 Melody Beattie, p. 33

154 Angelyn Miller, p. 25

155 Melody Beattie, pp. 37-45

156 Identity Problem is a subconscious diagnosis hypnoanalysts use in describing a complex of negative associations relating to the basic question of "Who am I?" A client's identity is frequently rooted in a powerful feeling of affinity with another person or group, which can involve regarding somebody or something as a model and adopting his or her beliefs, values, or other characteristics. What a person associates him or herself with is ultimately who that person is, for all identity is ultimately in relationship to something else. An American person identifies himself or herself as "American", for example, and that becomes part of that American person's identity. The same person might identify themselves as male (or female), a member of a particular religious group, a brother or sister, a child, an employee, etc. Even more personally, they may identify themselves as a loser, as someone who is helpless to influence the course of their lives, or as someone who needs to hate a particular religious group simply because that is what members of their own religious group are "supposed" to do. The underlying hypnoanalytic theory rests on the notion that we are all children of God and therefore when the subconscious diagnosis of Identity Problem is given, hypnoanalysts believe the client's identity as a child of God received a death suggestion and the treatment goal is to reestablish the broken or lost identification with God, Higher Power, The Universe, Jesus, or other deity consistent with the client's belief system.

157 John Bradshaw, *Homecoming, Reclaiming and Championing Your Inner Child* (New York: Bantam Books, 1992), pp. 8-9.

158 John Scott, Sr., hypnosis script on Identity Problems.

159 John Scott, Sr.

160 John Bradshaw, *Religious Addiction*, a cassette tape lecture.

161 John Bradshaw

162 John Bradshaw. One interesting comment about roles arises from the work of Eric Berne, M.D., the man behind transactional analysis and how he defines non-intimate transactions between and among people as "games." For more information, read *What Do You Say After You Say Hello* by Eric Berne, M.D.

163 John Bradshaw, *Healing the Shame that Binds You* (Recovery Classics Paperback, Oct 15, 2005) Healing shame is very important in becoming the person we want to be.

162 Tony Schirtzinger, therapist (http://helpyourselftherapy.com/topics/shame.html).

163 *ibid.*

164 Bradshaw, *Homecoming*, p. 21.

165 Joan Borysenko, Ph.D., "Getting Rid of Unhealthy Guilt," *Shape,* Aug. 1990, p. 75.

166 Joan Borysenko, Ph.D.

167 James F. Masterson, "The Hollow Self," *Self Magazine*, Aug. 1990, p. 123.

168 Marilyn Sargent, *Plain Talk About Depression*, (National Institute of Mental Health, Office of Scientific Information, Rockville, MD 1994.

169 *Headlines*, (Human Services, Inc., 4514 Travis, Suite 305, Dallas, Texas 75206. 1990).

170 Alcoholics Anonymous World Services, P.O. Box 459, Grand Central Station, New York, New York 10163. www.aa.org.

171 M. Amy, *Letting Go of the Need to Control*, (Hazelden Foundation, 1987, Center City, Minnesota 55012, p. 1).

172 www.codependents.org defines the group as: "Co-Dependents Anonymous is a fellowship of men and women whose common purpose is to develop healthy relationships. The only requirement for membership is a desire for healthy and loving relationships. We gather together to support and share with each other in a journey of self-discovery -- learning to love the self. Living the program allows each of us to become increasingly honest with ourselves about our personal histories and our own codependent behaviors. We rely upon the Twelve Steps and Twelve Traditions for knowledge and wisdom. These are the principles of our program and guides to developing honest and fulfilling relationships with ourselves and others. In CoDA, we each learn to build a bridge to a Higher Power of our own understanding, and we allow others the same privilege." This renewal process is a gift of healing for us. By actively working the program of Co-Dependents Anonymous, we can each realize a new joy, acceptance and serenity in our lives.

173 **The Twelve Traditions of Co-Dependents Anonymous**

1. Our common welfare should come first; personal recovery depends upon CoDA unity.
2. For our group purpose there is but one ultimate authority -- a loving higher power as expressed to our group conscience. Our leaders are but trusted servants; they do not govern.
3. The only requirement for membership in CoDA is a desire for healthy and loving relationships.

4. Each group should remain autonomous except in matters affecting other groups or CoDA as a whole.
5. Each group has but one primary purpose -- to carry its message to other codependents who still suffer.
6. A CoDA group ought never endorse, finance, or lend the CoDA name to any related facility or outside enterprise, lest problems of money, property and prestige divert us from our primary spiritual aim.
7. A CoDA group ought to be fully self-supporting, declining outside contributions.
8. Co-Dependents Anonymous should remain forever nonprofessional, but our service centers may employ special workers.
9. CoDA, as such, ought never be organized; but we may create service boards or committees directly responsible to those they serve.
10. CoDA has no opinion on outside issues; hence the CoDA name ought never be drawn into public controversy.
11. Our public relations policy is based on attraction rather than promotion; we need always maintain personal anonymity at the level of press, radio, and films.
12. Anonymity is the spiritual foundation of all our traditions; ever reminding us to place principles before personalities.

[174] Miller, *The Enabler*, p. 91.

[175] Robert F. Willard, Ph.D and Michael Gilbertini, Ph.D. *The Seven Jewels of Codependence* (7JOC Press, 2002).

[176] Gershen Kaufmann, *SHAME: The Power of Caring* (Cambridge, Massachusetts: Schenkman, 1992), p.37.

Chapter 13

[177] Joe Paterno with Bernard Asbell, *Paterno: By the Book* (New York: Random House, 1989), p. 81.

[178] I met and played in a pool tournament with Walter Payton after the Bears won the Super Bowl during the '80's.

Here' our picture: He seemed to possess an unlimited degree of optimism.

179 Thomas Bonk, "Tiger Woods' mental game is also unmatched" (*LA Times*, June 09, 2008).

180 Roger Kahn, "They Ain't Getting No Maiden," in *I Managed Good, But Boy Did They Play Bad*, eds. Jim Bouton with Neil Offen (Chicago: Playboy Press, 1973), p. 172.

181 Les Cunningham and Wayne Ralph, *Hypnosport: How You Can Improve Your Sporting Performances* (Glendale, California: Westwood Publishing Company, 1984).

182 Paterno with Asbell, *Paterno: By the Book*, pp. 129-30.

183 Paterno, p. 82.

184 Paterno, p. 94

185 Ed Temple with B'Lou Carter, *Only the Pure in Heart Survive* (Nashville, TN: Broadman Press, 1980), p. 54.

186 Willie Mays with Lou Sahadi, *Say Hey: The Autobiography of Willie Mays* (New York: Simon and Schuster, Inc., 1989), p. 15.

187 Willie Mays, pp. 72-73.

188 Cunningham and Ralph, *Hypnosport*, p. 140

189 *ibid.*

190 Cunningham and Ralph, pp. 140-141

191 *ibid.*

192 These principles are adapted from a script by the American Academy of Medical Hypnoanalysts.

193 Tim Gallwey, *The Inner Game of Tennis The Classic Guide to the Mental Side of Peak Performance* (New York: Random House, 1997).

194 James M. Rippe, M.D., and William Southmayd, M.D., *The Sports Performance Factors* (New York: Perigee Books, 1986).

195 Dr. Taylor, Medical Hypnoanalyst, told me about this case and gave me permission to use it.

196 Cunningham and Ralph, p. 142

197 Eric Berne, M.D., *What Do You Say after You Say Hello*" (New York: Bantam Books, 1984), p. 205.

Chapter 14

198 Gerald May, *Care of Mind-Care of Spirit: Psychiatric Dimensions of Spiritual Direction* (New York: Harper and Row, 1992).

199 Daniel A. Zelling, M.D., in an editorial in T*he Journal of the American Academy of Medical Hypnoanalysts* 1, no. 2 (Dec. 1986): p. 46.

200 Alan C. Anderson, *The Problem Is God* (Walpole, New Hampshire: Stillpoint Publishing, 1985), p. 242.

201 *ibid*

202 Sam Menahem, Ph.D. *When Therapy Isn't Enough: The Healing Power of Prayer* (Relaxed Books, Winfield, IL 1995*) p.79.*

203 Alan C. Anderson, p. 246

204 D. Scott Rogo, "Religion in America Today and the Vital Role of New Thought," *Science of Mind* (Oct. 1987): p. 10-12.

205 *ibid*

206 Between 50 to 60 percent of my clients are Catholics, recovering Catholics, or retired Catholics.

207 Cassie recalled having her vagina probed by her mother's fingers.

208 *The Thompson Chain-Reference Bible*, New International Version, Gen. 1:27-28 (Grand Rapids, Michigan: B.B. Kirkbride Bible Co., Inc., 2007).

209 Galatians 2:16

210 Galatians 2:21

211 Galatians 3:16

212 Galatians 3:16-18

213 Galatians 3:19

214 Galatians 3:24-26,29

215 I will not force a past-life regression or attempt to make a person believe in reincarnation. My job is not to proselytize but to analyze and remove negativity in pursuit of my client's goals. Frequently, clients ask and want to learn about past life, subconscious memories.

216 Henry Reid, Ph.D., ed., "Confession Is Good for You, *"Perspective on Consciousness and Psi Research 7,* no. 6 (April1986): p. 3.

[217] Thomas A. Ritzman, M.D., "Depression and the Nature of God," *Medical Hypnoanalysis* (Nov. 1982): p. 133.

[218] *Thompson Bible*, Matt. 22:37-40

[219] Alan C. Anderson, *The Problem Is God.*

[220] Ken Keyes, Jr., *The Hundredth Monkey* (Coos Bay, Oregon: Vision Books, Pocket Book ed., 1987).

Index

B

C

E

F

G

H

K

L

M

N

Q

R

S

W

Y

Z